ECUMENICAL DIALOGUE
AT HARVARD

THE ROMAN CATHOLIC—
PROTESTANT COLLOQUIUM

ECUMENICAL DIALOGUE AT HARVARD

THE ROMAN CATHOLIC– PROTESTANT COLLOQUIUM

Edited by Samuel H. Miller and G. Ernest Wright

THE BELKNAP PRESS OF
HARVARD UNIVERSITY PRESS

CAMBRIDGE, MASSACHUSETTS · 1964

65182

CONTENTS

EDITORS' INTRODUCTION

THE ROMAN Catholic-Protestant Colloquium at Harvard, meeting from March 27 through March 30, 1963, adds its own evidence to the mounting indication of a radical change in the religious climate of the world. Some one hundred and sixty scholars and specialists, divided equally between Protestants and Roman Catholics, met for three days of discussions about matters of mutual concern, and especially about those things on which we are divided. Separated into four seminars, the groups concerned themselves with such matters as Scripture, tradition and authority, public worship and liturgy, the meaning of reform, and the common ethical questions that our pluralistic and relativistic society thrusts upon us. This volume is presented in the hope that it may inspire other and similar adventures in understanding.

Ten years ago the Colloquium would have been an impossibility. Some of the mysteries of this change we can only ascribe to the work of God. The mounting urgency of ecumenicity marked the labors of many men in many places. For half a century Protestantism has been pressing deeper into ecumenical issues and has accomplished major gains in establishing a world council and continuing conversations among its many churches. The new forces and factors released in the "younger" churches, both Protestant and Catholic, were not content to remain in the patterns fixed by sixteenth- or seventeenth-century Europe. Secular powers created their own massive pressures toward unity, which could not be excluded from the realm of faith. Added to these elements were the changes wrought in Western culture during and since World War II, making one world a technological reality long before we were imaginative enough or mature enough to sustain it morally. Along with this imbalance, traumatic fears of demonic power had been unleashed both by the experience with totalitarian politics and nuclear fission, demanding a larger magnitude of spiritual unity for the moral judgment and control of the world. It was in this situation that Pope John announced the Second Vatican Council, and so conducted its first session as to give the world a hope that we had entered upon a new stage of historic development in the life of Christendom. A moment of authentic greatness in our time was the power of humane simplicity and humble integrity to be seen in the person of John XXIII. Ancient attitudes were so transformed as to make it possible for men to step out of the past into a new opportunity.

It was in this changed climate that the Colloquium was able to address itself realistically and with the surprise of great joy to the task of understanding ourselves and each other. Busy scholars, without very much warning, often at their own expense, and sometimes at considerable inconvenience, responded to invitations with alacrity and enthusiasm. Indeed, one had the feeling that these men had been hungering for this for a long time.

Whereas many confessed that they had presumed the Colloquium would be characterized by the gestures of academic courtesy, and that this, in itself, would assist in paving the way for mutual acquaintance among scholars in the same field of study or research, they were surprised that on all sides there was an immediate establishment of openness, in which concrete issues and historic dogma were considered with a marked lack of defensiveness or dogmatic rigidity. It was our common experience that we found ourselves, over and over again, not merely trying to understand another man's position, but looking at our own in a fresh way and trying to articulate what we ourselves had come to believe.

All of us present certainly had a sense of having lived through a most exhilarating encounter. We did not play down the differences or cover up the historical roots, but we were men of religion, nurtured by Christian faith, seeking both to know and to understand the nature of reality, as far as it had been revealed to us. That our expressions of it varied did not surprise us; but that with such diversity of opinion we could begin to see the common ground in Christ on which we were all striving to stand, brought an inner joy that obviously lends itself to no report. The truth is that we were conscious of having broken out of our schismatic separation and of having found in such freedom food for our souls.

The Colloquium was also a significant acknowledgment of the historic importance of Pope John's ecumenical intentions. Since the Reformation, Christians have been almost prisoners—in cages of their own making. There was a barrier that ran all through Western culture—a religious scandal of profound dimensions. How the bad habit and ill humor of three centuries can be changed or shifted is still to be seen. But a significant step was taken by a man of singular humanity, in whom faith had retained its warmth and penetration.

This was important, not only in the sense of breaking a deadlock of centuries, but equally in the sense of confronting the urgent conditions of our time. On all sides the structures of traditional religion have been under sustained attack; many have been demolished; others are held in contempt. Multitudes are disillusioned, their lives distorted and damaged by the harrowing of the wars and cursed by wild and demonic fears of unchecked power. Needs that have been released on a wide scale and at unprecedented depths of the human heart cannot be met or answered by the clichés of the past, or even by the Scriptures, which, however sacred, seem now to offer so little guidance in a strange new land of technical horror and urban sophistication. Faith stands at a crucial juncture; it is no longer simply a question of being Catholic or Protestant, but the deeper question of the possibility of faith itself.

In an age of excessive destruction and even of inhuman brutality, of disappearing moral and religious landmarks, of deep anxiety and a bewildering lostness, if there be any help in religion, any compassion, any hope, any assurance, then the Church, the whole Church, must find a way to make the ancient resources of faith available for a world that has long since grown doubtful even of our motives, sometimes of our concern, and very often of our ability to help. Unless the Church finds something sufficiently deep, sufficiently powerful, sufficiently comprehensive, by which it can pull itself together and reverse its trend toward fragmentation, it will not be able to save even its own life. Of more significance, it must manifest in its own nature and practice the unity of God's Will as the very reality of life itself, so that it may be worthy of mention in a time of enormous need. Indeed, if we can strive to answer Christ's prayer to the best of our ability, to be one in him and in the Father, we may also, please God, be able to answer the world's unspoken prayer that the people of God demonstrate in their life together the trust and faithfulness that are able to sustain the peace of the world for which all men hunger.

Any attempt to list those to whom we are indebted for whatever success the Colloquium achieved would involve listing the whole membership of the conference. The most remarkable generosity prevailed on all sides. Members assisted in a thousand ways to help every aspect of the Colloquium procedures. We must express our gratitude for the enthusiastic and earnest counsel of His Eminence, Richard Cardinal Cushing, and the assistance in many details of the conference by Father Joseph I. Collins and Father Robert F. Quinn.

It would have been impossible to have prepared for the conference had not members of the Faculty of the Divinity School taken on considerable burdens in addition to their regular duties. Professor Amos Wilder served as Chairman of the Colloquium Committee before he departed for Rice University as a Visiting Professor. Working closely with the Committee was a staff whose efficient labor and extraordinary loyalty to the project contributed in a very large measure to the success of the occasion. Among them the names of Elinor Bunn Thompson, Dorothea S. Willcomb, Kathleen F. McLaughlin, and William N. Feaster must be mentioned especially. We wish also to express our gratitude to Ann Orlov of the Harvard University Press and Ralph Lazzaro of the Divinity School for their unusually efficient assistance in seeing the manuscript through the press, and to the Rev. Richard Wertz for preparing the index.

Last in order, perhaps, but first in significance, we express our gratitude to Chauncey D. Stillman, whose foresight and generosity first made the Charles Chauncey Stillman Professorship of Roman Catholic Theological Studies possible, and then graciously liberated its use for this extraordinary purpose.

Samuel H. Miller

G. Ernest Wright

December 12, 1963

The reader will need to remember that the addresses and papers in this volume were written and presented before the death of Pope John in the interval between the first and second sessions of the Second Vatican Council. At certain points the emphasis might have been somewhat different, had the Colloquium taken place after the conclusion of the second session of the Council.

THE CHARLES CHAUNCEY STILLMAN
LECTURES ON THE UNITY OF CHRISTIANS

INTRODUCTION

THERE ARE three collections of the ecumenical writings and addresses of Augustin Cardinal Bea. The first is that of Eva Maria Jung-Inglessis, printed as an ample appendix to her sketch in German of the life of the eminent biblical scholar and ecumenist; the second is entitled *The Unity of Christians;* and the third constitutes the first part of the present volume.[1]

Although there are but three lectures in the present collection, they constitute a distinctive trilogy, notable both for the fact that they were the occasion of the extraordinary Roman Catholic-Protestant Colloquium, sponsored by the Dean and the Faculty of the Harvard Divinity School, and for the fact that the lectures, delivered in the presence of the Cardinal Archbishop of Boston and of the President of Harvard University, were composed and presented during a crucial phase between the close of the first session of the Second Vatican Council on December 8, 1962, and the opening of the second session on September 29, 1963, under Pope Paul VI.

During that first session, at the end of the climactic debate over the draft constitution (schema) "On the Sources of Revelation," Pope John had dramatically intervened; and, calling for a radical revision, he appointed Cardinal

[1] *Augustin Bea, Kardinal der Einheit* (Recklinghausen, 1962), with eight papers and bibliography, pp. 61–151. Only two of these, namely, "Diener des Sakramentes und Diener des Wortes" (1960) and "Die Bedeutung des 2. Vatikanischen Konzils für die Einheit der Christen" (1962), are not translated in *The Unity of Christians,* Bernard Leeming, S.J., ed. (New York, 1963), with an introduction by the late Apostolic Delegate in Great Britain, the American-born Archbishop Gerald P. O'Hara. This collection of twenty ecumenical titles, selected from the period 1960–1962, appears in several other languages.

Bea and Alfredo Cardinal Ottaviani as co-presidents of a
joint commission to prepare a new schema.[2] Here the president of the now-permanent Secretariat for Promoting Christian Unity, a biblical scholar and archaeologist, the former
rector of the Pontifical Biblical Institute in Rome, would
have the opportunity, with Cardinals Frings, Liénart, and
Meyer—and all the bishops belonging to his ecumenical
secretariat—to reformulate a basic theological document
of the Council. In helping to recast, in the light of contemporary Catholic biblical scholarship, the meaning of
Scripture in the mouth of the Church, Cardinal Bea and
his colleagues were called upon to construct the dogmatic
platform on which Catholics would be standing for perhaps
a long time to come in their ongoing dialogue with Protestants.

As though this immense task of clarifying the relation of
Scripture, tradition, and (by implication) the papal-episcopal *magisterium* were not enough, Cardinal Bea anticipated
another major contribution of his Secretariat for Promoting
Christian Unity on January 13, 1963, when he gave a
revolutionary talk "On Liberty of Conscience" before the
annual *agape* at Pro Deo University in Rome.[3]

It was evident to some, during Cardinal Bea's visit to
Harvard, that he was anxious about the possibly adverse
effect of his absence from Rome on the final formulation
concerning freedom of conscience in what he, perhaps
alone among us, knew would within a fortnight break forth
upon the world as John XXIII's great encyclical *Pacem in
terris* on April 11. This was addressed to Catholics and

---

[2] The Secretariat and the Theological Commission jointly prepared
the new text, "De divina Revelatione," which was to be approved by
Pope John on April 22, 1963, for presentation during the second session of the Council.

[3] The text is published in *The Catholic Messenger* (Davenport, Iowa),
January 31, 1963, and in *The Ecumenist* (Paulist Press, Toronto)
1:62 (April/May 1963). See reference below on page 9.

notably "to all men of good will," embodying, as it turned out, in all its fullness Cardinal's Bea's conviction about the dignity of every human conscience.

Cardinal Bea's three Stillman Lectures on Christian Unity can thus be read as the literary transcript of the mind of a major draftsman of the rapidly unfolding pattern of Catholic ecumenicity. In this pattern a dialogue or colloquium with Protestants is now possible from the Catholic side on what would appear to be a fivefold basis: the recognition by Catholics (1) that non-Catholic Christians individually and as religious communities belong with them to the same Mystical Body of Christ by virtue of a valid baptism; (2) that "Christian brethren," though jurisdictionally and in varying other ways separated, can, as Protestants, as Orthodox, or as members of the Lesser Eastern Churches, give valid testimony under the impulsion of the same Holy Spirit operative among churches in communion with the Holy See; (3) that, while visible unity with the successor of the Prince of the Apostles, in fulfillment of Jesus' prayer "ut omnes unum sint," is the unswerving aim of Catholic ecumenicity, the inviolability of every human conscience and the dignity of every Catholic communion must be vigorously defended in the fraternal dialogue; (4) that dogmatic truth should be practiced in love, which may well mean in our age restating truth in an idiom common to the participants in the dialogue and relevant to their era (*aggiornamento*); and (5) that Scripture is preeminent if heard in the mouth of the Church, the latter understood sometimes as the universal People of God or invisible Mystical Body, though more commonly as the Roman jurisdiction.

Cardinal Bea is the world-traveling embodiment of these five Catholic ecumenical principles. He was the confessor of Pius XII, the close advisor of John XXIII, and an early supporter of Paul VI. Near the threshold of his present mission, the octogenarian ecumenist, biblical scholar, and builder of schools looked back upon his career and declared, "My whole life has been a preparation for this."[4]

There is no full-length biography of the Cardinal.[5] Moreover, although his complete bibliography to date is available in *Biblica*,[6] it would be rash for one removed from the unpublished sources and the scenes of the Cardinal's labors to presume to trace his emergence as the chief official spokesman of Catholic ecumenicity. But, by way of introducing Cardinal Bea's three lectures, in which the five above-mentioned ecumenical principles are articulated or presupposed, it is of interest to look back at some of the biblical and other writings of the emergent ecumenist in order to take note of the background of his more fully developed ideas on religious freedom; love and conscience; unitive baptism; the universality of the operations of the Holy Spirit; revelation: Scripture, tradition and *magisterium*; the Church and university.

I. FREEDOM AND LOVE

The professionally engaged reader of Professor Bea's extensive textual, historical, and archaeological writings composed between 1910 and his elevation to the cardinalate in 1959 would scarcely have detected advance notice of his present preoccupations as president of the Secretariat for

---

4 Xavier Rynne, *Letters from Vatican City* (New York, 1963), p. 167: "The chief spokesman in the Curia for the new approach was unquestionably Cardinal Bea, whose efforts over the past two years had been nothing short of phenomenal. 'My whole life has been a preparation for this,' he has said."

5 Besides the very vivid sketch by Eva Maria Jung-Inglessis, recently summarized by her as "The Cardinal of Unity," in *The Catholic World* 196:157–164 (December 1962), see also the character sketch of the Cardinal and description of the Harvard Colloquium by Xavier Rynne, in *The New Yorker*, May 11, 1963, pp. 120ff *passim*; and for a profile sketched by a member of his Secretariat, see Monsignor Werner Becker, "Augustin Bea: Kardinal der Einheit," *Oekumenische Profile* (Stuttgart, 1963), II, 167–179.

6 *Biblica* 43:254–276 (1962), with a dedicatory preface by Bernard Cardinal Alfrink.

Promoting Christian Unity, as chief proponent of the ecumenical dialogue, and as defender of the freedom of conscience. Yet all his resident and teaching years in the Pontifical Biblical Institute of which he was rector, 1930–1949, were preparatory. Significantly, his last professorial lecture before he assumed his princely duties in the Curia was on a favorite theme, the doctrine of divine inspiration.[7]

Professor Bea had already served long as a *consultor* in several administrative Congregations of the Curia, notably in the Congregations of the Holy Office, of Rites, of Seminaries and Universities, and also of the Biblical Commission. It would appear that his daily contact with the problems and pressures registered from all over the world in these great bureaus of curial administration gradually altered his vision of his Church's mission in the world. And when, on the morning of November 16, 1959, Professor Bea learned to his immense surprise that John XXIII had announced his intention to make him a Cardinal and that the Superior General of the Jesuit Order had been apprised of the impending appointment,[8] it is plausible to conjecture that something of the experience of Saul on the Damascus Road was his, as the scope of his new mission flooded in upon him. Not, of course, that this solid Catholic scholar had been persecuting Protestants and Gentiles and had then become suddenly converted to their views! Since the International Congress of Old Testament scholars in Göttingen in 1935 he had been in increasing and always friendly contact with biblical colleagues outside his communion. But surely a new vision of his role and of the mission of the Catholic Church—to be freed from some of its heavy carapace of curial legalism—now energized the venerable scholar with a renewed devotion to the Christ who is the

[7] Jung-Inglessis, p. 34.
[8] The last Jesuit in the College of Cardinals died in 1946. The actual appointment took place in the Consistory on December 14.

Lord of Gentiles no less than of Catholics. As the motto for his coat of arms the new Cardinal took Colossians 3:17, "In nomine Domini Jesu."

On January 25 in that same year, Pope John had startled and cheered the ecumenical world with his announcement in the basilica of St. Paul's Outside the Walls that he proposed to summon a council. It is surely significant that the former professor's first publications as a Cardinal were two articles based on addresses given in Rome on Paul as the inwardly free "captive of Christ" and as "the herald and hero of liberty."[9]

Occasioned by the nineteen-hundredth anniversary of the arrival of Paul in Rome, these two essays illuminate for us not only the mind of Paul but also the mind of the biblicist Cardinal. Well launched upon his role as interpreter of Jesus—alike to the Godfearers and to the Gentiles of the modern world—Cardinal Bea was determined to construe the true freedom of the Catholic law in love. Curial and scholastic legalists and obscurantists within his communion[10] should no longer, he implied, any more than the Judaizers of old, imperil the divinely willed accommodation of the formulae of redemptive truth and of the structures of redemptive order to the larger, more complex, and precarious *oikoumene* of our day. Cardinal Bea's writings on Paul were programmatic in this sense. However allusively, they were also suggestively autobiographical. This can scarcely be overlooked in his passing observation that his patron saint Augustine, born a Christian, was taken captive by Christ in the fullness of time. One observes, too, the new Cardinal's specific reference in the two addresses to the ecumenical question and the missionary assignment, especially when

9 "Paolo 'Afferrato' da Cristo," *La Civiltà Cattolica,* May 21, 1960, pp. 337–352; "San Paolo araldo ed eroe della libertà," *ibid.,* October 1, 1960, pp. 3–14.

10 Note his reference to canon law and his sly citation of Cardinal Ottaviani in favor of *apertura* on page 38 following.

he noted that only four hundred seventy-five million of the eight hundred eighty million Christians, altogether a scant third of the world's population, belonged to the Roman Catholic Church and when he urged *all* the baptized to be united in the one apostolic Church and that "the Gentiles" be converted. At the same time, the Cardinal was clear about the inviolability of the individual conscience. Moreover, in characterizing Paul as the herald and hero of liberation from the tyranny and the insufficiency of law— for "if a man is able to save himself by means of observing the law . . . then Christ and his work and the grace of God become superfluous"—he implied the contemporary relevance of the profound Pauline perception of the relation of truth and love, of Christ's law and freedom.

The modern civic and ecclesiological applications of this idea were to become movingly explicit three years later in the already mentioned Pro Deo allocution of January 13, 1963: "Obviously, it is . . . not a question of making truth a relative and undetermined thing. It is, rather, a question of a real and *binding* love of truth, and it is precisely this love which admonishes us [Catholics] to bear in mind the limitations of our knowledge and recognize also *that side of truth which others see,* without denying, however, that which we ourselves really know about truth."[11]

In this allocution, in which he again conspicuously quoted both Paul and Augustine, a few weeks before his three Stillman Lectures for the Harvard Colloquium, Cardinal Bea made as explicit as perhaps anywhere up to that time the Catholic theological, ethical, and biblical basis for a *binding* or committed theological colloquy among separated Christians. He grounded such an exchange in Paul's conception of love as patient and kind and rejoicing in the truth (I Cor. 13:4–7), and in the acknowledgment in this

[11] *The Ecumenist* 1:62 (April/May 1963), and *The Catholic Messenger,* January 31, 1963, p. 9. Italics mine.

love of the right and of the duty of every man, Christian and non-Christian, "to follow his conscience, and [of] the right that this independence be respected by all." Having distinguished between abstract errors and persons who err, and having recognized that the jurisdictionally separated baptized may validly testify to a neglected aspect of truth, the Cardinal concluded his revolutionary allocution with a call to prayer without ceasing "that we will find the harmony, so hard to achieve, between the love of truth and the love of neighbor."

Cardinal Bea in his Stillman Lectures bases the ecumenical dialogue not only upon a common baptism and incorporation into the Mystical Body,[12] but also upon the Pauline conception of forthrightness in love. He appeals here to Ephesians 4:15 on "practising the truth in love."[13] At this point, one might add that the Vulgate text thus rendered in English is, by chance, more apposite for ecumenical interchange than the King James version. The latter has the merely verbal "*speaking* the truth in love." The (Catholic) Christian, the Cardinal goes on to say, "respects everyone, listens to all, and considers their problems as his own," and "takes into account further aspects of revealed truth which they [the separated brethren] consider important."[14] He urges specifically, with respect to the Council, that the observers "favor" the Council Fathers and *periti*, especially within the Secretariat, "with their complete confidence and frankness . . . their reactions and criticisms," "no longer merely observers!"[15]

[12] On the unity in baptism, see, for example, pages 30, 31, 39, 54, and 66. Cardinal Bea also cites Pius XII's encyclical *Mystici Corporis* (1956). He apparently first made ecumenical use of the operation of the Holy Spirit among all the baptized in his paper "Il cattolico di fronte al problema dell' unione" (1961); Jung-Inglessis, no. 3; Leeming, no. 1.

[13] "Veritatem autem facientes in charitate." See page 32.

[14] Pages 31, 38.

[15] Page 53.

II. SCRIPTURE AND TRADITION

If practising dogmatic truth in love (Eph. 4:15) is Cardinal Bea's scriptural ground for forthright, free, but committed, yet nonegalitarian dialogue, we may now note some of the Cardinal's earlier thought on the relation of tradition and scriptural science[16] touched upon anew in his three lectures and prominent in several of the colloquies and papers.

Professor Bea's initial work in his special field of Old Testament studies had been on the composition of the Pentateuch (1918/1928).[17] An abiding interest in the sources and divine inspiration led to his second book, *De scripturae sacrae inspiratione; quaestiones historicae et dogmaticae* (1930).[18] Herein he touched upon a succession of Protestant views on inspiration and canonicity, observing that the Protestant "internal testimony of the Holy Spirit" was a "psychological criterion." This criterion was to the fore especially in John Calvin, although in the *Institutes,* as Bea noted, Calvin recognized as supplementary such criteria as the consensus of the churches, the confession of pious and learned men, and the constancy of martyrs. As for Martin Luther, according to Bea, he so defined the inner testimony in terms of "solafideism" (by faith alone) that he considered himself at liberty to push the Epistle of James to the very margin of the canon.[19]

Turning to the historic basis of modern Protestant the-

---

[16] In a modified way the Catholic Church is doing concurrently in the twentieth century what Protestants did in two separated phases: in the sixteenth century by placing institutions under the judgment of Scripture, and notably since the opening of the nineteenth century in placing Scripture itself under the scrutiny of rational inquiry.

[17] "Deutsche Pentateuchforschung und Altertumskunde in den letzten vierzig Jahren," *Stimmen der Zeit* 94:584–595 (1918), and *De Pentateucho* (Rome, 1928).

[18] 2 ed. (Rome, 1935).

[19] *Ibid.,* pp. 121f, 127.

ology, Bea characterized the work of Friedrich Schleiermacher as semirationalist and charged him with inverting
the idea of scriptural inspiration by construing "the common spirit of the Church" (*spiritus communitatis chris-
tianae*) instead of the Third Person of the Trinity as the
source of inspiration.[20] He also charged him with construing the whole life and work of the Apostles and their community as inspired rather than the scriptural books.[21] These
strictures, though normal in such accounts, are of interest
when set over against Professor Bea's own Catholic view
that an alleged disintegration or flattening out of the Protestant understanding of inspiration and canonicity has been
due to neglect of the consensus of ecclesiastical Tradition.[22]
Elsewhere he added that when there is no consensus, the
Catholic Church necessarily eschews critical and scientific
investigation and depends upon the Holy Spirit to direct her
infallibly as to what was in fact, however obscurely, revealed by God to the Apostles from the beginning.[23]

But for the most part Bea has not been preoccupied with
the relatively few cases of the intervention of the *magisterium* in his field, but rather with the papal encouragement of provisionally free research. Much of Professor Bea's
interest in the instrumentalities of inspiration and much of
his concern for the original, literal sense of Scripture clearly
resound a dozen years after *De inspiratione* in the encyclical *Divino afflante Spiritu* of Pius XII in 1943. This encyclical, widely hailed as a charter of freedom in the realm of
biblical research,[24] is one in which Bea's influence as *consultor* of the Biblical Commission is clearly visible.

[20] See proposition 130 of Schleiermacher's *The Christian Faith*. Eng-
lish translation of the second German edition by H. R. Mackintosh and
J. S. Stewart (Edinburgh, 1956). Torchbook edition by Richard R.
Niebuhr (New York, 1963).

[21] Bea, *De inspiratione*, p. 12.

[22] *Ibid.*, p. 14.

[23] *Ibid.*, p. 136.

[24] See below, pages 100, 293, 294.

Then, in 1950, came Pius XII's doctrinally more comprehensive encyclical *Humani generis,* which, in its section on biblical research, seemed to many to pull back from the earlier charter. This encyclical came, indeed, as a *monitum* welcome to the more alert conservative biblicists, including some in the Roman Pontifical Theological Academy in the Piazza of St. John Lateran, where Pope John XXIII himself had once given a series of lectures.

The Lateran, in the first year of John's pontificate, was raised to the rank of Pontifical Lateran University. In celebration of this distinction, there were appropriate addresses and papers, published in the recently founded periodical of the Theological Academy, *Divinitas.* And at the end of the summer of 1959, writing still as Pater Bea, the authoritative biblicist, and the key figure in any discussion as to whether *Divino afflante Spiritu* had, in fact, represented a major turning point in Catholic biblical scholarship, brought out in *Divinitas* a magisterial survey of Catholic biblical science from Leo XIII through Pius XII.[25]

In this survey Bea insisted on the essential continuity in Catholic biblical science under recent pontiffs and also vindicated against Protestant detractors the Catholic claim to an important place in the development of the historico-critical method. Bea cited, among others, Richard Simon

---

[25] "La scienza biblica da Leone XIII a Pio XII," *Divinitas* 4:590–634 (1959). See also his earlier "L'enciclica 'Humani generis' e gli studi biblici," in *La Civiltà Cattolica,* November 18, 1950, pp. 417–430, in which he agreed that the *Nouvelle Théologie* had taken some of the earlier directives in an improper sense; and "Il progresso nell' interpretazione della Sacra Scrittura," in *Gregorianum* 33:85–105 (1952), in which he showed that allegorical and mystical meaning prevailed among the Fathers and the Schoolmen, and that the present age was discovering the superior richness of the original literal meanings. At this point Catholic hermeneutics, in giving enhanced *religious* significance to the literal or historical sense (among the four senses) of Scripture, seems to be going through an awakening comparable to that of Luther.

(d. 1715). Taking as his own the axiom of Leo XIII, *Verum vero adversari haudquam potest,* Bea found that the key freedom in biblical scholarship lay in distinguishing sharply between the work of biblical science and the task of the dogmatic or systematic theologian. He underscored in *Divino afflante Spiritu* the fact that Pius XII had authorized careful textual criticism "because of that very reverence which is due to the Divine Oracles," sent by God "as so many paternal letters to His own children." Hence the Pope's recognition that the original languages of the sacred writers should take precedence over subsequent versions, and accordingly that the Vulgate, having juridical value in the Latin Church, should not exercise a critical role in Catholic biblical scholarship (though on a very few controverted points it would still be valid for the faith of the Church). Moreover, while the postbiblical, nonliteral meanings were not to be excluded, they were emphatically to be subordinated to the original literal sense: "for the Sacred Pages, written under the inspiration of the Spirit of God, are themselves rich in original meaning, endowed with divine power." In ascertaining the literal sense, Catholic scholars were thereupon encouraged by the Pope, Bea pointed out, to get all possible help from the disciplines of palaeography, archaeology, and even comparative culture. The quest for the literal sense, Bea remarked, was almost completely open; for, as the encyclical had observed, only a few texts had ever been defined by the ecclesiastical *magisterium,* and only a few more had ever been unanimously agreed upon by the Fathers in the tradition. In defending *Divino afflante Spiritu* in this essay against detractors and minimizers in the Roman circle of biblical scholars, Bea chose to occupy the vantage point of defending it also against a series of Protestant scholars who had allegedly also misconceived its import.[26] Bea was willing, moreover, to concur

26 *Divinitas* 4:626–632 (1959).

in what must have been a very strong sentiment among most of the subscribers of *Divinitas*, that the proponents of the New Theology had, for their part, misconstrued the positive directives of the encyclical, which therefore had rightly to be further safeguarded by the subsequent strictures in *Humani generis.*

It is evident from his essay that Professor Bea had come to feel more at home with sober biblical exegetes and archaeologists than with the exponents of the New Theology. Many of the latter were drawing inspiration from *nonliteral* patristic and monastic theology, and from patristic, biblical, and extrabiblical texts. Their ecumenical enthusiasm for the community of faith, East and West, patristic and modern, he might well have regarded suspiciously as "a transplant" of Schleiermacher's "common spirit of the Church."[27] Bea's scholarly concern for establishing the meaning of the ancient text as it was originally intended no doubt brought him, in effect, closer to the feeling of many Protestants but perhaps, unwittingly, further from the feeling of the Orthodox. He concluded his essay on an ecumenical note, confident that Catholic biblical science would contribute its part in realizing the desire of Christ, that they all might be one. Within a few weeks of the appearance of his *Divinitas* article, Professor Bea was the new Jesuit Cardinal.

In the course of the same academic year (1959/1960) Pope John delivered a discourse on biblical scholarship. The occasion was the fiftieth anniversary of the Pontifical Biblical Institute (1909), linked with the much older Jesuit Gregorian University (1552). In the papal discourse, while recognizing on the horizon the dark clouds of impending storm, due to biblical criticism, John yet gave his

[27] *Ibid.*, p. 605. The image of transplantation is here employed in connection with Catholic Modernism, but that Bea may have seen a similar spirit in the New Theology is suggested in "Il modernismo biblico secondo l'enciclica 'Pascendi,'" *Divinitas* 2:9–24 (1958), esp. p. 24.

full encouragement to critical labor in the service of truth, and enjoined scholars both to be loyal to the high standards of international biblical scholarship and faithful to the sacred deposit and the magisterial infallibility of their Church.[28]

This papal discourse called forth a spate of articles which constitute the immediate intellectual and institutional background of the polarization on Scripture and tradition in the minds of the Council Fathers at the first session. In Rome the conflict seemed to be a struggle not only between conservative and progressive Catholic exegesis and hermeneutics but also, alas, a struggle between two Roman universities, the Lateran and the Gregorian. In the ensuing bitterness, Cardinal Bea discharged the role of irenic conservative. It had long been said of him: "Pater Bea always finds a solution."

A key document in the controversy was that of Alonso Schökel, S.J., "Where is Catholic Exegesis Going?"[29] This article by Professor Schökel of the Pontifical Biblical Institute appears to have been sent out in offprint to all the bishops of Italy as expressive of the views of the institute. To Schökel and other progressivists Antonio Romeo of the Lateran University retorted at length in *Divinitas,* arguing against "the invasion of progressivism" and "its corollaries, relativism and subversion," with its spurious appeal to the Holy Spirit on the part of the "illuminists" and by other protagonists of *mutamento, novità,* and *apertura!*[30] Romeo was at pains to adduce solely those utterances of the new Jesuit Cardinal and former rector of the institute which

---

28 The papal address was delivered on February 17, 1960. It is printed along with Cardinal Bea's discourse on the history of the Institute in *Biblica* 41:1–8 (1960), and also in *Acta Apostolicae Sedis* 52:40 (1960).

29 "Dove va l'esegesi cattolica?" *La Civiltà Cattolica,* September 3, 1960, pp. 449–460.

30 "L'enciclica 'Divino afflante Spiritu,'" *Divinitas* 4:387–456 (1960).

could be construed in favor of the more integralist view of biblical scholarship.[31]

To the issues raised by Romeo both Cardinal Bea, for himself, and the Biblical Institute corporately replied. Cardinal Bea at the close of the annual *Settimana Biblica Italiana* at the institute on September 24, 1960, took the occasion to strike the balance between true progress in biblical scholarship and fidelity to dogma.[32] Appealing to I Timothy 3:15, he reminded his hearers that, amidst the claims, counterclaims, hypotheses, and excesses (for example, Rudolf Bultmann) of modern biblical scholarship, the Church of the *living* God is ever "the pillar and bulwark of the truth"; and he insisted that, while Catholic exegetes should be open to insights from all quarters, enjoying as scholars "the true liberty of the sons of God," and should accordingly always be judged or restrained solely by maternal love, still the Catholic scholars themselves should, for their part, never forget, amidst all their researches and hypotheses, that the original and abiding purpose of the Word they study so assiduously is the healing of the souls of men.

Presently the Pontifical Biblical Institute, using as its organ *Verbum Domini* (its periodical designed primarily for the clergy) rather than *Biblica* (its international periodical for biblical specialists), corporately defended Schökel and his colleagues from Romeo's attack.[33] Because of the rising tension, especially intense within the circle of biblical scholars in Rome itself, the Holy Office published a *monitum* on June 20, 1961,[34] which, in allusion to the form-critical method (*Formgeschichte*), enjoined all Catholic centers of

[31] For example, *ibid.*, p. 408n53 and p. 412n65.

[32] "Parole di Chiusura del Card. Agostino Bea alla Settimana Biblica Italiana," *La Civiltà Cattolica*, November 5, 1960, pp. 291–295.

[33] A collective statement, signed P.I.B., "Pontificium Institutum Biblicum et recens libellus R.mi D.ni A. Romeo," *Verbum Domini* 39:3–17 (1961).

[34] *Acta Apostolicae Sedis* 53:507 (1961).

biblical learning to beware of bringing into doubt the
historical and objective truth of Scripture, particularly with
reference to the New Testament, and especially with respect
to the words and acts of Jesus Christ. By this time Professor
Francesco Spadafora, a pupil of Romeo and himself intimately acquainted with the instruction that had been going on at the Biblical Institute under Bea's successor, Rector
Ernst Vogt, entered the conflict with a number of articles,
destined to be widely distributed in off-print. He endeav-
ored tendentiously to show that the recent *monitum* had
been a rebuke to the Pontifical Biblical Institute.[35]

It is against the background of acrimonious polarization
within the Roman circle of biblical scholars closest to the
Holy See, near the outset of John's pontificate, that we must
understand the significance of an action three years later.
This was the rejection by nearly a two-thirds majority of
the Vatican Council of the schema on Scripture and tradition prepared by the preconciliar theological commission
presided over by Cardinal Ottaviani. Cardinal Bea, exegete
and ecumenist, outspoken opponent of the scholastic, not
to say manualistic, earlier schema to which his group had
been apparently permitted to contribute almost nothing, was
able, with his biblical confrères among the Fathers, to carry
the day in the Council, and this because he had never
alienated the more alert and responsible spokesmen of
biblical conservatism at the Lateran and elsewhere.[36] It is
against this background also that, in the lectures before us,

35 The most notable pieces were "Un documento notevolissimo [the
monitum] per l'esegesi cattolica," *Palestra del Clero*, no. 18, September
15, 1961, and *Razionalismo, esegesi cattolica e Magistero* (Rome,
1962).

36 In fact, with the biblical conservatives he has shared anxieties
about the dogmatic and perhaps constitutional implications of the New
Theology. Nevertheless, though by age, temperament, and professional
training and *specialization*, he is somewhat removed from the new
circle, he has, instinctively magnanimous, included a number of exponents of the New Theology among the bishops and especially the
consultores and the staff of his Secretariat.

we must understand Cardinal Bea's allusions to "the sources . . . common to us all, to Holy Scripture and its authentic development in the ancient tradition of the Church."[37]

The diplomatic phrasing of the lectures of Cardinal Bea in the present volume may well reflect a formulation in the revised schema entitled, not "On the (two) Sources of Revelation," but "On Divine Revelation," with an anticipated gesture to the sensibilities of the scholarly spokesmen of the classical Protestant principle of *sola Scriptura,* themselves now also much preoccupied with the significance of tradition in the light of their own form-critical methods in New Testament research.

III. REVELATION AND MAGISTERIUM

Primarily concerned as a scholar to establish the ancient, literal sense of Scripture, Cardinal Bea has, especially in the latest phase of his scholarly work, come close to his Protestant colleagues in the biblical field and helped level the terrain for an emerging ecumenical exegesis. At the same time Cardinal Bea has been able to carry his more conservative Catholic colleagues deep into the ecumenical dialogue because of his unequivocal reliance upon the authoritative *magisterium* in the harmonization of exegetical findings and dogmatic formulations. Clearly open to some fresh formulation of the relation of Scripture and tradition as aspects of the one divine revelation, Cardinal Bea in his Stillman Lectures broaches with restrained confidence the impending ecumenical task of facing, as he says, "head-on," the problem of Scripture and dogma, revelation and *magisterium.*

It is of interest that in his extensive bibliography the first work in which Professor Bea expressly took cognizance

---

[37] The further development of Cardinal Bea's thought is to be found in the mimeographed booklet *The Historicity of the Gospels* ([Rome], 1962) distributed to Council Fathers and their *periti* during the first session of the Council.

of the effect upon the ecumenical dialogue of new papal formulation within the tradition was in 1954, when he commented on the repercussions of *Munificentissimus Deus* (1950) with its definition of the dogma of the bodily Assumption of the Virgin.[38] It was quite characteristic of Professor Bea that he should have chosen to set forth his views on the possibly adverse effects of the infallible definition precisely in a Marian periodical. It was equally characteristic of him that, after carefully surveying Protestant reactions to the dogma, he should have chosen to interpret the widespread Protestant and Anglican agitation in a positive sense, as "truly noble and worthy of praise," precisely because it was a clear sign that the separated brethren "in all the Christian Churches" had come to feel profoundly involved in the doctrinal commitments of the Roman Catholic Church as a consequence of the ground swell of mutual, ecumenical concern. He then went on to note an increased appreciation and love of Mary in Protestantism and expressed the hope that the other churches might in due course recognize the legitimate role of the "living *magisterium* of the Church" in the "legitimate progress of dogma" "under the illumination of the Holy Spirit." He took heart also from the fact, once the Catholic Church had in *Munificentissimus Deus* and *Humani generis* rejected a "false irenicism" and a "disloyal palliation of differences," that Protestants soon resumed the dialogue with Catholics after having momentarily withdrawn in theological shock from the numerous and promising interconfessional exchanges that had been in progress, especially on the Continent, all during the preceding Nazi-seared decade.

Since the Cardinal has not chosen to go into any of the details of the relation among Scripture, tradition, and the

---

38 "La definizione dell'Assunta e i Protestanti," *Echi e Commenti della Proclamazione del Domma della Assunzione, Studia Mariana* 8:75–92 (1954).

papal-episcopal *magisterium* interpretative of the contemporary consensus,[39]—although we might expect him, as an ecumenist by his present vocation and as a harmonist by disposition, to be responsive to new trends in the consensus —we may appreciatively note his recurrent fondness for Luke 24:32: "Was not our heart burning within us, whilst he opened to us the Scriptures?" And we may refer specifically in his lectures to his serene confidence that all Christians who "read Scripture in prayerful meditation and incorporate its teaching . . . will not only be drawn closer to Christ, but also inevitably closer to one another . . . in reaching an *objective* interpretation of those texts which are presently the subject of divergent interpretation."[40]

IV. CHURCH AND UNIVERSITY

It was at the instigation of Pius XII that Professor Bea was at one period in his biblical career most concerned with establishing the literal sense of the Psalms. A critical edition of the Latin Psalter, translated afresh from the Hebrew text, was the corporate fruit of the Pontifical Biblical Institute under his rectorship.

[39] These relations are of intense local interest at the Harvard Divinity School because of the current work of two members of its faculty. Professor Heiko Oberman has incisively distinguished three meanings of tradition: (1) the ancient exegetical tradition, alone acceptable to *classical* Protestantism; (2) that connected with the two-source theory of revelation, canonized at the Council of Trent and now under review by some exponents of the New Theology; and (3) according to some, that called above the magisterially interpreted consensus: see "Quo Vadis, Petre?" *Harvard Divinity Bulletin* 26:1–25 (July 1962), reprinted in the *Scottish Journal of Theology* 16:225–265 (1963). See also Oberman, *The Harvest of Medieval Theology* (Cambridge, Mass., 1963), pp. 365–393. Professor Georges Florovsky, who under the auspices of the Faith and Order Commission of the World Council of Churches served as the vice-chairman of the American study commission on tradition and traditions (which reported at Montreal in July 1963), has stated his views summarily in "Scripture and Tradition: An Orthodox Point of View," *Dialog* 2:288 293 (Autumn, 1963), and more amply in "The Function of Tradition in the Ancient Church," *The Greek Orthodox Theological Review* 9:153–166 (1963/64).

[40] See page 37.

In the early spring of 1945, before the Nazi and Fascist armies had completely pulled back or had collapsed in Northern Italy, Pius XII in the Piazza of St. Peter's exhorted the throng to devote themselves to true repentance and to the work of Christian reconciliation among the nations. In this Lenten allocution[41] he cited the psalm for the day, 94:7-9 (R.S.V. 95:7-9): *"Oh, that you may hear God's voice this day*: 'Harden not your hearts as in the wilderness, where your fathers tempted me . . . although they had seen my works.' "* For those in the throng who had ears to hear, the Pope was already using the Latin version of the Psalm from the new, critically edited Latin Psalter which would not be promulgated for adoption in the liturgy and in the breviary until the following Palm Sunday. Father Bea, confessor of Pius XII and sometime *consultor* of both the Biblical Commission and the Congregation of Rites, had long pressed hard for textual accuracy even when this meant alterations in the sonorities of traditional liturgical formularies. In this instance the ancient text spoke with enhanced urgency.

Cardinal Bea, the scholar, is today the leading Catholic symbol of the importance of biblical scholarship, in particular, and of theological and scientific-humanistic learning, in general, in the present stage of ecumenical interchange and in the common Christian encounter with the world of conscientious but unbelieving scholarship. It was as a scholar, as a teacher, and as builder of several Jesuit schools around the world that Father Bea became one of the advisors of Pope Pius XI in the drafting of the papal constitution on higher education, *Deus scientiarum Dominus* (1931). Significantly, therefore, after being much later

---

[41] "Nella trepida attesa di una cristiana riconciliazione dei popoli," March 18, 1945; *Discorsi e Radiomessaggi di Sua Santità Pio XII* 7:11-18, esp. p. 13 (Vatican City, 1945-1946). The occasion was the conclusion of an exceptional and popular course on the inner mission in Rome, instigated by the Pope.

placed by John XXIII in charge of the representatives of the non-Roman churches at the Council, Cardinal Bea found that by far the majority of the observers were drawn from the ranks of scholarly churchmen. To theological scholarship has clearly been assigned, as Cardinal Bea rightly points out, an ecumenical role.[42]

It will not, therefore, go unnoticed by the future chroniclers of the development of Christendom in our age that major New World responses to the Second Vatican Council should have taken the form of an ecumenically-motivated centenary convocation at Boston College and of the four-day Stillman Colloquium in our venerable seat of Puritan learning. Under the presidency of one whose services as an ecumenical churchman are known world-wide, Harvard University has, as it were, momentarily repossessed an important role once discharged by the medieval university, providing the reasonable context in which we may corporately think through some of the moral, political, and theological issues of the day. Not that the university enters directly upon the realm of faith nor that professors presume to discharge the office of priests, but our university has in a notable endeavor been able to foster the dialogue among scholars of good will, standing in disparate but, as we hope, reconverging traditions.

We in Harvard University on the Protestant side would like to believe that our academic forebears who once sought to *reform* the *Reformation* in a new Cambridge in a New England will have looked down upon our proceedings without misapprehension, as also those more recent founders of our theological faculty, who sought to establish within the university a nonsectarian School of Divinity, however much we have *reconceived* the instrumentality of their larger purpose. Indeed, we trust that Increase Mather and William Channing, now even better informed, can join us

[42] See pages 32–38.

in saluting Augustin Cardinal Bea on the occasion of the publication of his Stillman Lectures. For they, too, would heed the warning of Psalm 95: "Harden not your hearts as . . . in the wilderness, where your fathers tempted me . . . although they had seen my works."

Many of us, as we first heeded the heartening words carefully shaped on the lips of a revered scholar and beloved prince of his Church, listening to his words each night in the favoring presence of the Cardinal Archbishop of Boston, perceived that we of this ancient academic community, dedicated to the preservation and the clarification of the *Veritas* which sets men free, had *personally,* and with a sense of solemn joy, entered now upon a new age of the Church.

George H. Williams
Harvard Divinity School
December 1963

THE LECTURES

THE ACADEMIC PURSUITS
AND CHRISTIAN UNITY

AUGUSTIN CARDINAL BEA

Distinguished Gentlemen:

Allow me, first of all, to express my sincere appreciation and deep joy for being able today to address such a select audience, here at Harvard University, on the theme of Christian Unity. My joy is still greater because I regard my lectures here as somehow representative of the many others that have been asked of me, but which I could not deliver because of the pressing demands of the Second Vatican Council. I do not think I am wrong in saying that this event—especially as your invitation is not the only one which I received—would have been inconceivable only a few years ago. This authentic Christian openness and readiness to listen to one another surely bears witness to the fruits of the working of God's Spirit among those who bear the name of Christ. This event is therefore one more encouragement to persevere and to advance further along that path to unity which has already been taken.

In addressing you may I make my own the words of the Apostle to the Gentiles, who writes to the Romans: "For I long to see you, that I may impart some spiritual grace unto you to strengthen you; that is, that among you I may be comforted together with you by that faith which is common to us both, your faith and mine" (Rom. 1:11–12). On this privileged occasion, we are conscious of the gigantic task, common to us all, of fostering unity among all who believe in Christ; at the same time, we respect the proper aims of a theological faculty. Thus, we want to consider specific ways in which we can correspond in our daily work to the profound desire of the Divine Saviour "that they all may be one" (John 17:21).

What is, then, the very object of this lecture, this exchange of a spiritual gift, this opportunity of a mutual strengthening? No doubt you would like to have first-hand impressions and news about the Second Vatican Council and its progress to date, and especially what are the ecumenical concerns of the Council and what we expect the Council Fathers to decide on ecumenical questions. But as I shall deal in detail with this subject in two other lectures, it seems more appropriate here to look even beyond the Council. Pope John XXIII has had such foresight, for in a recent audience with him he outlined for me several of his plans for the period after the Council.

But this looking beyond the Council has still a more profound reason. Today everyone knows that the Council is not meant to be a Council of reunion; that is, it does not aim to negotiate or draw up final reunion plans with one or more Christian communities. Rather, the Council intends, in its own way, to prepare the way for an eventual reunion; it is long-range planning.

In this long-term perspective the Council has already surprised all of us. Nobody could have imagined that already in the Council there would be that widespread and intense ecumenical attitude and concern that we all witnessed. This surprising fact was above all influenced by the presence of the delegated observers from so many non-Catholic communities. We have every reason to take for granted that this atmosphere will still remain. We can even hope that this genuine spirit will grow more intense, especially if there be present more delegated observers from the venerable Orthodox churches of the East.

The Council also will definitely give its position on

various important unity questions: for example, the problem of what is the Church and what is her proper unity; the doctrinal foundation and general pastoral direction for her ecumenical work; and the problem of religious liberty. The Council will also treat many practical questions, for example, the pastoral handling of mixed marriages.

But, in spite of all these encouraging signs within the Council, the truly largest and hardest work toward unity itself can be done only after the Council, a work built upon the wide basis provided by the Council itself. This is the reason we must ask ourselves: What can we do for unity in our day-by-day activities as scholars and teachers? Concretely, what bearing have scientific research and university training upon the urgent and delicate task of promoting Christian Unity?[1]

1. First of all, may I urge that we become more conscious that our day-by-day work *does* have a profound and *basic importance* for the ecumenical movement. Without exaggeration one can say that scientific research and university training exercise a decisive and leading function in forming *spiritual attitudes* for ecumenical work. By this exacting activity nearly all the attitudes, outlooks, and convictions for the work of unity are carefully worked out and handed on to others. Ecumenical work rests on this foundation; it lives on it, is nourished by it, and is orientated by it. Moreover, by the same activity all those are formed and trained who in the future will exercise the same spiritual function. Thus, one can say, without hesitation, that as far as God's design for Christian unity depends upon human cooperation—and no doubt it depends much upon it—the ecumenical movement will be, or will not be, well orientated

[1] For more details about this important and interesting topic see Augustin Cardinal Bea, *The Unity of Christians,* ed. Bernard Leeming, S.J. (New York, 1963), pp. 94–110.

to the degree that persevering scholars have convincingly proved its meaning and intentions, its urgency, and its proper methods in work and deed.

2. In order to be able to offer our contribution to the noble cause of Christian unity, we ourselves must first possess an authentic ecumenical *attitude* and let it penetrate and direct our whole teaching and research.

a) What more precisely, then, do we mean by this ecumenical attitude? It consists simply in the fact that we seriously accept the New Testament teaching of baptism and its consequences. Each baptism, validly conferred, makes one a member of the Mystical Body of Christ. It therefore effects an organic union with Christ and an intimate relationship with all the other baptized. As children of God and brothers in Christ, all the baptized form the one, unique Family of God and therefore should try to come to an ever increasing family unity. The degree of unity that is to be reached is nothing less than the unity of the Father and Son in the Blessed Trinity: "That they may be one, *as thou, Father, in me, and I in thee*" (John 17:21); it is the unity in believing and loving, the unity in living and acting. As Christ asked of his disciples, "You therefore are to be perfect as your heavenly Father is perfect" (Mt. 5:48), so Christ also prayerfully implored the Father to give to the disciples, during the time when Christ would no longer be visibly among them, that gift of perfect unity, which should be an image of the unity of the Son with the Father.

In what does this unity concretely consist? Today, it is being more and more asserted, even by non-Catholic Christians, that the perfect unity of all Christians consists not only in the invisible union of faith and love, but also in the external profession and witness of the same faith, in the use of the same sacraments, and at least somehow in the direction of the same Church ministry and order. We need refer only to the resolution submitted by the Faith and

Order Commission to the Third General Assembly of the World Council of Churches at New Delhi in November 1961, and accepted by the same Assembly.[2]

But how far, how very far is Christianity today from such a unity! The present torn and tattered condition is necessarily for everyone who loves Christ a painful sting, an open wound that goes on bleeding and hurting. Such pain produces a strong desire and a firm resolution to do and to suffer everything in union with Christ the High Priest to bring relief, to heal this wound little by little. The Spirit of God has given a special grace to the Christians of our time in letting us experience intensively and vividly the scandal of wounding separation and the urgency of the healing work for unity.

b) Whoever possesses this ecumenical mentality puts it into practice in his scientific research and university training. He has a constant vision of the whole of Christianity in the whole world and in all confessions, and shapes his work according to this vision. He respects everyone, listens to all, and considers their problems as his own. From such consideration of all those who are baptized in Christ or who at least believe in him, we become more and more conscious of the problems presented by the wounded condition of a divided Christianity. The spirit, then, which should animate ecumenical efforts is characterized by the well-known norm of St. Paul, in fact written in connection with

---

[2] "We believe that the unity which is both God's will and his gift to his church is being made visible as all in each place who are baptized into Jesus Christ and confess him as Lord and Saviour are brought by the Holy Spirit into one fully committed fellowship, holding the one apostolic faith, preaching the one Gospel, breaking the one bread, joining in common prayer, and having a corporate life reaching out in witness and service to all, and who at the same time are united with the whole Christian fellowship in all places and all ages in such wise that ministry and members are accepted by all, and that all can act and speak together as occasion requires for the tasks to which God calls his people." This is paragraph 2 of the report of the Section on Unity, *The New Delhi Report* (New York, 1962), p. 116.

the idea of Church unity: "practicing the truth in love" (Eph. 4:15). The truth in charity! Truth and charity must be ever present in our ecumenical work hand-in-hand, because truth without charity is intolerant and repulsive, and charity without truth is blind and will not endure.

3. What specifically can we do in certain areas of research, once we possess this ecumenical attitude and are animated by a spirit of absolute fidelity to the laws of truth and the demands of charity?

a) We have, first of all, exactly to determine and to work out what the different confessions have *in common*. Often we shy away from this inquiry and from the exposition of the common Christian patrimony, in the fear that it *necessarily* means concealing or glossing over our differences. Such is not the case. Speaking for himself, Pope John XXIII recently said that he always preferred to emphasize that which tends to unite men, and to accompany every man as far along his way as he can without betraying the demands of justice and truth.[3] Besides, it is a well-known principle of method that in obscure questions one starts from what is clear, advancing step by step into the obscure. In the same way, the exact discovery of the Christian goods we have in common is a help in distinguishing clearly the differences, in seeing them in the right light and proportion and also in gradually overcoming them. Moreover, the establishment of what we have in common will make us rejoice in what we already share, and this joy helps to increase our mutual appreciation and fraternal love. And love will drive us to come always closer and closer to each other. Finally, a firmly established Christian heritage forms the basis for cooperation in the very appreciation, exercise, and witnessing of goods common to several Christian communities and confessions. This cooperation will not only bring

---

[3] Words of greeting to a "Pax Christi" Movement Pilgrimage, July 26, 1961, as reported in *L'Osservatore Romano*, July 27, 1961, p. 1.

about concrete results; it will also effect in all those who so cooperate a further coming together in ways of thinking and in love, with the consequence that gradually they will begin to understand one another in many other points.

b) On the other hand, an authentic love for the truth demands that our differences are not concealed or glossed over, but that they are boldly ascertained and clearly stated. Nevertheless, a love for the truth refuses to rest contentedly with this clear delineation of differences; rather it tries to overcome the differences. Indeed, it is here that the difficulty lies. It stands to reason that overcoming the differences is not a search for compromises. Faith must not be confused with politics. Charity without truth will flicker but briefly. Love for the truth, the absolutely unbroken love for the truth is for all of us simply fidelity to Christ and to his Church. The Church is not the controller, the master of the truth, but its minister, its servant. She preaches the truth she has received from Christ, explains it, keeps it undefiled. If this be so, can every endeavor to overcome our differences be unquestionably doomed to failure?

Experience proves the opposite. The theological dialogues that have been going on for some time, for example, in Belgium, France, Switzerland, Germany, and more recently also in Great Britain, Canada, and the United States, have shown that it is possible, with much patience on both parts, and in serene objective discussions, to come to a greater understanding and deeper esteem of each other. The problem we face together is this: to go back with an open mind, and to investigate calmly the sources that are common to us all, to Holy Scripture and its authentic development in the ancient tradition of the Church.

I mention but one example for this coming nearer. From the Protestant side today mention is often made of a "rediscovery of the Church." A ministry is demanded that clarifies and obliges our profession of faith. Whereas some time ago (and still somewhat today) many Protestant theologians were willing to accept only an *invisible* Church and with it only an *invisible* unity, the Faith and Order Commission of the World Council of Churches, in the resolution already mentioned, has enumerated a number of signs by which the unity of the Church appears visible, for example, the profession of the same faith and the use of the same sacraments.[4]

c) How are these theological advancements possible without betraying the truth? They are possible because in these differences which are found among the confessions, the points in question are often due to a *lack of understanding*, to ignorance and misconceptions on both sides. How often and how long, for example, has papal infallibility been understood—yes, even by Catholic theologians—as though the Pope could pronounce nothing but the truth in any of his words and make no mistake in any of his judgments. Sometimes it was even thought that the Pope is freed from human weaknesses and cannot sin, instead of the true Catholic position: the Pope pronounces unerring judgments in a few very clearly circumscribed, divinely protected cases.

In other cases of misunderstanding, we find the cause in the *shifting accentuations* or in the all-too-exclusive stress on one aspect of the Christian mystery, forgetting or even denying the other aspects. An excellent example is the doctrine of the Church. Because the Protestants of the sixteenth century disavowed the social and hierarchical structure of the Church, the Council of Trent felt obliged to clarify this proper dimension, with the consequence that later many Catholic theologians became quite suspicious and wary about any accentuation on the mystical-spiritual

---

4 This part of the resolution may be found in the *Ecumenical Review* 14:299 (1962). For many other examples of the drawing nearer of different points of view, see "The Council and Christian Unity," in *The Unity of Christians*, pp. 111–128.

aspect of the Church. They imagined that such accentuation would signify a denial of the visible social-hierarchical structure of the Church. Only our own times have seen the delicate work of forming a profound synthesis of both aspects—in the extraordinary encyclical of Pope Pius XII on the Mystical Body. And now we are looking forward to the second period of the Council, when we hope the Council Fathers will deepen this synthesis and proclaim it clearly and warmly to us.

As in this example from ecclesiology, so there are on the whole many explanations or *formulations* of the councils that are bound to their own times and have to be explained in their contemporary setting. The council formulas often highlight that aspect of reality which was in discussion at a specific time and needed a special answer. The above-mentioned example of the doctrine of the Church shows how carefully such formulations have to be understood and how they may not be considered to exhaust the whole of reality. Otherwise, there is danger that the aspect *not* mentioned in a council declaration may be ignored or even denied. The Church can never exhaust the truth entrusted to her, wrote Pius XII in his encyclical *Humani generis.*[5]

Another source of difficulty and misunderstanding among Christians is the language which is used. In his opening address to the Council, Pope John stated that the truth, of which the Church is the custodian and servant, must be proclaimed to the world by means of the literary forms of modern thought, the only forms which the modern world understands. The substance of the doctrine is one thing, the Holy Father said; the manner in which it is expressed is another. Fidelity to the precision of doctrine is not compromised by the use of contemporary terminology which is understood and accepted by the common people.[6] Many

---

[5] *Acta Apostolicae Sedis* 42:568 (1950).
[6] *Ibid.*, 54:792 (1962).

of the disagreements within the Christian family today are traceable to differences of terminology. In every age, philosophical systems express the thoughts and mentality of the men of that age, equally as much as they contribute to the formation of that thought. Similarly, the theology of any given age, as well as the way in which that theology is expressed, is bound to be influenced by such systems. And this is all the more true when a theology has no strong linkage with an established tradition. With this in mind it is easy to see how Catholic and non-Catholic theology have developed along divergent lines through the centuries.

Is there nothing which can be done about this? Surely much can be done, provided only that both sides exercise Christian charity and patience. We must trace the history of human thought and its development. We must seek out its origin, inquire into the circumstances from which it came and the influences to which it was exposed as it made its way to us. In this way we shall be able to face head-on the problem of the conformity of theological truths with Holy Scripture and tradition, and determine the meaning of these several truths as understood here and now.

Such a theological undertaking will surely bear abundant fruit; theological dialogues among experts of different confessions will undoubtedly yield good results. The way will be long and hard, but the spirit of Christ and his grace are omnipotent and can smooth the way and shorten the time.

4. Perhaps an example will bring out more clearly the ecumenical possibilities of this kind which are present in our work.[7]

a) Great strides are being made in the field of Church history by men who are guided by the motto "truth in charity." Scholars are clearing away the many misunderstandings and prejudices which led to and continued the

[7] For more detailed explanation of such examples, see *The Unity of Christians*, pp. 96–104.

separation of Eastern and Western Christendom and later of the Christian family of the West. There remains, however, much to be done in this field. It will require patient and persevering work, and it will not be completed until the results of this scientific work have penetrated to the level of school books and other scholarly publications, bringing the truth to the hearts and the minds of the Christian people.

b) Another example of this type of progress lies in the biblical sciences, especially biblical theology. We are happy to note the significant progress which has been made in the past twenty-five years. Again, however, there remains much to be done. Holy Scripture is the common ground of all Christians. If all who believe in Christ will read Scripture in prayerful meditation and incorporate its teaching into their lives, they will not only be drawn closer to Christ, but inevitably closer to one another. This penetration into the spirit of Christ which brings together human hearts and minds will aid us enormously in reaching objective interpretation of those texts which are presently the subject of divergent interpretations.

The principles which we have been discussing are particularly applicable in the field of the history of dogma and of what is called systematic or dogmatic theology.

c) The history of dogma investigates the origin of theological ideas, the pronouncements of Church councils, and the characteristics of the times in which they were conceived, as well as the concrete problems which they tried to answer. It indicates the particular areas of revealed truth which a given age emphasized. These particular areas are then worked out clearly by systematic theology which places them in the framework of the fullness of revealed truth, and in this way sheds further light upon them.

These theological sciences, furthermore, must always remain receptive to the different voices of Christians from other confessions, listening with attention and sympathy to their problems and interests, and taking into account further aspects of revealed truth which they consider important.

d) A few more examples from the field of canon law. His Eminence Cardinal Ottaviani, Secretary of the Vatican's Holy Office, has said: "When truth has once been acknowledged, that truth to which the Church cannot make any concessions, all those who want to unite with her will find her as the Mother, disposed to grant whatever she can on the liturgical, traditional, disciplinary and purely human levels."[8] We see immediately what scholarly work is needed to apply this principle. To take this position presupposes that, with the exception of an occasional dogmatic norm, the vast body of ecclesiastical law has been formulated on the basis of concrete situations and necessities, and these laws are by no means to be considered as absolute. A collection of scholarly theses on disciplinary measures of the councils—for example, the penitential practices of different times, surveys of the varieties of matrimonial law, or administrative organization—would permit us to demonstrate how juridical decisions are tied to historical circumstances. The professor of canon law should never cease to point out how the demands of pastoral care are the reason for many juridical directives. Since the same directive of the past may lead to quite different results in different times, the scholar should study how and what legislation should change today in fidelity to the principle of all canon law: *salus animarum,* the care of souls.

In conclusion, I hope these reflections—so brief in the short time at our disposal—have shown that our scientific research and university training definitely offer rich and varied possibilities for the work of Christian unity. But these same reflections also have revealed the many difficulties lying on this way, so many indeed that it will take a

[8] Quoted in *La Civiltà Cattolica,* October 7, 1961, p. 78.

long time to overcome them; such undertakings require much patience and perseverance. It would not be good to delude ourselves on this matter. But it would be worse to give in to discouragement and to resign.

The unity of all the baptized is the will of God, as it also was the object of Christ's unceasing, pleading prayer to the Father on the eve of his death on the Cross. We shall collaborate with all our strength and talents to fulfil his will, but we may not forget what St. Paul wrote to the Corinthians about this apostolic work: "I have planted, Apollos watered, but *God has given the growth* . . . we are God's helpers" (1 Cor. 3:6,9).

The success, the increase, the fruits of our labor for Christian unity is God's concern. But God is omnipotent. Recall the Lord's reply to an objection of the frightened disciples: "With men this is impossible; but with God all things are possible" (Matt. 19:26). So, confidently and fearlessly, in love, prayer, and action, we go the way that leads to the unity of all those who are baptized in Christ, mindful of St. Paul's word: "For it is God who of his good pleasure works in you both the will and the performance" (Phil. 2:13).

THE SECOND VATICAN COUNCIL AND NON-CATHOLIC CHRISTIANS: PREPARATION AND THE WORK IN THE FIRST PERIOD

AUGUSTIN CARDINAL BEA

I AM VERY pleased, indeed, to have been invited to speak at Harvard in the interval between the first and second session of the Second Vatican Council. The reasons for my pleasure are many. Foremost is the esteem which this university enjoys, not only in America but abroad as well. I need not dwell on this. My personal experience during many years as an exegete and professor of archaeology made me aware how often Harvard was credited with outstanding achievements in both these sciences and especially in archaeology. Why, quite recently the university has participated in excavating the cult site of Abraham and of Jacob at Shechem. The prestige of the university, therefore, imparts special significance to this invitation which will not go unnoticed in the international scientific world.

But the opportunity to speak here gives me another reason for joy. Apart from yesterday's address to the university, today is the first time that I have had the opportunity to address a non-Catholic secular institution on the Council and Christian Unity. I, therefore, welcome this opportunity to enter into direct contact with very many of my Christian brethren and to speak to them sincerely, lovingly, and frankly, as Christians should. My thanks go, therefore, first and foremost to the authorities of the university for having afforded me this opportunity.

My subject, of course, can only be that event which more than any other has fascinated and moved Catholics and non-Catholics in recent months: the Council. In its review of the year nineteen hundred and sixty-two, *The Christian Century* said of the Council: "It was the year's only religious event which can be compared with the other big events of the same year."[1] The Executive Secretary of the World Council of Churches in the United States, Dr. Roswell P. Barnes, agreed with this judgment when he said: "The most notable extension of interest in unity was demonstrated in the attendance of Protestant and Orthodox observers at the Second Vatican Council."[2] Indeed, no one can deny that the Council is a great religious event not only in itself but also when seen from the viewpoint of the ecumenical movement. Each of its plenary sessions was attended not only by the more than two thousand conciliar bishops, but by some forty non-Catholic observers as well. These came from every corner of the globe and represented almost all the religious denominations that stemmed from the Reformation. In addition, a goodly number of the ancient churches of the East who do not belong to the Orthodox Church sent representatives. The Orthodox Church itself was represented by observers from the Moscow Patriarchate, and from the Russian Church outside the Soviet Union. The observers belonged to eight great World Alliances of the Protestant Churches, the Anglican Communion, six Oriental Churches and the Utrecht Union of Old Catholics. Today the presence of non-Catholic observers at the Council has begun to appear to many as something almost self-evident. Yet, if one reflects on the reserve with which the first announcement of the Council was received, he will see that we have traveled a long and difficult path to reach the present satisfactory result. But this result, I must say,

[1] December 26, 1962, p. 1576.
[2] *Ecumenical Press Service* (Geneva), January 12, 1963, p. 1.

is only the beginning of another long and laborious journey which lies before us. Yet it is a significant and happy beginning, one full of promise for the future.

It is now about four years since Pope John first announced the Council in the Basilica of St. Paul's in Rome. This is a sufficient lapse of time to permit us to look back and assess all that has happened in the interval. I do not look back complacently to marvel at our own accomplishments. For we are really talking about the gifts of the infinite mercy of God and the effects of the wonderful and irresistible influence of Christ and his spirit in the Church. In so far as human cooperation was associated with the influence of Christ, we must gratefully recognize that the success obtained up to now is due to many many prayers and to the sacrifices of generations of faithful Christians. It is above all the fruit of the manifold, silent and hidden sufferings of Christians throughout the world, especially during the terrible years of World War II. We can fittingly apply to ourselves what Christ said long ago to his disciples: "I have sent you to reap a harvest for which you have not toiled. Others toiled and you have come in for the harvest of their toil" (John 4:38).

The meaning and purpose of this survey of recent developments is, therefore, to thank the Father of Lights and the Lord of the Church for what he has given us and to strengthen our confidence in his goodness and mercy. Thus we will go forward to work for the unity of all those baptized in Christ with an unlimited faith which moves mountains. But this survey will also permit us to hearken to the still but unmistakable voice of the Lord of the Church speaking to us through the events of recent times, and thus obediently subject our work to his will.

To facilitate our examination we will divide our report into three parts. The first part will deal with the events between the public announcement of the Council and the establishment of the various preparatory commissions (among them, the Secretariat for Promoting Christian Unity). This lasted about a year and a half, from January 25, 1959, until the end of May 1960. The characteristic note of this first stage was the misunderstanding about the ecumenicity of the Council which arose at the moment of the proclamation, and the disappointment which was caused when this misunderstanding was cleared up.

I

In his announcement of the Council, the Pope spoke of an "ecumenical council" and explained that it should be considered as an invitation to all Christians who were separated from the Apostolic See to seek even more eagerly than before that unity for which Christ prayed on the eve of his sufferings.[3] Now the term "ecumenical" has been used for the last fifty years to signify that which is common to all Christians. This meaning derived from recent usage caused many to think that the Pope had in prospect a council to which representatives of all the Christian denominations would come in order to discuss the question of unity. But the Pope did not intend to use the word "ecumenical" in this sense. He gave it the meaning which it had for many hundreds of years in the terminology of Catholic canon law, namely: a council to which all the bishops of the *oikumene* (the whole world) who were in communion with the See of Peter were invited.[4] The Pope, therefore, was not thinking of a reunion council such as the Council of Lyons in 1274 and that of Ferrara-Florence in 1438–1442 had been. Indeed, such a council, given the present-

---

[3] See *Acta Apostolicae Sedis* 51:68 (1959); the same document also appears in *Acta et documenta Concilio Oecumenico Vaticano II apparando,* series 1 (Città del Vaticano, 1960), I, 5ff.

[4] See *Codex Juris Canonici,* canon 222f. See also *The Unity of Christians,* ed. Bernard Leeming, S.J. (New York, 1963), p. 129.

day condition of the various denominations, would be a utopian idea, as anyone with even a superficial acquaintance with the situation regretfully realizes. For though much has been accomplished on both sides of the "Great Divide," a sufficient spiritual preparation has not yet been achieved and an attempt to call a reunion council at this time would do more harm than good. In addition, the Pope could hardly summon an assembly of all the Christian churches before treating with them beforehand.

In the period following the announcement of the Council, therefore, the Pope insisted again and again that it would serve the purpose of Christian unity only indirectly, in so far as it would offer a precious picture of the truth, unity, and love which reigned in the Catholic Church, and thus spur on all Christians who are separated from the See of Peter to strive even more than heretofore for the unity which Christ intended his Church to have.[5] But, as is wont to happen when hopes are dashed, the Holy Father's clarification left a bitter taste in the mouths of many non-Catholics. This initial misunderstanding certainly did not improve relations between the Catholics and the other Christians. In fact, during this period of disillusionment the opinion was often expressed that the Council was really an internal Catholic affair which was of no interest to non-Catholics. So the situation immediately following the announcement of the Council was anything but encouraging. But the "miracles" which the Lord worked afterward against this dark background were all the more remarkable.

We must also note with joy that even during this unpleasant period a number of highly respected non-Catholic leaders had the breadth of vision which allowed them to

---

[5] See *Discorso . . . coprare del volume Unione*, p. 113, nota 8 in basso; see also *Encyclica Ad Petri Cathedram*, June 29, 1959, in *Acta Apostolicae Sedis* 51:511 (1959).

speak Christian words of love and solidarity. In this vein, the Archbishop of Canterbury and Primate of All England said: "The present Pope possesses, it seems to me, much Christian good will and great charity. Wherever charity is present no one can reckon the results."[6] And, as if he had foreseen the developments to come here in America, Bishop Pardue of the Protestant Episcopal Church in Pittsburgh, wrote a pastoral letter on the subject of unity and Pope John, in which he declared that he had high hopes about what the Council would do in this regard. The Central Committee of the World Council of Churches stated during its meeting in Rhodes in August, 1959: "that the leaders of the ecumenical movement cannot remain indifferent to such an event as the council. For it cannot fail to have important consequence for mutual relations between the Churches." On this account, the same Central Committee requested that prayers be offered for the Council so that it might serve for the mutual *rapprochement* of the Christian communities.[7] Leaders of various churches similarly requested prayers.

Even if some rays of light were present, in this first stage, the situation taken as a whole was quite dark and unpredictable. However, during the second stage things became much brighter.

II

The second stage of pre-Council developments lasted from the time when the Secretariat for Christian Unity was founded until the inauguration of the Council itself. This was from June 1960 until the beginning of October 1962. This stage is marked by a hectic course of events which improved very quickly the climate between the vari-

[6] Quoted by B. Sketchley, "Le Concile oecumenique et les Anglicans," in *Unitas* (Paris), 13:298 (1960).
[7] *The Ecumenical Review* 12:60 (1959–1960).

ous denominations and made possible the sending of non-Catholic observers to the Council.

The founding of the Secretariat for the Promotion of Christian Unity on Pentecost, June 5, 1960, was one of the most important of these events. It was a magnanimous and courageous gesture on the part of the Pope to add this Secretariat to the number of preparatory commissions instituted the same day. It was meant to be, as the Pope expressly stated, a sign of his love and his good will toward all his non-Catholic brethren. It was also meant, he added, to help them to follow more easily the events of the Council.[8] The founding of this Secretariat was warmly welcomed by non-Catholic opinion where it was seen as proffering valuable cooperation in the task of bringing the idea of unity to realization. The Executive Committee of the World Council of Churches explicitly stated this at the meeting of the Central Committee at St. Andrews in Scotland in 1960, shortly after the establishment of the Secretariat: "We warmly welcome the fact that a dialogue with the Roman Catholic Church is now possible. The opportunity to discuss matters together must be seized." The Committee added that the World Council of Churches would avail itself of this opportunity to bring certain fundamental convictions already proposed either by the General Assembly or the Executive Committee to the attention of the Secretariat: for example, their ideas on religious liberty, on Christian social action, etc.[9]

Through the establishment of the Secretariat the Holy Father's interest in the question of unity and in the ecumenical movement received concrete, tangible expression. As an immediate result, from that point onward interest in Christian unity spread ever more and more widely in both

8 "Motu proprio 'Superno Dei nutu,' " no. 9, in *Acta Apostolicae Sedis* 52:436 (1960).
9 *The Ecumenical Review* 13:46 (1960).

Catholic and non-Catholic circles. I could say much on this subject. It may be enough, however, to refer to the large number of requests for lectures, articles, press-radio-and-television interviews with which I, as president of the Secretariat, was deluged. Just to give you an idea of this, let me tell you that I was able to give over twenty-five lectures in six different countries, while in the year 1962 alone I gave twenty-five interviews. Nevertheless, I was far from satisfying all the requests which came in! These lectures and interviews were published in Italian six months ago. An English edition is shortly to appear, and in the next months they will appear in six other languages![10] This is surely a sign of a great and widespread interest in the question of unity.

The establishment of the Secretariat was taken as a pledge of good will and desire for accommodation on the part of the Catholic Church; it called forth reciprocal action from non-Catholics. Many of these initiatives were truly surprising. The most important, of course, were the well-known visits of highly placed non-Catholic personalities to Pope John. I shall mention here only the first and the most important of these: the visit of Dr. Geoffrey Fisher, Archbishop of Canterbury and Primate of the Church of England in December 1960. In November of the following year, another personality visited His Holiness, the Presiding Bishop of the Protestant Episcopal Church of the United States, Dr. Arthur Lichtenberger. In December 1961 His Holiness received Dr. Joseph H. Jackson, President of the National Baptist Convention of the United States. Last of all, in April 1962, Dr. Archibald Craig, Moderator of the General Assembly of the Church of Scotland, visited Pope John.

Yet all the initiatives did not come from one side. In November 1961 official Catholic observers attended the

---

[10] *The Unity of Christians.*

General Assembly of the World Council of Churches at New Delhi. Later, two other Catholic observers were present at the Paris meeting of the Central Committee of the same World Council. As President of the Secretariat, I met many important persons outside Rome—apart from my numerous contacts with the important personalities who had come to the Eternal City. Thus I met many Reformed and Orthodox leaders on the occasion of a lecture in Paris in January 1962. In April of the same year I met Dr. Otto Dibelius, the Bishop of Berlin-Brandenburg, and Dr. Kurt Scharf, President of the German Evangelical Church Conference. Last October I had conversations with Bishop Fred Pierre Corson, President of the World Methodist Council. But of all these meetings I must single out the courtesy visit which it was my privilege to pay Dr. Michael Ramsey in Lambeth Palace, London. This was our way of returning the compliment paid to the Catholic Church by the visit of his predecessor, Dr. Geoffrey Fisher, in Rome.

It is clear that these and similar meetings could not at one stroke remove all the obstacles that lay on the path to unity. But you will understand immediately that these contacts and conversations helped enormously to arouse non-Catholic interest in the coming Council. It also stirred the desire among them to be represented in some measure at the Council by the presence of their own official observers.

The official document by which the Council was convoked appeared on Christmas 1961. It contained two points of interest for the ecumenical movement. Firstly, it explicitly stated that it was within the competence of the Council to review the complex of doctrinal and practical questions which had a bearing on Church unity.[11] Among these were numbered the language of the liturgy, mixed marriages, re-

---

[11] See the bull *Humanae salutis,* of December 25, 1961, in *Acta Apostolicae Sedis* 54:12 (1962).

ligious freedom, the nature of the Church, and other similar questions.

Secondly, the document entrusted to the Secretariat for Unity the task of establishing relations also with the non-Catholic churches of the East. As a consequence, our efforts to bring non-Catholic observers to the Council took on greater dimensions. These contacts formed the chief activity of the Secretariat once the preparation of the doctrinal and practical proposals for the Council deliberations had been completed. We can, therefore, turn now to consider the third stage, the ecumenical aspect of the Council itself.

III

This is not the place to sketch the inner events of the Council which had no direct bearing on the ecumenical movement. This has been already sufficiently reported by the press, radio, and television. We pass over also the personal impressions of individual observers who shared in those experiences. It would hardly be tactful to mention in public what we learned from the observers in our frequent personal meetings with them. They themselves have the right to publish or not to publish their reactions. However, I must underline the deep impression made by the presence of these non-Catholic Christian observers at the Council.

The majority of the observers publicly declared that the audience they had with the Holy Father made a deep impression on them because of the Pope's simplicity and kindness. On the other hand, Pope John made it clear in his conversation with the observers that the sight of this group at the opening ceremony of the Council in St. Peter's was a source of encouragement and consolation to himself. He then added: "For the moment, let us be content with what we have done. It is sufficient that we have achieved so much. Perhaps you can see into my heart. If so, you can read and understand there much more than my words themselves express."[12] Permit me to mention here my own reaction: while talking immediately after the audience with some of the Catholics present, I found myself saying: "This is a miracle, a genuine miracle!" I was thinking not merely of the audience but of all the events of that memorable day.

Let us leave these impressions aside and concentrate on the facts which are significant for the problem of unity. The first of these facts is undoubtedly the common prayer which Christians of all persuasions offered for the Council. The Ecumenical Press Service of Geneva was able to announce on October 12: "Christians around the World, Orthodox, Anglicans, and Protestants—as well as Roman Catholics, are praying that the second Vatican Council which opened in Rome on Thursday may advance the cause of Christian unity. Prayers are being offered in response to appeals by leaders of Churches, and national and international bodies."[13] One week later the same press service added: "The number of non-Roman Catholics praying for the Vatican Council continues to grow."[14] Two weeks before this, Lord Fisher of Lambeth stated in San Francisco's Grace Cathedral: "All over the world, people of every church will be praying, as we pray here, for the Second Vatican Council of the Church of Rome as it begins its labours." During his sermon, the Archbishop said: "No council of the Church of Rome has ever met, so surrounded by the prayers of other churches. Prayers in no sense against them, but for them and with them." It is truly surprising and stirring to read and reflect upon the expressions and formulas used in these appeals. One example will be cited: The Old Catholic bishop, Dr. Urs Küry of Bern, Switzerland, said: "Let us unite ourselves with the whole of Christendom in sincere

[12] *Ecumenical Press Service,* October 19, 1962, pp. 26–27.
[13] *Ibid.,* October 12, 1962, p. 6.
[14] *Ibid.,* October 19, 1962, p. 3.

prayer for the important Church assembly in Rome." Archbishop Iakovos, Primate of the Greek Orthodox Church of North and South America, requested prayers for unity. He prayed the Founder of the Church: "Look upon the Second Vatican Council of our Catholic brethren and grant unto them Thy mercy and compassion."[15]

When we scan the names, the numerous names, of the religious bodies who requested such prayers for the Council, we notice the diversity of the denominations. To mention only the names of a few, there were: the Orthodox and other Eastern Churches, the Old Catholics, the Anglicans, the Baptists, the Evangelical and Lutheran Christians, the Methodists, Presbyterians, the Reformed Churches. To these we must add the various church groups, for example, the Young Men's Christian Association and the World Council of Churches. This last body at the meeting of its executive committee in Paris in August 1962 requested the various churches to offer prayers. There went all over the world such requests, to Africa, Australia, India, Japan, as well as to England, France, Holland, Austria, Switzerland, Germany, Canada, and the United States. The American reaction was enthusiastic.

So far we have mentioned only those calls for prayer which were publicly made. I could list also a whole series of lesser groups who assured us directly or indirectly of the help of their prayers. I should like to mention in this context sixty-six Anglican organizations which on their own initiative assured us in writing that their prayers were with us in our work.

This common prayer is very important. We perceive how differently people reacted to the First and to this the Second Vatican Council. This mutual prayer is also religiously important, because it recalls the saying of the Lord: "Again I tell you this: if two of you agree on earth about any request

[15] *Ibid.*

you have to make, that request will be granted by my heavenly Father" (Mt. 18:19). Is not this communion in prayer the first beginning—full of promise—of the unity to come?

A second fact concerns the work of the observers and their participation in the Council itself. In this connection, I should like to state clearly that all the observers without any exception manifested genuine and sincere religious and ecumenical sentiments. The first contacts between the observers themselves were undertaken in this spirit. The observers also followed the work of the Council in the same spirit. With regard to this work, it would be false to conclude from the many journalistic descriptions of the events of the Council that the observers were merely present at the celebrations or that they were merely top-dressing to the pomp and splendor of the occasion. Such an idea would not do justice to the objective truth.

These were certainly days of genuine brotherhood and exciting meetings. But they were above all days of really hard and tiring work. The observers received the same secret documents as the bishops of the Council. I know that this confidence in them made a deep impression. At the reception given by the Secretariat in honor of the observers, Professor E. Schlink of Heidelberg University voiced the thanks of all present for this manifestation of confidence. You should know that these Council documents consisted of two volumes, one of two hundred and fifty folio pages, the other of about one hundred and twenty folio pages, both written in Latin and full of quotations and notes. The two volumes were stiff-going, which presumed rather fundamental theological knowledge and demanded earnest study. In order to help this study and to help overcome the hurdle of Latin especially, the Secretariat provided a team of professional theologians and counsellors to assist the observers.

We must then mention the plenary assemblies, five of them every week, of over two thousand bishops. These began with the divine service celebrated each time in a different rite and language. Immediately afterward about three hours of discussion followed which was almost exclusively carried on in Latin. The observers were able to follow all that went on during the plenary sessions through the help of the interpreters which the Secretariat supplied.

In addition to all this there was the very important work which the observers carried on outside the Council sessions. The Secretariat organized—at least once a week—a private session for the observers. Here they were able to discuss matters among themselves. They could also speak with professional theologians from the Secretariat and with one of Council bishops or theologians who had been particularly active in the discussion then on the floor of the Council. Here the observers could express their ideas and proffer criticisms. I myself asked them, during the reception held in their honor, to favor us with their complete confidence and frankness, to speak their minds freely, even when they thought that what they had to say might displease us, to share with us all their reactions and criticisms. I must admit my satisfaction that they did so to a great extent and that in this way many observations made by the observers reached beyond the Secretariat and penetrated even into the discussion on the floor of the Council where they were most useful.

We must add to these official occasions the series of private contacts and meetings which took place outside the Council sessions. Many observers confessed that in this way they were able to establish fruitful relations with not a few Council bishops. Many of the latter, on the other hand, had the same comment to make. The situation was such that the General Secretary of the World Council of Churches, Dr. Visser 't Hooft, was able to say that the observers were no longer merely observers since so many contacts and so many conversations had taken place between them and the bishops in the Council.

We shall speak in detail later about the observers' reactions to the Council. Today we must close our remarks with the grateful comment that already the preparation of the Council and its discussions have brought a divine blessing on all Christians. It has in fact clearly shown how Christians of every denomination desire unity intensely.

It is true—as was noted in many statements made after the closing of the first period—that no concrete question was solved; all the problems between the different confessions are still there. But the atmosphere has come to be quite a different one. The Council has also shown the consciousness which all the baptized possess of belonging to each other and manifested the common will to let this unity take concrete and objective shape. We can say that this consciousness and the desire for unity has been mightily strengthened through what has happened at the Council. We also admit that this desire and its various external expressions have taken on gigantic proportions in a relatively short time. We see, too, how swiftly events have caught up with our hopes. The realization that we are all members of Christ has really spread like wildfire. All this is the sign of the overflowing grace which the Father of mercies has granted to his children. It is the sign of the powerful influence of his spirit, of the spirit of Christ, over the broad field of Christianity. Thus, the events which we have portrayed constitute a gentle but insistent invitation to us to raise our hearts in gratitude to him, to place all our hope in him, and, finally, to work for unity with that faith which can move mountains.

THE SECOND VATICAN
COUNCIL AND NON-CATHOLIC
CHRISTIANS: EVALUATION
AND PROGNOSIS

AUGUSTIN CARDINAL BEA

THE FORMER Archbishop of Canterbury, Lord Fisher of Lambeth, in a sermon preached some days before the opening of the Vatican Council, described his visit to Pope John and His Holiness' attitude made manifest in the establishment of the Secretariat for Unity, as the most significant ecumenical event of the past few years. He went on to say: "All this leadership cannot be reversed. All this spontaneous outflowing of goodwill between the Churches has happened. It cannot now be undone. In that context of wonder and thankfulness for what God has done for us all, the Council will meet."[1] His successor to the See of Canterbury echoed this statement in an even warmer manner when he said: "We thank God for the new spirit of brotherly love which is noticeable throughout the whole of Christianity. The Christian world is watching the Council in Rome with interest."[2] The same sentiments were expressed from still another sector of divided Christianity when the Ecumenical Patriarch, His Holiness, Athenagoras of Constantinople, made the following statement during an interview on the Italian television: "The announcement of the Council has aroused a wave of sympathy for the Catholic Church and,

[1] Sermon in Grace Cathedral, San Francisco, on September 30, 1962.
[2] Related by the Austrian Catholic news agency, *Kathpress*, October 10, 1962, p. 7.

in particular, for Pope John XXIII. This sympathy has been aroused not merely by his kindliness and simplicity but also because again and again he has described himself as the Bishop of Rome and the brother of all bishops of the world. And even more, notwithstanding the privilege of Infallibility which the first Vatican Council recognized as his, he none the less summoned the Council."[3]

I. REVIEW OF THE FIRST PERIOD

Today we can say confidently that these anticipatory and positive evaluations of the Council have been fully verified by what took place. After the Council, that well-known weekly, *The Christian Century*, wrote: "While only the first session of the Second Vatican Council has been completed, it is already evident that the Council may prove to be the most important religious event of our time . . ." After remarking that, of course, the continuation of the Council depends on the health of the Pope, the author went on to say: "Even without the present Pope, forces long pent-up in the Roman Catholic Church and loosed by him through the Council would surely continue to make their influence felt. The renewal of the Church which the Council was summoned to undertake has already visibly begun."[4] President Kurt Scharf, Chairman of the Council of the German Evangelical Church, used equally optimistic tones in saying that it was impossible to judge the Second Vatican Council too positively. Indeed a decisive step has already been taken, no matter what the further developments may be. The flame enkindled during the first session cannot be extinguished and represents a gain for the whole ecumenical world.[5] Another German Church leader, who has not always appeared so well disposed toward Catholics, Dr. Martin Niemöller,

[3] Related by the Italian news agency Ansa, *Informazioni religiose,* September 15, 1962.
[4] January 2, 1963, p. 3.
[5] Related by the *Esslinger Zeitung,* February 12, 1963.

said: "Perhaps we are nearer to the one Christian Church than we thought even a short while ago." And he added that: "The great change within the Catholic Church under Pope John XXIII, which none of us had dared to believe in, gives me hope."[6]

The broad perspective of the World Council of Churches permitted Dr. W. A. Visser 't Hooft, its General Secretary, to deliver the following judgment of the Second Vatican Council in his official report to the Executive Committee. Notwithstanding many reservations he stated that "the Council has shown that the Roman Catholic Church is discovering its true position in the modern world . . . and is beginning to take up the challenge of the modern situation seriously." He said further that the Council has shown that the Church has "a greater capacity for renewal than most non-Roman Christians and in fact many Roman Catholics considered possible." He added that "until now the Roman Catholic Church has left all initiatives in ecumenical matters to the World Council of Churches and other ecumenical bodies. Now," he said, "the Church of Rome has become a source of ecumenical initiative."[7]

Here, perhaps, it will not be without interest to cite still another verdict, or rather the total impression of one of the non-Catholic observers. Professor Edmund Schlink was present at the Council as the official observer for the German Evangelical Church. He wrote as follows: "Positively speaking one must say of the Council that a genuine synodal event has taken place in an atmosphere which permitted free speech and free decisions. Although the order of business and the appointment of the Council Presidency were in the Pope's hands and not in the Council's, it is clear that the Pope in no way imposed his own will on conciliar discussions as in the First Vatican Council. The discussions of the

[6] Related by the *Stuttgarter Nachrichten,* February 1, 1963, p. 17.
[7] *Ecumenical Press Service,* February 12, 1963, p. 1.

draft schema on the Church saw the facing of new problems
and a surprisingly open attitude toward other Christians.
Here strong ecumenical currents broke through. Here doors
were thrown open to admit the rest of Christianity and the
world, doors which previously have been shut, and the inter-
denominational atmosphere changed tremendously, as we
were able to learn during our many conversations with
bishops and theologians."[8] May I repeat the impression of
still one more observer, Dr. Vilmos Vajta, director of the
Theological Section of the Lutheran World Council. He
wrote: "The fact that non-Catholic observers were invited
is often considered from one side only as if the Catholic
Church alone had opened doors . . . But we should also
point out that the sending of observers by the non-Catholic
Churches was not something that could be taken for granted
. . . There are still groups in both the Oriental and the Protestant Churches who cannot understand the acceptance of
the Pope's invitation because they can still conceive the life
of divided Christianity only as the coexistence of hostile
bodies."[9]

These judgments are based, for the most part, on the impressions which the Council made on non-Catholic observers. Time does not permit me to dwell longer on these
impressions which, of course, are now in the public domain.
Permit me, however, to adduce just two testimonies closer to
home, that is, from American observers. The first was given
by the Rev. George Williams, Professor of Church History
at this university. Speaking of his experiences, he com-
mented: "It is a new climate, a climate of trust, of mutual
respect, which touches on the miraculous. A student of
ecclesiastical annals, I have found an atmosphere such as
this only at this moment of history, at this first Council of

---

[8] *Evangelische Welt: Informationsblatt für die Evangelische Kirche
in Deutschland,* December 1962, pp. 729ff.
[9] *Lutherischer Weltbund,* January 4, 1963, p. 2.

the twentieth century."[10] Another witness is Professor James H. Nichols of The Princeton Theological Seminary. He said: "I had not realized that anything like this existed . . . I thought the Roman Catholic Church was a very closed, complacent, and sectarian body that had nothing to learn from anybody else. I know now that this is no longer accurate, if it ever was." And he added: "All the differences (between the Catholic Church and us) are still there. I do not think that any major problem is in any sense solved. Nevertheless, the whole atmosphere is so different that, as Cardinal Bea says, it is a 'real miracle.' "[11]

In general terms, it is true to say that the majority of the observers were impressed above all by the freedom of discussion that reigned at the Council. Most of them arrived in Rome with the usual conception of the monolithic structure of the Catholic Church and in particular of the Catholic bishops. But from the very first session they were able to see for themselves that there were real discussions in which great differences of opinion were expressed—though no one questioned any dogma. They realized that the bishops felt free to open their minds and that the Pope was the first to watch over and protect this freedom. The course of events made clear that the bishops were not considered or treated merely as those who should execute the decrees of a centralized authority. They appeared as successors of the Apostles who together with the successor of Peter bore the responsibility for the good of the *entire* Church. What happened revealed that the principle of Catholic canon law was true, namely that it is the Council in union with the successor of Peter which represents the highest authority of the Church.[12] The Council met as a college, aware of its unity, not only in faith but also in solicitude, imposed by

[10] Interview given to a great Italian magazine, *Famiglia cristiana,* November 11, 1962, p. 21.

[11] *Ecumenical Press Service,* January 18, 1963, p. 6.

[12] *Codex Juris Canonici,* canon 228.

duty for the Universal Church of five hundred millions and
its grave needs and undertakings.

We cannot, however, be satisfied with these evaluations
of the Council, significant as they and their authors undoubtedly are. We must discover the basis for the positive
judgments we have mentioned. Our question, therefore, is
as follows: *What positive results, what concrete fruits have
come forth from the Council from its convocation up to the
end of the first session?*

(1) A first and highly important result was the establishment of a permanent organ of the Holy See devoted to the
search for unity; I mean, the Secretariat for Christian Unity.
This Secretariat first prepared a series of draft constitutions
which dealt with various aspects of the problem of unity.
These draft constitutions were then examined by the preparatory central commission and will be presented to the Council. It is also significant that while all the other preparatory
commissions (with the exception of those purely functional bodies occupied with the technical organization and
the maintenance of the Council) ceased to exist before the
Council opened, the Secretariat for Unity remained in
existence and was placed on an equal footing with the other
conciliar commissions. It has now been entrusted with the
task of contacting not only the Protestant but the Eastern
churches as well. It now possesses two sections: one for
Western churches, the other for the churches of the East.
The historical significance of the establishment of the Secretariat as a permanent organization can be justly compared
to the creation of the Congregation for the Missions, back
in the seventeenth century.

The basis for this comparison naturally does not lie in
the fact that non-Catholic Christians are considered in the
same way as non-Christians—for certainly they are not—
but only in this: as was true of that Congregation then, now
we can say that a gigantic undertaking which concerns the

fundamental mission of the Church and for which no permanent organization had previously existed has now been entrusted to the Secretariat for Unity. An organization now exists, therefore, which will give unity of purpose and set clear goals for this entire field of activity. The Church could not have supplied a more striking proof of its heartfelt interest in the ecumenical movement and its sincere quest for unity.

(2) The invitation of non-Catholic observers to the working sessions of the Second Vatican Council imposed on the Council itself a clearly ecumenical outlook. A continuous interchange between the Council bishops and the group of observers started quite early. Because the latter were few in number compared to the mass of two thousand conciliar bishops, the mutual communication of ideas between the two groups was all the more unexpected. Several bishops declared publicly that the presence of the observers definitely affected the climate of the Council. Their very presence kept the ecumenical task of the Church in the forefront of their consciousness as the bishops discussed their problems. Whether the Council was debating the teaching of the Church or its practice in, for example, divine worship, warnings were loudly voiced that the Council must not close any doors which would facilitate contact with non-Catholics.

(3) There is, however, one result of the Council which must be reckoned as the most precious, because, of all recent happenings, this touches most closely the very heart of Christianity. That is the new realization that all Christians of any and every denomination belong to each other. We should say, perhaps, that the consciousness of all Christians has been sharpened to this realization, because such a consciousness has always existed. Even when the Council was judged negatively as a mere display of the pomp and glory of the Roman Church, even there its critics were forced to admit that the Council had already exerted both direct and

indirect influence on the whole of Christianity.[13] They felt that what had happened in one part of Christianity was the concern of the other parts of Christianity, and that it necessarily called for a response from them.[14] Every Christian as well as every denomination has an interest in the Second Vatican Council—this is the opinion of Professor G. Bornkamm of Heidelberg, President of the German Evangelical Union.[15]

During his 1962 Christmas message Pope John expressed a hope which was based on this new realization. He said: "The characteristic result of the ecumenical council was this: spontaneously, in a manner which the majority almost did not expect, a feeling of unity manifested itself. I can describe it better as a clear, conscious, accepted attraction toward the brotherhood of Christians, as the Apostles' Creed expressed it in giving the notes of the Church as One, Holy, Catholic, and Apostolic. Not that the Church so characterized should tend to dominate men. On the contrary She is at the service of all those who desire to bring to realization the designs of Christ, even if they do not seize clearly its plan and its meaning."[16]

I must add here that this awakening sense of unity was accompanied by a desire for unity, as the Pope stressed in his talk. According to the Pope, the sensitivity shown by our contemporaries for religious problems when the Council got under way tended to group those who felt it around the image of the one fold and the one shepherd. This coming together is as yet tentative, hindered as it is by prejudices nourished by fears. We are able to understand these fears.

---

[13] Note the statement of Bishop Dietzfelbinger of Munich in *Katholische Nachrichtenagentur*, August 6, 1962.

[14] *Ibid.*, September 25, 1962, statement of Oberkirchenrat Dr. Sucker.

[15] *Ibid.*, October 5, 1962, p. 8.

[16] *Acta Apostolicae Sedis* 55:17 (1963).

We wish to understand them in order that they may be removed by the grace of God.

II. PROSPECTS FOR THE FUTURE

Naturally I have no intention of playing the prophet here. I wish to indicate how, in my opinion, further developments may go. I do this on the basis of what has been achieved up to this time.

(1) The achievements of the Council thus far provide us with a most significant starting point. The Preparatory Commission for the Oriental Churches has laid before the Council a proposal which not only concerns the Eastern Churches separated from the Roman See, but which also contains many elements of general ecumenical interest. The bishops have approved the fundamental outline of this proposal with moral unanimity. Furthermore, they voted that this proposal be incorporated in a more comprehensive document containing other proposals on the same matter. These other proposals came from the Secretariat for Christian Unity and from the Theological Commission. Thus the Council has given its highest approval to the fundamental lines of approach which the Catholic ecumenical movement should follow. It has, therefore, manifested its intention to give concrete form to this ecumenical work. We have an assurance that the Council will pursue this, with God's grace, in the ecumenical climate referred to already which reigned throughout the first session.

(2) What concrete steps is the Council likely to take in this regard?

a) First and foremost the fundamental teaching of the Catholic Church will not be changed. Compromise on points of faith which have already been defined is impossible. It would be quite unfair to our non-Catholic brethren to stir up false hopes of this nature. Nor is there a possibility that the Church—even in its zeal for eventual union—will ever be content with a recognition only of "essential dogmas," or that she will reverse or withdraw the dogmatic decrees drawn up at the Council of Trent. Again it would be simply dishonest to suggest that there is any likelihood that the dogmas of the primacy or the Infallibility of the Pope will be revised. The Church has solemnly proclaimed all these doctrines to be of faith, that is to say, truths revealed by God himself and necessary for salvation. Precisely because of these solemn declarations made under the guidance of the Holy Spirit, the action of the Church in this field is severely limited. She must guard these truths, explain them, preach them, but she cannot compromise them. For the Church founded by Christ cannot tamper with the Word of God which he preached and entrusted to her care. She must humbly subject herself to him with whom she is inalterably united.

I am sure that my non-Catholic brethren will understand this. For they maintain, just as strongly as we, that unity cannot be achieved at the expense of truth. As Dr. Ben Mohr Herbster, the President of the United Churches of Christ, put it: "A unity based on the least common denominator would be a curse and not a blessing."[17]

Are the hands of the Catholic Church, therefore, completely tied? Not at all. First, the traditional formulae which express points of doctrine of interest to non-Catholic Christians have often been misunderstood. The Council, therefore, can restate them in a manner more intelligible to the modern mind. As the Pope explicitly stated in his opening speech to the Council, "the *substance* of the ancient teaching of the deposit of faith is one thing, the *manner* in which it is expressed is another. It is, therefore, not only possible but necessary to clothe this teaching in forms which are ac-

[17] *Ecumenical Press Service,* December 7, 1962, p. 2.

cessible and attractive to the way men think today."[18] The points of doctrine I am thinking of here concern the nature of the Church, Church authority, the apostolic succession, the Petrine office and the authoritative teaching mission of the Church.

But the points of doctrine which have been irrevocably fixed are far from exhausting the treasure-trove of divine revelation. Besides these there are many questions which have not yet been proclaimed as binding on all. Among these are many doctrines which have great significance for the modern ecumenical movement. Here I draw your attention to the problems of the union of all Christians with Christ, of the membership of non-Catholic Christians in the Church and many other questions which deal with the constitution of the Church, where the mutual relations among the various ecclesiastical authorities, and between these and the Holy See, have not been definitively decided. The Council will certainly tackle at least some of these questions and will try to decide them accordingly as both the revealed word of God and the needs and tasks of our time demand. Besides this there is the vast field of Church practice where often divine revelation has not given specific directives and whose determination therefore has been left to the discretion of the authorities of the Church: for example, many matters which concern the public worship of the Church, its language and its rites. The Council has already begun to act in this field.

b) As things are developing at present, the Council will also undertake the task of setting guidelines for ecumenical activity and, above all, it will strive to foster this activity itself. It will emphasize the heavy responsibility which lies on every Catholic to be interested in, and to work for, the welfare of his separated brethren and the union of all the

[18] *Acta Apostolicae Sedis* 54:791–792 (1962).

baptized in Christ. Catholics take it for granted that they should pray and should make sacrifices to forward the work of foreign missions, the Church's work for the non-Christians. This is as it should be. But are not our brothers who like us believe in Christ and have been baptized in his name, are they not much closer to us than non-Christians, even though they are divided among themselves and separated from the Apostolic See? Moreover, the Council will point out in detail how the individual believer and, indeed, the whole Christian family may share in the work for unity. Above all else, it will lay stress on the means which every son of the Church should employ in this task: prayer and sacrifice. The Council will recall to all our minds the duty of displaying to our Christian brethren a love which is understanding and truly Christian both in word and in action. It will, moreover, point out the possibilities for wholehearted cooperation with our non-Catholic brethren in areas of activity where differences in belief do not enter, where all can cooperate to ensure the concrete realization of natural law concepts which all Christians hold in common and of the laws of the Gospel common to us all, for example, for the relief of our suffering and oppressed fellow men. The Council will promote serious, orderly, theological dialogue and will take measures to ensure that future Catholic priests will be instructed during their years of training in the importance and the practice of ecumenical undertakings.

Let us conclude: I said at the beginning that the goal of this survey was to fill our hearts with thanks to God our Lord, with total trust in his grace and with renewed zeal. My second purpose was to subject this our human striving for unity to the action which the Lord of the Church has set in motion. We have seen that we have many reasons, so many reasons indeed, to be grateful for what God our Lord has accomplished for his Church up to now through this Council. This miraculous activity has revealed already how irresistible are his grace and his spirit and so has renewed our trust and our courage. This activity is a tremendous challenge to all of us, a challenge to pray, to suffer and to work for the Council itself, and afterward for everything which can contribute to the achievement of Christian unity. This is what our High Priest, Jesus Christ, wills and prays for: that all may be one and that the world may know that the heavenly Father has sent him and has loved us even as he had loved him, our Saviour and Redeemer.

ADDRESSES AND PAPERS

THEOLOGICAL REFLECTIONS ON
THE SECOND VATICAN COUNCIL

GREGORY BAUM, O.S.A.

T O DERIVE theological implications from the Second
Vatican Council, we must first try to understand its
place in the history of the Church. Events in Roman
Catholicism, whether they belong to the order of teaching
or administration, reveal their significance only when we
consider them as a part of a development taking place in
the Church. This is true for the councils of the past, and
this is true for the Council of our own day.

Since the convocation of the Vatican Council by Pope
John has, almost overnight, changed the atmosphere between Catholics and Protestants on this continent and
created a new and happier image of the Catholic Church in
the minds of many people, it may appear to some that this
Council is a gift fallen from the sky, a sudden and unprecedented boon, due to the initiative of one man intent
on renewing and reforming the Church. It is only when we
consider the life of the Church over this century that we
discover that the Council is not the starting point of a new
movement but, rather, the culminating point of an evolution which has gone on in the Church for several generations. To understand the Council, therefore, we must turn
to the movements of renewal which have characterized the
Catholic Church in the twentieth century.

The first of these is the liturgical movement. This movement aims at leading the Christian people to a greater appreciation of the sacramental mysteries celebrated in the
Church and, therefore, puts great emphasis on the euchar-

istic worship as the center of Christian life. It is there that we encounter our redemption. It is there, in the liturgy, that we meet Christ in his perfect self-surrender to the Father and are able to join him, with the whole Christian community, in a unity produced by the Holy Ghost. It is there, likewise, that we experience the forgiveness and transforming grace which Christ constantly offers to his Church. In order to bring out the engagement of each Christian in the worship of the Church and to renew the consciousness of community or fellowship, the liturgical movement has, from the beginning, sought a greater participation of the faithful in the celebration of the Mass and the other sacramental rites.

The liturgical movement began in France, at least for a spiritual elite, in the last century. The famous name in this connection is Dom Guéranger. No one, as yet, has found the origin of the term "liturgical movement," but we know that it was used already before 1880. From France the movement made its way to Belgium, and under the influence of Cardinal Mercier and Dom Baudouin achieved wider proportions and aimed at renewing pastoral life in the Church. From there the leadership shifted to Germany and Austria, and, through the liturgical research of Dom Casel and the extraordinary liturgical apostolate of Father Pius Parsch, the movement began to reach all areas of ecclesiastical life in central Europe, the parishes, the clergy, the teaching of theology, and the diocesan bishops. As with all movements of renewal in the Church, there was no lack of opposition on the part of ecclesiastical superiors. Though many countries, especially the Latin ones, were hardly touched by the liturgical movement, it finally obtained official status in the Church universal through an encyclical of Pius XII, *Mediator Dei* (1947), which approved and gave strong impetus to the whole endeavor. After this encyclical, the liturgical renewal was carried on by the Holy See itself: new rituals in the vernacular were approved, a new translation of the Psalter was made, the liturgy of Holy Week was renewed and the ancient Easter vigil restored, evening Masses were permitted and the eucharistic fast simplified. At a liturgical congress celebrated in Assisi, Italy, in 1956, Pius XII called the liturgical movement "the passage of the Holy Ghost through the Church."

Since the liturgy of the Church is made up of texts from the Scriptures, the liturgical movement drew attention to the Scriptures as a source of spiritual life in the Church. It therefore encouraged a second movement arising in the Catholic Church, the so-called biblical movement. The concern of this movement was not only to achieve greater scholarly interest in matters biblical and deeper insight into scriptural doctrine, but, at the same time, to renew, with this biblical emphasis, the whole of Catholic theology and Christian teaching. The movement stood for a new relation to the Word of God. It broadcast the rediscovery that, according to ancient Catholic doctrine, the Word of God, announced and received in the Church, is not simply a message addressed to man's understanding but also, and especially, a way of divine grace, a living power in the Church exercised by God to transform the human heart.

In several countries this movement was officially established in centers of the biblical apostolate that advocated greater love for the Scriptures, the reading of the Bible by the people, and the application of the Scriptures to a theology which was too much preoccupied with philosophical categories.

In this connection we should mention the contribution made to this movement by Protestant scholarship and the ecumenical dialogue. The insights of the form-critical school of biblical interpretation have established beyond question that the text of the Scriptures reflects the faith and the liturgy of the believing community in which it was composed. The biblical accounts are not simply historical records of the past, but more especially the annunciation and application of the marvellous works of God to the situation of a particular community. Regarded in this way, Scripture became the mediator between the divine acts of the past and the human need in the present. The Word of God as contained in the Bible renders present to the man of faith the redemptive acts of God in Israel and in Jesus Christ. Through his Word God continues to act today.

The biblical movement encouraged another reforming trend, the so-called catechetical renewal. This began two generations ago on the continent of Europe. Catholic educators had always studied the question of the best way of teaching religion, but usually their concern had been to find methods which would be psychologically more efficient, either by introducing a new pedagogy or by rearranging the material to be taught. The catechetical renewal, on the other hand, took another look at the content to be taught, examined the very nature of what the Church is teaching, and regained the insight that the teaching of the Church is always the good news of salvation. The doctrine of the Church is not simply a summary of dogmatic propositions, it is, at the same time, and more especially, the good news addressed by God to man, to the community, as well as to each person individually, and for this reason our catechisms, whether for children or adults, must take on the form of the Gospel.

This transformation was achieved in several ways. First of all, Catholic doctrine was taught in greater continuity with the Scriptures. Then a greater unification and simplification of doctrine was sought so that each separate article of faith could be announced in a way that would imply, or at least suggest, the total redemptive doctrine of the Church. Through every element of doctrine, the Christian should be able to encounter the whole Lord. A third principle of this catechetical renewal was derived from the clearer understanding that the divine revelation took place in history, and transformed history, and that it must, therefore, be announced, not in totally abstract formulations, but within the context of its own history. This principle at once made Christian doctrine more Christological. It also gave more meaning to the period of preparation in Israel and the time of fulfillment promised for the Last Day.

In many countries the catechetical renewal has left the stage of experiment. It has been adopted by the national hierarchies and has produced the official new catechisms in such countries as France, Germany, Austria, Belgium, and Holland.

The movements we have mentioned so far have partly been the result of, and partly a stimulation for, a more profound theological approach to divine revelation. Catholic theology has undergone a considerable evolution in the last few generations, an evolution determined by a more resolute Christology and the emergence of an historical and eschatological emphasis. One important factor in this theological development was undoubtedly the ecumenical movement which, ever since World War I, has encouraged dialogue on unity between Catholics and Protestants. Through this movement both parties began to realize the one-sidedness of the polemical approach. They became aware that by constantly engaging in arguments against one another and emphasizing in their own tradition what distinguished them from the others, they had lost much of their own substance and acquired an unbalanced possession of the Gospel. Ecumenical dialogue, therefore, initiated a movement of recovery and renewal in theology and pastoral life in all the Christian Churches. To give an example, one may mention that Protestant writers, influenced by ecumenism, approached the sacramental and liturgical realities of the Gospel with a new openness, and Catholic theologians, exposed to the same influence, would attribute a more positive and active role to the Word of God in the worship and the total life of the Church.

In addition to these four movements, one can mention a few others. There was, for instance, a clearly defined missionary movement which reexamined the Church's relation to the world and began to understand in more profound terms than ever before the mission or function of the Christian Church in the world. What is our relation to other religions? To non-Western cultures? And how must the mission of the Church be carried out among non-Christian nations? This movement was responsible for much theological insight into the universality of the Church and the realization that divine grace is present in the whole of humanity preparing the ground for the establishment of God's kingdom. One also might mention the lay movement in the Catholic Church, born of a greater apostolic consciousness on the one hand, and of the realization, brought home by the liturgy, that not only the priest or the bishop but every believer is an active member of the Church, with his own part to play. This is true in the liturgy, and this should be true in the general life of the Church.

These movements in the Catholic Church must be appreciated if we want to understand the theological significance of the Council. I will add that at the moment when the Council opened in October of last year we did not know whether the Council would actually succeed in making these new movements more universal in the Church, encourage them in areas where they exist and establish them where they are little known, or whether—and this was a frightening thought—the Council would crush these movements or, at least, impede their advance. The latter was a real possibility. I remember that on arriving in Rome in October we discovered that a pamphlet called "Rationalism and Catholic Exegesis" had just been published by a professor at the Lateran University and distributed to the Council

bishops. This pamphlet sought to discredit the biblical movement in the Church. In particular, it accused Catholic authors of denying the historicity of the divine events of salvation. The author of this pamphlet interpreted the common
conviction of modern exegetes that the text of the Scriptures
reflects the faith of the community in which it was announced as if they wished thereby to deny or reject the
historicity of the events which are announced in these texts.
Needless to say, the pamphlet was answered immediately
by a number of Catholic biblical scholars. New pamphlets
were made which, again, were distributed to the bishops.
But no one knew at that time whether the movements of
renewal had already been strong enough in the Church to
reach the majority of the bishops gathered at the Council.
It was only on November 21, more than a month after the
opening of the Council, that it became clear to everyone
through an important election that two-thirds of the bishops
gathered in Rome approved of the new movements, and
defended them, and desired their universal extension in the
Roman Church.

I do not wish to describe at this point the various factors
which produced this majority among the bishops. It may
safely be said that if the test had been made at the beginning
of the Council the result might well have been less favorable
to the movements of renewal. The strongest factor was undoubtedly the position taken by Pope John XXIII. In his
opening speech on October 11, Pope John had made it quite
clear, gently, subtly, but firmly, that he approved of the new
movements and that the time had come when the Church
should act courageously and respond positively to the
challenges of the twentieth century.

The movements of renewal I have mentioned could all
be characterized by a single term, which has become a
standing phrase—especially in France—"return to the
sources." This term suggests that the renewal of the whole

Church, whether in the area of theology, of religious instruction, of pastoral life, or even of forms of government, must always return to the source of faith, which means, to the Scriptures and the authentic liturgical tradition. The word "return" must not be understood in this connection as an attempt to copy patterns of the past or to long for the golden age of days gone by; it has nothing to do with archeological zeal or the desire to make the Church into a beautiful museum of antiquity. The return to the sources means that we approach the Scriptures and the authentic liturgical tradition with modern questions, listening anew to the Word of God and creatively applying the solutions found in biblical revelation to our own time. This return gives expression to the faith that God continues to speak to his Church in his Word, and that in this Word, as heard within the context of the believing community, we find the strength to reform, inspiration for renewal, and the insight and sense of urgency to bring the life of the Church into greater conformity with the will of the Lord.

This is the background we must take into account if we want to understand the controversy at the Council concerning the famous document on Scripture and tradition. The controversy was just the echo of the conflict among Catholic theologians concerning the relation of Scripture and tradition, and unless we consider the historical situation of the conciliar debate, we may be tempted to regard it as the quibbling of scholars.

All Catholics agree that there is a close connection and a basic agreement between the Scriptures and the Church's tradition, but we find two distinct tendencies when it comes to defining this relation more precisely. Some Catholic theologians stress the constitutive role of the Scriptures in the Church and look upon tradition as the witness of the Spirit to the Scriptures throughout the ages. For these Catholic theologians there is only *one* source of revelation, God's self-disclosure, which is present to us in the Scriptures and expressed in the tradition of the Church. Revelation is wholly present in Scripture and wholly in tradition; it is present in Scripture as voice, and present in tradition as teaching, present in Scripture and wholly in tradition; it is present in doctrine and life. Tradition, according to this view, is the unique way of faithfully listening to the Word of God. While all that is necessary for salvation is contained in the Sacred Scriptures, the genuine understanding of this is obtained only when they are read, and listened to, and accepted within the believing community that is the Church.

Theologians of the other viewpoint prefer to speak of *two* sources of revelation, of Scripture and tradition, and they believe that of the doctrines which God has revealed to his people, some are contained in the Scriptures and some in the tradition of the Church. God's revealed Word, according to these theologians, is present to us partly in Scripture and partly in tradition. These writers think of tradition as being supplementary to the Scriptures and relatively independent from them.

I may mention here that the Council of Trent left this question quite open. This Council taught that the Gospel of salvation is contained in Scripture and tradition, but refused to specify what the relation between these two organs of the Spirit were. Today a great deal of research has been done by Catholic and Protestant scholars in order to elucidate the authentic doctrine of this Council on tradition, but what has happened is that those who tried to show that the Council proclaimed a very definite concept of tradition, really proved too much and hence failed to convince. These writers began with the premise that a council of the Church always defines precise theological concepts, such as we find them in confessional documents of the Reformed and the Lutheran Churches. This, however, is not really so. The definitions of councils usually reject or refute what

they regard as an error, but in condemning the error the
positive declarations always leave room for several tendencies and theological positions to exist within the orthodoxy
of Catholic faith. Hence a council does not usually define a
single position but, rather, indicates the limits of Catholic
orthodoxy beyond which the theologian may not go. Of
this we have become very conscious during the present
Council! Many of the formulations were broad enough to
admit various theological outlooks and hence did not have
a uniquely defined meaning. This is unavoidable in a
Church which claims to be universal and leaves room for
several theological traditions. For this reason, then, the
modern scholar who attributes one single meaning to the
doctrine of tradition at the Council of Trent misjudges the
character of conciliar documents.

The two theological positions we have just described
basically determine two distinct attitudes to ecclesiastical
life and the ways of renewing it. If we believe that Scripture and tradition are intimately related and compenetrate
one another, then every renewal of ecclesiastical life will
imply a return to the Scriptures. It is precisely through this
return to the Word of God that the tradition of the Church
is constantly purified and made more authentically Christian; it is through this return to the Word of God that we
can distinguish within the life of the Church the elements
which are of divine origin and those which represent purely
human and hence conditional developments. It is by listening to the Word that the holy tradition of the Church is
generated. Tradition may be regarded as the response of the
whole Church, and especially of those who are pastors in
the Church, to the Word of God.

If, however, theologians regard Scripture and tradition
as relatively distinct and assert that tradition has its own
life independent of the Scriptures, then there is no need to
"return to the source" for renewal; renewal and reform may

then be considered as a process in which bishops make more demanding legislation and exhort the faithful to be more obedient. These theologians would claim that the Spirit is always with his Church and hence will renew the Church's life by asserting more vigorously the principle of authority. But if tradition is regarded as in some way independent from the Scriptures, we have no principle by which to purify Catholic life, to distinguish what is healthy from what is unhealthy in it, and every effort of renewal will ultimately be an attempt at restoration.

With this situation in mind, it is easy to see why the document on the two sources of revelation caused such a vehement controversy. The title alone implied the viewpoint separating tradition from Scripture, and therefore suggested restoration. The majority of bishops felt that greater stress should be put on the coinherence and compenetration of Scripture and tradition in the Church, since in the unity of these two modes of transmitting the Gospel we have the basis of all the movements of renewal existing in the Church. Even though the arguments at the Council were couched in theoretical terms, the real heart of the matter was whether the movements of renewal were to be approved and advanced or whether they were to be curtailed. In the course of the first session it became clear that the spirit of renewal was constantly gaining ground.

We now turn to a second result of the first session of the Vatican Council, one which is related to the organizational structure of the Church. The Church as society was not formally discussed in the first session, but even apart from definitive decisions, certain significant structures have emerged which point the way to future developments.

One may feel that ecclesiastical organization is not a very exciting subject; what counts, ultimately, is the spiritual, our union with God in Christ. This is undoubtedly true, but even on the external and organizational level, the

Church of Christ must present an authentic image of what she was meant to be, namely the family of God.

The first remarkable development at the Council's first session was the emergence of the national episcopal conferences. How did this happen? At the beginning of the Council, the bishops were asked to elect the members who were to constitute various conciliar working commissions. The curial organizers of the Council had prepared lists from which the bishops were to make their choice. However, Cardinal Lienart of Lille, France, and Cardinal Frings of Cologne, Germany, stood up and asked that the bishops be given a chance to become acquainted. They suggested that the election of these working commissions be postponed for a few days. This unexpected move was successful. Three days were granted, and in these three days the national hierarchies organized, set up their own secretariates, proposed lists of names, and sent these around to other national hierarchies. The understanding among the bishops was mediated through these episcopal conferences. After three days of ceaseless activity, the bishops walked into the Council with lists of their own, ready to elect working commissions which were truly representative.

The national hierarchies remained organized. Many of them held regular meetings, either to discuss the issues of the Council, or to listen to episcopal or nonepiscopal theologians giving the scholarly background of the issues at stake. It must be added here that there was no hint of nationalism in all this. The national tensions which had played such a great part in former councils of the Church simply did not exist at the Second Vatican. If there were tensions at this Council they were between those who desired reform and renewal and others whose ideal was, rather, restoration and preservation.

Perhaps I should explain that, until now, the episcopal

conferences existing in many countries do not have a legal status in the organization of the Church. They are not legislative bodies. They do not teach with authority. Their whole concern has been with what is vaguely called "pastoral matters." Until now, everything that was important was decided at Rome.

This highly centralized government has not really been in harmony with Catholic ideals. To ward off totalitarianism in any form, the social teachings of the Church affirm *the principle of subsidiarity.* This principle states that a higher authority in a society should not usurp a function that could be exercised by smaller units in its care. For instance, the state should not arrogate to itself what could be adequately handled by the family, or the municipality, or professional societies. The interference of the highest authority is justified and necessary when the lower organs cannot take care of the problem, or when the well-being of society as a whole is touched.

Recent popes have often declared that this principle of subsidiarity is also valid in the Church. The present legislation in the Church, however, does not make many provisions for its application. The emergence of the episcopal conferences at the Council was of such great significance, since it was a spontaneous manifestation of this principle of subsidiarity. Even before the whole subject was specifically discussed at the Council, the episcopal conferences became active in the life of the Council itself. The Pope acknowledged this fact. When, on December 5, 1962, he published the directives for the work between the two sessions, he specified that the documents, corrected and rewritten, be sent to the bishops of the world *through* the presidents of the episcopal conferences. Until now such documents from Rome were always sent through the apostolic delegates. Pope John, in touch with the developments at the Council, altered this. The episcopal conferences are beginning to have a status in the Church even before the legislation is actually changed.

What is the significance of this? The place which the episcopal conferences are likely to have will decentralize the life of the Catholic Church.

Here is a concrete example of this process. The liturgical document which the Vatican Council has discussed and, in part at least, accepted specifies the general principles of liturgical renewal. It does not go into detail. There was the general conviction that the life of the Church was so varied, so dependent on local situations and national traditions, that it would be absurd to seek an identical legislation for the universal Catholic community. The general norms of the liturgical document will therefore be applied and adapted to the needs of national or linguistic regions by episcopal conferences. In some countries all the possibilities of adaptation will be made use of, and in others liturgical changes will be introduced rather slowly. All this means decentralization, diversity, flexibility.

The picture of the Church we have so often drawn, whereby all power and all teaching authority remains with the pope, is certainly inadequate. We must not forget that bishops are successors of the Apostles, and hence, in union with the pope, *they also* teach with authority and exercise supreme power.

The first Vatican Council in 1870 defined the supreme authority of the pope in the Catholic Church, but it did not spell out in precise terms the role of the other bishops and their relation to the successor of St. Peter. The prerogatives of bishops are not derived from Peter or his successors but, rather, from the body of the Twelve, the so-called Apostolic College.

This leads us to a doctrine called "the collegiality of the bishops." This word and the idea behind it are probably quite new to many Catholics. We are so used to regarding the pope as the sole ruler and teacher in the Church that the bishops have become for us the heads of their dioceses and nothing more. We have almost lost the ancient notion of the unity of the episcopal college. We tend to consider a bishop as an individual successor of an Apostle, instead of regarding him as a member of the episcopal college which, as a body, succeeds the Apostolic College. The Twelve were created by Christ as a body. Together they were prepared (Matt. 10), together they were sent on their mission (Matt. 28), together they were called to be witnesses (Acts 1), and together they received the Holy Ghost (Acts 2). We read that the Apostles are the foundation of the Church (Eph. 2:20) and have received the power of the keys together (John 20:23). As a body they are indefectible (Matt. 28:20). This, at least, is the Catholic faith. The supreme role of Peter within the Twelve did not invalidate their common calling as the foundation of the Church.

Now, just as the pope, according to Catholic faith, is the successor of St. Peter, so the bishops in their totality, the episcopal college, are the successors of the Twelve. The role of the Apostles was certainly unique and inimitable. They had seen the Lord Jesus, they had been witnesses of the wonderful things God had done in Jesus Christ. But their office of preaching and interpreting the message once-for-all delivered to the Church, of perpetuating the deeds of salvation in a sacramental liturgy, and of ordering the community—this was passed on to their successors. In this sense, the bishops, as a body, are the heirs of the Twelve.

This doctrine has immediate practical consequences. A bishop in the Catholic Church is not only the head of his diocese, he is also, and first of all, a member of that body which has the care of the Universal Church. He is co-responsible for the life of the whole Church. His eyes are not simply turned to his own diocese; he looks, rather, at the whole Church, conscious that he has a real responsibility for its teaching, its liturgy, and its life everywhere. This ancient doctrine appears new to many. In the present legislation of the Church where the care of the universal community is almost exclusively in the hands of the See of Rome, the bishops hardly ever have the opportunity of expressing their coresponsibility for the total mission of the Church. At the Council, however, the bishops rediscovered this mission again. They realized again what the apostolic office to which they are appointed means and they exercised their sacred ministry in union with the pope, their head, for the good of the universal Catholic community. At the Council the collegiality of the bishops has become a meaningful term again.

We may ask if this coresponsibility for the Church universal could not find expression in an organizational structure after the Council. The following suggestion has been made by many bishops: if an ecclesiastical body were created at Rome, convening every one or two years, made up of the pope and bishops delegated by the various episcopal conferences, the pope and these bishops together would then be in a position to discuss and determine the ways of the Church and the adaptation of Catholic life to the needs of the day. In this way the collegiality of the bishops would be constantly exercised. In this way, moreover, the Roman curia would be made responsible to the whole college of bishops.

From this description it becomes obvious that there is a certain dialogue structure in the exercise of supreme authority in the Church. While the pope, as the successor of St. Peter, has supreme jurisdiction in the Church, he is, at the same time, a member of the episcopal college and, as such, engaged in dialogue with his brethren, the bishops. A greater consciousness of this dialogue structure, such as the bishops gained at the Vatican Council, will change considerably the quality of Catholic life. There will be greater diversity. Greater freedom will be granted to the initiative of men whom the Spirit inspires. Until now, so many good ideas, so many ways of pastoral renewal, could not be translated into action because the Church was so completely centralized. The Council is initiating a structure which will facilitate communication, dialogue, diversity, and adaptation.

I must now make a very frank observation. Repeatedly I have been asked by people whether such a decentralization is a good thing. These people have suggested that the Roman authorities are more universal in outlook than the local bishops and that if more power were given to the bishops, Catholic life might become more parochial in certain areas. A bishop might use his newly gained power to dominate his diocese, to impose his will, to close himself to the wider perspectives which have always characterized the teaching of the popes. The question is a valid one. Will this new trend in the Church, which has begun successfully at the Vatican Council, make our bishops into single-handed rulers? It is well known that the movements of renewal of which I have spoken have not always found encouragement from local bishops. The local hierarchy have not always understood the theological dimensions of the liturgical movement. In some places the bishops, overwhelmed with the many problems of a growing community, have had to sacrifice themselves and become, in the first place, administrators. They have been often out of touch with the vital movements in the Church. Will not the new trend, then, threaten the forces of renewal in the Church?

The question deserves careful consideration. Our first observation is this. It has become apparent at the Vatican Council that decentralization will not mean more power for the individual bishop in his diocese but, rather, more independence for the episcopal conference and legislative power to apply and adapt the general norms valid for the Church Universal. In the application of the liturgical renewal, regional bodies of bishops will determine the path to be followed. There will be a real conciliar atmosphere at these episcopal conferences. Papers will be read, various views will be proposed and discussed, specialists will be asked to make their comments, and the bishops who are less in contact with the vital currents in the Church will be brought up to date. The bishops will learn to feel co-responsible for Catholic life in the whole area entrusted to them. We need not fear, therefore, that a bishop brought up on the ideas of the recent past and not in touch with the movements of the Church will have more power to impose his will. On the contrary, there will be ecclesiastical forces at work making the bishops more conscious that they are teachers and leaders in the Church.

The second observation is a little more delicate, but I must make it. When modern Catholic books and articles speak of reemphasizing the episcopal office, they do not have in mind the increase of episcopal power in regard to the people over whom the bishops are placed, but rather the increase of power in regard to the central authority of the Church. Bishops become more powerful when they are able to orientate and adapt Catholic life in their churches to the needs of the people, without the handicap of a uniform legislation destined for the Church Universal. More power in the bishops then, does not mean greater dominance in their dioceses. On the contrary, I am convinced that the dialogue structure within the exercise of supreme authority in the Church, brought out at the Vatican Council, will qualify the relation of superior and subject throughout the Catholic Church. The bishops, engaged in dialogue among themselves and with the central supreme authority, will find it natural to enter into dialogue with the people for whom they are responsible.

This process, I believe, cannot be stopped. When bishops, conscious of the collegial responsibility for the whole Church, meet to discuss the ways of the Church, engage in constructive criticism of the central authority, make their personal suggestions, and seek to influence public opinion among the bishops in favor of their own ideas, then it is natural that they will not be upset, but rather take it for granted, when people in their churches also offer constructive criticism in the press, propose their ideas, and seek to influence public opinion. *All this is in no way opposed to ecclesiastical obedience*; for the papal and episcopal authority which, according to Catholic faith, comes from Christ will indeed make decisions that are binding for Catholics, but in the process of making these decisions there is much room for dialogue and the exchange of ideas.

The movements of renewal, together with the structural changes described above, fostered and created by the Council, will teach us to make use of all the gifts of the Spirit that come to us, and become more effective instruments in the hands of the Lord announcing and establishing his kingdom of holiness.

Postscript: The second session of the Vatican Council took place in the same spirit as the first. The unanimity among the bishops in favor of renewal and reform, of the ecumenical movement and collegial responsibility has been constantly growing. Though the second session has not succeeded in formulating any of these things in approved documents—and this is cause for some disappointment—the movements of renewal described in this paper have acquired the approval of the overwhelming majority of the Council, and the principle of episcopal collegiality as part of the Church's

God-given structure was approved by over eighty percent of the bishops in an important vote on October 30, 1963. Unless the small opposition to the reform of the Church, concentrated in the Roman Curia, succeeds in blocking documents and issues from coming on the floor of the Council—since curial cardinals are involved in the organization of the Council, this is a real possibility— the Vatican Council will make the movements of renewal universal in the Catholic Church and begin a tendency toward the sharing of responsibility and conscientious dialogue among the members of the Church, papal, episcopal, clerical, and lay.

INTERPRETATION OF SCRIPTURE
IN BIBLICAL STUDIES TODAY

JAMES M. ROBINSON

YESTERDAY at this hour we listened to Father Gregory Baum present "Theological Reflections on the Second Vatican Council." This afternoon, as the Protestant *pendant,* I am presenting a paper on the "Interpretation of Scripture in Biblical Studies Today." Thus, the two confessions seem at first glance to be talking past each other again, rather than entering into dialogue. Would it not have been better for the Protestant speaker to present, for example, "Theological Reflections on the Third Assembly of the World Council of Churches" that took place at New Delhi just a year before the Second Vatican Council? The Protestant Assembly and the Roman Catholic Council could then have been compared structure for structure, and it would not have been hard to identify the points at which they converge and diverge.

I would like to suggest that such a comparison, so strikingly fitting as it may at first glance seem to be, would itself be an instance of talking past each other, in that it would begin by obscuring a basic structural problem of the dialogue in which we are here seeking to enter. Perhaps you will permit me to draw attention to this structural problem by calling it the problem as to the appropriate hermeneutical principle for interpreting each of the confessions. By a hermeneutical principle one means the situation in which one places a person or thing to see what it really is, or that with which one confronts a text in order to elicit its meaning. If you want to find out what a cat is, put it in front of a mouse.[1] Such a hermeneutical principle is the nearest the humanities get to the experiment so central to the natural sciences. Perhaps the Second Vatican Council is a suitable hermeneutical principle for bringing to expression what the Roman Catholic Church is, in that such a Council is the situation in which the Church is the Church and shows what it is to be the Church.

If, then, to some extent one may say that the Second Vatican Council is an appropriate hermeneutical principle for understanding the Roman Catholic Church, one can to much less an extent maintain that the Third Assembly of the World Council of Churches is the model for analyzing the nature of Protestantism. Protestantism's hermeneutical principle must be located elsewhere. Recently a Protestant theologian, in trying to define the nature of Church history as a discipline distinct from history in general, said that Church history is the history of the interpretation of Scripture.[2] That is to say, wherever in history people understand what they are doing as interpreting the Scriptures, there one has to do with the Church. In this sense apostolic succession would consist in the successive translation of biblical meaning from generation to generation, from culture to culture; the Church's tradition would be the successive interpretation of Scripture, that is to say, tradition would be *traditio*, the transmission of biblical meaning. To be sure, such interpretation of Scripture is not confined to the technical work of the biblical scholar. In a recent article in the *Harvard Divinity Bulletin* on "New Testament Study in the Divinity School," Professor Wilder quotes his predecessor, Henry J. Cadbury, when asked whether the transition from the scholar's study to the chairmanship of the American

[1] The definition and illustration derive from Ernst Fuchs, *Hermeneutik* (Bad Cannstatt, 1954), pp. 103–118, esp. p. 109.

[2] Gerhard Ebeling, *Kirchengeschichte als Geschichte der Auslegung der Heiligen Schrift* (Tübingen, 1947).

Friends Service Committee was not rather abrupt, as reply-
ing: "I am still trying to translate the New Testament."[3]

It is this wide spectrum of interpretation of Scripture that
in Protestant thought is where the Church is the Church.
As Protestantism classically formulated it, *sola scriptura*
is the formal principle of the Reformation. If then we focus
our attention upon the interpretation of Scripture taking
place in biblical studies today, we have directed ourselves
to as concrete an instance of where Protestantism reveals
itself as is the Second Vatican Council an instance of where
Roman Catholicism reveals itself. It is indeed the interpretation of Scripture, rather than the Third Assembly of the
World Council of Churches, that is the hermeneutical principle of Protestantism most appropriate to serve as a *pendant*
to the Second Vatican Council.

Interpretation of all kinds is constantly being carried on
without calling attention to itself, as people seek to understand each other and make themselves understood. Only
when normal communication breaks down, as a result of
some serious impediment in understanding (such as a language barrier), is attention drawn to the process of understanding itself in such a way as to call forth reflection upon
the theory of interpretation. Such theorizing about interpretation has been traditionally called hermeneutics.

Theorizing about interpretation has, in fact, been called
forth primarily by one particular kind of crisis for understanding that has recurred at characteristic periods in Western civilization. It is first the importance of what is to be
understood that has led to hermeneutical theory. The history of the theory of interpretation has had its center in the
study of classical and canonical literatures, the authority of
which is binding and the meaning of which is therefore
crucial. This first ingredient in the emergence of hermeneutical theory has been augmented by another factor: a new

[3] 25:9 (January 1961).

situation to which the normative literature no longer directly speaks, and into which it must be translated if it is to be heard at all. It is this necessity for translation that has been the *agens* in the history of hermeneutical theorizing.

In antiquity, on the one hand, the authority of classical Greek literature, of basic importance aesthetically, morally and religiously, was put in question by enlightenment, but was vindicated in the allegorical method of the Stoics. On the other hand, the canonical authority of the Old Testament for Jew and Christian was to be vindicated—in spite of the replacement of theocracy and temple by synagogue and church—by its translation into Rabbinic casuistry, by Qumranian and primitive Christian eschatological exegesis, and by the allegory of Philo and Origen. The necessity to interpret the *corpus juris* so as to reach a legal decision in cases to which that body of law does not directly speak has, along with Homer and the Bible, provided the third main subject matter for hermeneutical reflection over the years. Thus, the history of hermeneutical theory has in each case been determined by a very practical dimension, the necessity of man to act in the present, and yet to act correctly in terms of traditional norms. For interpretation itself is rooted in man's place in history, the call placed upon him to make full use of the past, and yet in such a way as not to deny his own present and future responsibility.

When the Renaissance and the Reformation coupled a revival of the authority of the classics and the Bible with a sense of the newness of the times, the hermeneutical question again became a focus of attention, from which the modern science of literary interpretation emerged. Indeed, Wilhelm Dilthey, who more than any other has clarified the history of hermeneutics, attributed to efforts at biblical interpretation the role of "finally constituting hermeneutics" as a discipline, in the context of the Roman Catholic-Protestant debate of the sixteenth Century. In fact, he identified the *Clavis scripturae sacrae* of Flacius Illyricus of 1567 as the first such systematic hermeneutic. Dilthey describes this situation in which hermeneutic emerged as follows:

> Flacius had to oppose two fronts. Both the Anabaptists and restored Catholicism insisted upon the obscurity of Holy Scripture. In opposing this Flacius learned especially from Calvin's exegesis, which often moved back from interpretation to its principles. The most urgent business for a Lutheran at that time was the disproving of the Catholic doctrine of tradition, that had at that time just been formed anew. The right of tradition to determine the interpretation of Scripture [over against the Protestant scriptural principle] could only be based upon the position that an adequate and universally valid interpretation could not be derived from the biblical writings themselves. The Council of Trent, meeting from 1545 to 1563, handled these matters from its fourth session on, and in 1564 the first authentic publication of the decree appeared. It was most acutely Bellarmin, the representative of Tridentine Catholicism, who, in a polemical document of 1581 [a bit later than Flacius], opposed the intelligibility of the Bible and tried in this way to prove the necessity of tradition for supplementing Scripture. In the context of such struggles Flacius undertook to show hermeneutically the possibility of universally valid interpretation. And in wrestling with this task he brought to consciousness methods and rules for its solution that no previous hermeneutic had worked out.[4]

If Dilthey published this essay on "The Origin of Hermeneutic" in 1900, it was appropriate that two years later Pope Leo XIII in the Apostolic Letter *Vigilantiae* instituting the Commission for Biblical Studies asserted:

> As we were saying, the nature of the divine books is such that in order to dissipate the religious obscurity with which they are shrouded we must never count on the laws of hermeneutics, but must address ourselves to the Church, which has been given by God to mankind as a guide and teacher. In brief, the legiti-

---

[4] "Die Entstehung der Hermeneutik," *Gesammelte Schriften*, V (Leipzig and Berlin, 1924), 324–325.

mate sense of the divine Scriptures ought not to be found outside the Church nor be pronounced by those who have repudi-
ated its teaching and authority.[5]

Yet, even if on such fundamental issues the situation at
the turn of the century had hardly changed since the sixteenth century, it is all the more significant to observe that
within our century the situation *has* begun to change. This
can be illustrated in terms of one of the rules Flacius developed to establish the clear meaning of a scriptural passage. Dilthey describes Flacius' discovery as follows:

Flacius was first to grasp . . . the significance of the psychological or technical principle of interpretation, according to
which the individual passage must be interpreted in terms of
the intention and composition of the whole work. And he was
first to use methodically for this technical interpretation insights of rhetoric as to the inner connection of a literary product,
its composition, and the elements at work in it. The ground-
work has been laid for him by the revision of Aristotelian
rhetoric by Melanchthon. Flacius, himself, is aware of having
first made methodical use of this aid for the clear determining
[of the meaning] of passages, an aid to be found in the context,
the goal, the proportion, the congruence of the individual parts.
He brings the hermeneutical value of such aspects under the
general viewpoint of methodology: "It is everywhere the case
that individual aspects of a whole get their meaning from their
connection to this whole and its other parts." He traces this
inner form of a work into its style and the individual ingredi-
ents at work in it and achieves already acute characterizations
of Pauline and Johannine style.[6]

If then stylistic or formal analysis of literary documents was
first recognized in its basic hermeneutical relevance in the
Protestant effort to demonstrate the clarity of Scripture and
thus the interpreter's independence of tradition and ecclesiastical authority in determining the meaning of Scripture,

5 *Rome and the Study of Scripture: A Collection of Papal Enactments
on the Study of Holy Scripture together with the Decisions of the
Biblical Commission*, 7 ed. (St. Meinrad, Indiana, 1962), p. 32.
6 Dilthey, V, 325.

it is significant to note the large role that such stylistic or formal analysis plays in Roman Catholic hermeneutics in our day, of which I will speak in a few moments. I mention the fact here merely to document the extent to which Catholicism today has appropriated hermeneutical insights that were first worked out as a Protestant alternative to the Tridentine dependence on tradition.

Another instance of an aspect of biblical scholarship beginning within the partisanship of the Roman Catholic-Protestant debate of former centuries and today becoming the shared heritage of Roman Catholic and Protestant alike is the discipline known as textual criticism, the comparison of manuscripts in the attempt to reconstruct a wording as near to the original as possible. Richard Simon, a French Catholic scholar of the seventeenth century, is the recognized father of textual criticism. In the preface to the second edition of his *Histoire critique du texte du Vieux Testament* of 1685 he defends the Catholicity of his work against the stringent polemic of Bossuet as follows:

The sizable alterations that were carried through in the manuscripts of the Bible after the original manuscripts were lost—as we have shown in the first volume of this work—destroy the principle of the Protestants and Socinians completely, who only investigate these same manuscripts of the Bible, and indeed in their present condition. If the truth of religion had not remained in the Church, it would not be secure to seek it now in books that were subjected to such great alterations and that in many respects were dependent on the will of copyists. It is certain that the Jews who copied these books took for themselves the freedom of introducing certain letters here and erasing others there, just as they thought best—although the meaning of the text is often dependent on these letters.[7]

---

[7] W. G. Kummel, *Das Neue Testament: Geschichte der Erforschung seiner Probleme* (Freiburg and Munich, 1958), in the series *Orbis Academicus: Problemgeschichten der Wissenschaft in Dokumenten und Darstellungen,* Fritz Wagner and Richard Brodführer, eds., vol. III, part 3, p. 42.

Yet the discipline of textual criticism is today shared by
Roman Catholic and Protestant alike, and Pope Leo XIII
could have been speaking for both when in the Encyclical
Letter *Providentissimus Deus* of 1893 he affirmed: "It is
true no doubt, that copyists have made mistakes in the text
of the Bible; this question, when it arises, should be carefully
considered on its merits, and the fact not too easily admitted, but only in those passages where the proof is clear."[8]
Père Lagrange, in his *Critique Textuelle* of 1935, maintained that "the 'B text,' though *légèrement revisé,* is the
original text pure and simple."[9] The most recent study of
the text of the Pauline epistles by the classicist G. Zuntz
confirms this general position.[10] Thus the controversial
overtones dominant in previous centuries at the dawn of
modern scholarship have in our century often given way to
a common scholarly *rapport* that is ecumenically far beyond
the first steps being taken gingerly by ecclesiastical authorities.

It is perhaps the emergence of the critical-historical
method as the touchstone of Protestant liberalism that
provided the last stage in the acute antithesis between Roman
Catholic and Protestant hermeneutics. It is just fifty-five
years ago that Alfred Loisy was excommunicated for modernism, that is to say, for the application of the critical-
historical method in a way comparable to that of leading
Protestants of his day. The mood of this antithesis is well
expressed in *Providentissimus Deus:*

> For although the studies of non-Catholics, used with pru-
> dence, may sometimes be of use to the Catholic student, he
> should, nevertheless, bear well in mind—as the Fathers also
> teach in numerous passages—that the sense of Holy Scripture

---

[8] *Rome and the Study of Scripture,* p. 23.
[9] M. J. Lagrange, *Introduction à l'Etude du Nouveau Testament,*
Vol. II: *Critique Textuelle* (Paris, 1935), p. 657.
[10] G. Zuntz, *The Text of the Epistles* (London, 1953), p. 274, cites
Lagrange p. 655.

can [nowhere] be found incorrupt outside the Church, and cannot be expected to be found in writers who, being without the
true faith, only gnaw the bark of sacred Scripture and never
attain its pith.[11]

Although such a formulation seems a blanket condemnation
of Protestant biblical scholarship of all times, the Protestant
can at least hope that the intricate interpretation of papal
pronouncements at which their Catholic colleagues are
masters will make it possible to understand such a blanket
statement as a historically conditioned evaluation, applicable
primarily to the situation at that time. In that case one
could then draw attention to a remarkable parallel to the
position of Pope Leo XIII in Karl Barth's criticism in the
preface to the first edition of his *Commentary on Romans*.

The critical-historical method of biblical research has its
validity. It points to the preparation for understanding that is
never superfluous. But if I had to choose between it and the old
doctrine of inspiration, I would decidedly lay hold of the latter.
It has the greater, deeper, more important validity, for it points
to the actual work of understanding, without which all preparation is useless. I am happy not to have to choose between the
two.[12]

If the emerging Protestant recognition of the superficiality
of much critical-historical exegesis in the past has something

[11] *Rome and the Study of Scripture*, p. 17. I am indebted to Father
John J. Collins, S.J., for a clarification of the translation cited above
from *Rome and the Study of Scripture*. The Latin text, available in the
*Enchiridion Biblicum: Documenta ecclesiastica sacram scripturam
spectantia auctoritate Pontificiae commissionis de re biblica edita*, 2 ed.
(Rome, 1954), p. 47, reads as follows: "Licet enim heterodoxorum
studiis, prudenter adhibitis, juvari interdum possit interpres catholicus,
meminerit tamen, ex crebris quoque veterum documentis, incorruptum
Sacrarum Litterarum sensum extra Ecclesiam neutiquam reperiri, neque
ab eis tradi posse, qui verae fidei experes, Scripturae, non medullam
attingunt, sed corticem rodunt." Father Collins points out: " 'Neutiquam'
means 'by no means,' 'not at all,' 'not entirely.' Numquam would mean
never."

[12] *Der Römerbrief* (Bern, 1919; reprinted 1963, Zürich), p. v.

in common with *Providentissimus Deus,* it does include aspects that the Encyclical of 1893, with its strictures against "higher criticism," did not seem to concede: the validity of the critical-historical method and the assertion that one does not have to choose in an either-or fashion between that method and a concern for the pith of the matter.

Yet it is precisely here that a development has taken place in Catholicism that should not be ignored. *Providentissimus Deus* did advocate "the study of the Oriental languages and of the art of criticism," even if on the rather *ad hominem* grounds that "these acquirements are in these days held in high estimation" and we must be "all things to all men."[13] Yet *Providentissimus Deus* did exhort the exegete "not to depart from the literal and obvious sense, except only where reason makes it untenable or necessity requires."[14] This is an emphasis which the Reformation had made over against the plurality of meanings typical of much medieval exegesis, and it is one which in our time has come to the center of Roman Catholic exegesis, especially since the Papal Encyclical *Divino afflante Spiritu* of 1943, which has been called "the Magna Charta of the literal sense."[15] Now this new emphasis upon the *sensus literalis* seems to open a door to critical scholarship. Indeed as early as 1906 the Biblical Commission answered in the affirmative the question:

Whether it may be granted, without prejudice to the Mosaic authenticity of the Pentateuch, that Moses employed sources in the production of his work, that is, written documents or oral traditions, from which, to suit his special purpose and under the influence of divine inspiration, he selected some

13 *Rome and the Study of Scripture,* p. 20.
14 *Ibid.,* p. 17.
15 Gustave Lambert, S.J., "L'encyclique 'Humani Generis' et l'Ecriture sainte," *L'Encyclique "Humani Generis,"* Cahiers de la Nouvelle Revue Théologique 8 (Paris, 1951), p. 58.

things and inserted them in his work, either literally or in substance, summarized or amplified.[16]

Although this would seem to necessitate a rather unique dating of the sources of the Pentateuch, it does sound more like the Graf-Wellhausen hypothesis than either of those gentlemen would probably have expected.

If Roman Catholic emphasis upon the *sensus literalis* and the Protestant relativizing of the ultimacy of the critical historical method have provided the basis for a gradual *rapprochement* among biblical scholars of the two confessions—indeed, as one outstanding feature of our situation today—this first step has been implemented on both sides by another factor of equal significance. Protestantism's relativizing of the literary criticism of liberalism in favor of a more explicit concern for theological meaning was complemented by a concentration upon oral forms as a key to meaning. Thus form criticism and the history of tradition in the Old Testament and form criticism in the New Testament became the new traits of Protestant biblical scholarship in the first half of the century, and comprise the technical method presupposed in outstanding works on biblical theology in our day. Yet Roman Catholic hermeneutics, in implementing the priority of the *sensus literalis,* has also accorded a new and in some respects decisive prominence to the "forms or kinds of speech" and "literary mode" of the biblical material. The Encyclical Letter *Divino afflante Spiritu* of 1943 states:

By this knowledge and exact appreciation of the modes of speaking and writing in use among the ancients can be solved many difficulties, which are raised against the veracity and historical value of the Divine Scriptures, and no less efficaciously does this study contribute to a fuller and more luminous understanding of the mind of the Sacred Writer.[17]

[16] *Rome and the Study of Scripture*, p. 119.   [17] *Ibid.*, p. 99.

Such an apologetic-sounding statement does not fully reveal
to the uninitiated what is involved. The way this hermeneutical principle works in practice can be illustrated from a
recent article in *The Catholic Biblical Quarterly* by Myles
M. Bourke on "The Literary Genus of Matthew 1–2."[18] The
article begins by repudiating Alfred Loisy's argument that
since Matthew 1–2 is a haggadic commentary it does not
have "the slightest historical basis." But then the article goes
on to use the fact that the infancy narrative belongs to the
literary genre of the haggadic commentary to explain away
the historicity of many items in the story, and then to conclude:

> Admittedly, the gospel presents Jesus' ministry, death and
> resurrection as events which really happened. But that the
> author of such a work might have introduced it by a midrash of
> deep theological insight, in which Jesus appears as the true
> Israel and the new Moses (thus containing the theme of the
> entire gospel), and in which the historical element is very
> slight seems to be a thoroughly probable hypothesis.[19]

The main difference between Bourke and Renan on this
point would seem to be that Renan lived at a time when this
position was inadmissible within the Roman Catholic
Church and Bourke is living in a time when it is admissible.
Form criticism has made it possible for the Catholic scholar
to assert that the literal sense of a given passage is not to
present a true story but rather a story conveying truth.

Of course this loosening of the reins should not be taken
too far, and the papal encyclical *Humani generis* of 1950
seemed again to restrict this liberty:

> In a particular way must be deplored a certain too free inter-
> pretation of the historical books of the Old Testament. Those
> who favor this system, in order to defend their cause, wrongly

[18] *Catholic Biblical Quarterly* 22:160–175 (1960).
[19] *Ibid.*, p. 175.

refer to the Letter which was sent not long ago to the Archbishop of Paris by the Pontifical Commission on Biblical Studies. This Letter, in fact, clearly points out that the first eleven chapters of Genesis, although properly speaking not conforming to the historical method used by the best Greek and Latin writers or by competent authors of our time, do nevertheless pertain to history in a true sense, which however must be further studied and determined by exegetes; the same chapters [the letter points out], in simple and metaphorical language adapted to the mentality of a people but little cultured, both state the principal truths which are fundamental for our salvation, and also give a popular description of the origin of the human race and chosen people. If, however, the ancient sacred writers have taken anything from popular narrations [and this may be conceded], it must never be forgotten that they did so with the help of divine inspiration, through which they were rendered immune from any error in selecting and evaluating those documents.

Therefore, whatever of the popular narrations have been inserted into the Sacred Scriptures must in no way be considered on a par with myths or other such things, which are more the product of an extravagant imagination than of that striving for truth and simplicity which in the Sacred Books, also of the Old Testament, is so apparent that our ancient sacred writers must be admitted to be clearly superior to the ancient profane writers.[20]

Whereas such a statement seems to draw back from the openness of the previous period, an approved interpretation of *Humanis generis* by the Jesuit scholar Gustave Lambert asserts that this is not the case, and he himself presents a summary of views on Genesis 1–11 that interpret some stories more as fiction conveying truths than as historical fact.[21]

Although such uncertainties as to just how much freedom is or is not accorded the scholar and the blunt statement of Pope Pius X on setting up the Biblical Commission

[20] *Rome and the Study of Scripture*, p. 115.
[21] Lambert, pp. 56–74.

that "all are bound in conscience to submit to the decisions
of the Biblical Commission"[22] do not quite coincide with
the Protestant's concept of the freedom of the conscience
and the university's concept of academic freedom derived
from it, it is none the less unmistakable that the Roman
Catholic scholar finds himself in a new position today,
which makes it possible for him to work in much closer
rapport with Protestant scholarship. And, indeed, the Protestant biblical scholar can only welcome the fact that the
manpower available for critical biblical scholarship has
doubled within the last generation thanks to the entry into
this category of so many Roman Catholic scholars.

Protestant biblical scholarship in our century has had
a newly awakened concern for the theological meaning of
the text. Needless to say interpretations have varied widely,
from Oscar Cullmann's *Christ and Time,* whose *Heilsgeschichte* has been widely accepted in Roman Catholic circles,
on through various shades of biblical theology, to the Bult-
mannian demythologizing or existentialist interpretation at
the other end of the spectrum. Krister Stendahl has pointed
out that this newly awakened interest in translating into
contemporary meaning is to some extent a byproduct of the
purely descriptive work of the historian. The latter by stating the meaning which the text had in its own day and
time draws attention to its distance, its foreignness in our
time, and thus poses acutely the question as to its meaning
for today.[23] If, then, it has been paradoxically the critical-
historical method that has posed the hermeneutical problem
for Protestantism, I suspect that it may be the emphasis
upon the *sensus literalis* that has led to the emergence of a
somewhat parallel movement in Roman Catholic scholar-

[22] Motu Proprio of November 17, 1907, published in *Acta Apostolicae Sedis* 40:724 (1907). Also published in the *Ecclesiastical Review* 38:63 (1908).
[23] *The Interpreter's Dictionary of the Bible* (New York and Nashville, 1962), I, 427.

ship—the concern for the *sensus plenior,* the fuller sense, of Scripture—a theme inextricably associated with the name of Father Raymond E. Brown, whose dissertation *The Sensus Plenior of Sacred Scripture* has since its publication in 1955 been at the center of Roman Catholic hermeneutical discussion.[24] And, once one begins to see what is being discussed under the Latin term *sensus plenior,* one recognizes that it is in various respects the same kind of hermeneutical problem with which modern literary criticism and Protestant hermeneutics are also involved. For example, the turning away from the psychologizing concern for the author behind the text and the concentration upon the subject matter that comes to expression in the language of the text have corollaries both in modern literary criticism and in Protestantism's new hermeneutic. And the interest in *sensus plenior* has some affinities with Gerhard von Rad's interest in the successive reinterpretation of the Old Testament *Heilsgeschichte* within the successive oral and written layers of the Old Testament itself, or with Rudolf Bultmann's detection that the Christology implicit in Jesus' mission becomes explicit in the Christological titles attributed to him after Easter. Furthermore Father Brown's insistence over against Père Benoit that the *sensus plenior* is not to be subsumed under the *sensus literalis* is reminiscent of Krister Stendahl's clear distinction between a purely descriptive Biblical theology that "yields the original in its own terms, limiting the interpretation to what it meant in its own setting," and the task of systematic theology to translate that meaning into the language of our day.[25] Of course, just as such Protestant translation for our day poses problems of distortion, modernization, and dogmatic prejudice,

[24] Published at Baltimore, Maryland, by St. Mary's University. See also his article "The *Sensus Plenior* in the Last Ten Years," forthcoming in the *Catholic Biblical Quarterly.*

[25] *The Interpreter's Dictionary of the Bible,* I, 427.

just so the criteria of *sensus plenior* are an area of unfinished business, as the Catholic critic John L. McKenzie has pointed out.[26] The Protestant, for example, looks with mixed feelings upon the more congenial wing of the Vatican Council's effort to merge Tradition and Scripture, if that involves defining as Scriptural such items as some Mariological beliefs which in fact lack adequate support in any sense of Scripture. It is to be hoped, however, that the discussion of *sensus plenior* will provide a controlled and responsible hermeneutical context for doing justice to the contemporary relevance of the biblical message without such excesses as in past ages characterized the practical interpretation of Scripture in Protestantism as well as Catholicism.

I have just alluded to a further aspect distinctive of contemporary Protestant hermeneutic, its concentration upon the deeper hermeneutical significance of the phenomenon of translation. This emphasis, originally oriented simply to making the Bible available in the vernacular, has recently been seen to involve the basic task of systematic theology, the translation of the meaning of the Bible into the thought world, the culture, the life, in which it is proclaimed and believed. Indeed, one is reviving an archaic meaning of the word "translate," signifying to "transfer" from one place to the other. This is a meaning confined largely to certain ecclesiastical usages, such as the "translation" of a saint to heaven or of his bones to the sanctuary, or, even before his death, his "translation" from one see to another. Translation as such a transfer of meaning involves much more than simply finding so-called equivalent terms for words in a foreign language. It is the whole broad task of contemporary theology, the problem sometimes referred to as "Christianity and culture." The task is fraught with the necessity of such

[26] "Problems of Hermeneutics in Roman Catholic Exegesis," *Journal of Biblical Literature* 77:197–204 (1958), esp. pp. 201–202.

correlation if the message is to "get across" and the inherent danger of its simply dissolving into the culture is avoided. In Roman Catholicism there has at times been an astounding assimilation, which has aroused the Puritanical opposition of Protestant biblicists who naively assumed that one could in our day and age do and think just as one could in biblical times. Here the Protestant has lacked tolerance even for legitimate Roman Catholic translational innovations. In other instances it has been Roman Catholicism that has resisted various trends toward Gallicanism, Anglicanism, or Americanism within the Church, so as to give to its tradition an untranslatedness of which the continued use of Latin in the liturgy is merely a symbol. Thus the vote by the Second Vatican Council to permit parts of the mass to be said in the vernacular is not only a translation from Latin into modern tongues; rather the vesting of the decision on such matters in the hands of the national colleges of bishops is to some extent a translation of the authority of the *curia* into the hands of the bishops around the world. A considerable portion of the Roman Catholic-Protestant dialogue must be devoted to this broader issue of translation in its relation to tradition, with the Protestant investigating the possibility that tradition may in many instances have been a valid translation of biblical meaning into a non-biblical culture, the Roman Catholic investigating the possibility that such a valid tradition, valid because it was a good translation into an earlier period of the Church's history, need not for that reason be valid for the Church's life today where a new translation is required.

If, then, there are various specific points where, in distinction from previous centuries, our century can note with gratification a *rapprochement* between Roman Catholic and Protestant hermeneutic, the bearing of all this upon the wider concerns of the Roman Catholic-Protestant dialogue is somewhat ambiguous—precisely for the reason suggested at the opening of my paper—in pointing to the varying position of biblical interpretation within the two confessions. Perhaps one can pose the problem by inquiring as to whether for Roman Catholicism there is really any hermeneutical problem at all. If for Protestantism the Church's being the Church depends upon the valid proclamation of the Word, then the hermeneutical problem is ultimately *the* problem of the Church. For it is in the proclaimed word that Jesus Christ, the reality of salvation, is present. In the Roman Catholic understanding the situation would seem to be different, in that the contemporaneity of the reality of salvation is mediated through the ecclesiastical institution. Hence, the Protestant theologian Gerhard Ebeling makes the provocative assertion:

> The hermeneutic problem of the present actualization of the historically unique event is here [for example, in the transubstantiated host] solved in such a radical way that a hermeneutic question in the narrower sense really no longer exists at all. For the question that arises primarily in regard to the exposition of Scripture—the question how far what is therein attested as the event of revelation has decisive significance for the present—is taken out of the context of Scripture exposition and answered by the objective event of the sacrament.[27]

One may wonder whether the hermeneutical freedom emerging gradually within the Roman Catholic Church is really parallel to that of Protestantism, where for Protestantism the true interpretation of Scripture is the essence of the Church but for Catholicism it would seem to be more an appendix to an already achieved contemporaneity of salvation in the Church as institution. Is it because hermeneutics is not the hermeneutical principle of Catholicism (which is to be found rather in the councils of the Church hierarchy), that Roman Catholic hermeneutics in our day has been per-

[27] *Word and Faith* (Philadelphia, 1963), p. 35.

mitted to run with loosened reins in a way often parallel to that of Protestantism?

It is perhaps significant that the Dutch convert to Catholicism, Willem Hendrik van de Pol, in his book "Reformation Christianity Viewed Phenomenologically,"[28] defines Protestantism as having only a derivative reality, in its concentration upon the word, whereas reality in a genuine, ontological sense is confined to Catholicism. Here one sees, stated in pro-Catholic terminology—and for the converse terminology one may consult Heinz Liebing's reply[29]—two antithetic concepts of reality confronting each other, one in which reality happens as Word, the other where reality is metaphysically institutionalized. These two contrary concepts of reality form the basic incompatibility of the two confessions, an incompatibility which gives their two hermeneutics, in spite of the many parallels to which I have sought to draw attention, a basic incongruence as yet unresolved. That this incompatibility can be resolved is a hope toward which every Christian in his faith may look. Just as the Roman Catholic can hope that the Protestant ecumenical movement will come to accept the validity of the renewed Roman Catholic institution, the Protestant can hope that the Second Vatican Council will provide ecclesiastical structures granting the biblical hermeneutics of Roman Catholic scholarship a *constitutive* role in defining the nature of the Church.

[28] *Das reformatorische Christentum in phänomenologischer Betrachtung* (Einsiedeln, 1956).

[29] " 'Proprie' und 'translate'. Erwägungen zur Hermeneutik der konfessionellen Auseinandersetzung," *Zeitschrift für Theologie und Kirche,* 59:168–181 (1962).

CHALLENGE TO DIALOGUE
IN THE NEW TESTAMENT*

W. D. DAVIES

I CONSIDER it a very great honor to have been asked
by the Harvard Divinity School to address its auspicious
Colloquium, but I am extremely conscious that I am not
equipped to deal with the many issues which it must pro-
voke. I have, therefore, decided merely to share with you
some reflections which my work as a biblical critic have
prompted in relation to the rapprochement which, like a
thaw after a long winter, seems to be cracking the icy barriers which have long plagued Christendom. My method
will be to point out certain areas where, it seems to me, a
challenge to dialogue is issued by recent study of the New
Testament. But instead of enlarging on these, as I had first
intended, I have been asked to illustrate some of them by a
treatment of one particularly pertinent theme in detail.

We have been reminded recently that the early fathers
were concerned to understand the Gospel tradition critically
and historically.[1] But historical criticism in the modern
sense stems mainly from two sources, the Reformation and
the Enlightenment. The spirit of rationalism and inquiry,
which invaded many forms of human awareness in the
eighteenth century, in the religious field questioned especially a basic concept of all Christendom—that of an authoritative canon of Scripture—and it thus fostered the rise

---

* The Scripture quotations in this paper are from the Revised Standard Version of the Bible, copyrighted 1946 and 1952 by the Division
of Christian Education, National Council of Churches, and used by
permission.
1 R. M. Grant, *The Earliest Lives of Jesus* (New York, 1961).

of criticism. It has sometimes been suggested that the criticism which was stimulated by the Enlightenment and in which we are still engaged, should not be taken too seriously. It has been, and is, merely a passing phase of Christian history, a phenomenon of recent centuries, which a long perspective upon Christian history will relegate to its properly subordinate place. Such a position I find difficult to accept. The Enlightenment was a major crisis in the history of the world as well as of the Church; and even though the Church may seek to ignore its acids, the world will not long allow it to do so: historical criticism is here to stay. Since it is not necessary to insist on this in the present Colloquium, I merely note in this connection that the questions raised by the Enlightenment are still with us and will remain with us. They constitute the ultimately crucial issues that have to be faced; for example, the question of the validity of the historical ground of our faith will always be asked by the world if not by us.

But it is the problems posed by the other source of historical criticism, the Reformation, that mainly concern this Colloquium. The Reformation was important for many reasons, but primarily because it returned, through the study of Hebrew and Greek, to the Scriptures and thus rediscovered aspects of Christianity which were endangered. With the positive, beneficial consequences of the Reformation, however, I am not concerned but rather with its negative impact. The churches that derived from the Reformation adopted the principle of *sola scriptura*. But as this came to be applied within the divisions of Protestantism, it usually came to mean "Scripture according to our tradition." There was no escape from tradition in the reading of Scripture. In time each of the Protestant groups—Congregationalists, Presbyterians, Baptists, and others—came to use Scripture for the justification of its own tradition. Each came to claim for its own polity a ground in the New Testament. But the very multiplicity of polities could not but, finally, compel the quest for what the New Testament actually taught. By provoking this quest the churches born of the Reformation prepared the way both for the Enlightenment and for higher criticism. The divisiveness of Protestantism was historically beneficial to scholarship. Today the situation is reversed. That very divisiveness is being challenged by the scholarship to which it gave birth. I venture to think that the issues raised by the Reformation within Protestantism are in process of being met in terms of a biblical criticism which is now delivering us from sectarian provincialism. By establishing for us a point of reference more fundamental than the various traditions have allowed, historical criticism is providing a check to the fissiparous tendencies within Protestantism. It is no longer possible for any one Protestant group to claim the sole authority of Scripture for its own polity. Criticism has compelled a reassessment of our particular traditions in the light of Christian origins, and, in this sense, has turned out to be a reconciling force: it is wrenching us away from loyalties to the partial, the local, and the merely traditional.

So far I have only mentioned the healing impact of criticism within Protestantism. Is that same criticism taking us further, not only behind Protestant provincialism, but also behind the Reformation itself, to a unity which can embrace both Protestantism and Catholicism?

In reply to this question, I can only state that the study of the New Testament has had repercussions for me outside Protestantism. These came primarily from an attempt to understand the interaction between Christianity and its mother faith, Judaism. Here certainly criticism has played a reconciling role, and has issued not only in a deeper appreciation of Judaism, but in the conviction that the renewal of Christendom is tied up with the rediscovery of its roots in Judaism. If I may be allowed to say so, we can only hope that a cry may go forth from Rome and elsewhere, not only that Christians may be one, but to remind the churches everywhere of their specifically Judaic inheritance. This would not only help to atone for the guilt of Christendom but help it to rediscover its own soul. This is a subject in itself, but I must emphasize that it is from a reappraisal of the relation of Christianity to Judaism in the New Testament that I have been led to a new openness toward Catholicism. In three spheres, it seems to me, recent New Testament studies are making it possible for Protestants to look with more understanding at what has divided us.

I

First, there is the question of order and ardor, office and charisma. Recent study is forcing upon us a new appreciation of elements of order in the primitive Church which Protestantism has often been loathe to recognize. Sohm argued that the organized structure of the Church not merely had no dogmatic significance, but actually involved a departure from the pristine purity of the primitive community, which was a purely spiritual fellowship of saints. Not all Protestants went as far as Sohm, but it has always been difficult for us to do justice to organizational principles that might have been at work in the primitive communities, for example, the authority of the Apostolate.[2] In two ways, at least, scholarship is leading us to a new awareness at this point.

In the first place, we are being compelled to give greater recognition to what I may be allowed to call, loosely, the intellectual aspect of primitive Christianity. We now know that the early Church displayed prodigious intellectual activity in an attempt to set the New Dispensation in the light

[2] See my *Christian Origins and Judaism* (Philadelphia, 1962), pp. 199ff, for a survey of the problem, and a review by T. M. Parker, *The Church Times,* April 1950, and by B. C. Butler, *The Downside Review,* October 1962, pp. 367ff, for correctives to this.

of the Old, and sought to interpret its Lord in terms of the Scriptures of the Old Testament. The use of the Old Testament in the New, to supply what Dr. Dodd[3] taught us to call the substructure of primitive Christian theology, was a task of immense intellectual industry and penetration. Dr. Stendahl's work, for example, on the School of Matthew, has opened our eyes in a direct way to the "scholastic" character of some, at least, of the primitive communities. But such biblical exegesis as the New Testament reveals could not have taken place in a vacuum: it presupposes communities which, deeply moved as they were by the Spirit, were also disciplined in the study of the Scriptures. The scriptural acumen and application of the primitive communities, not to speak of their possible liturgical sophistication, demands a clear recognition of their organized existence. If the primitive Church bears so many marks of a school, was it not more structured than much Protestant thinking has previously allowed?

That the exegetical activity of the primitive Church requires a greater recognition of its "scholasticism," so to speak, has been directly reinforced by the Dead Sea Scrolls. These have enhanced the likelihood that the early Church was born in a milieu which made a concern for order a natural one from the very beginning. The extent to which primitive Christianity was influenced by Essene ideology and organization is still in dispute. Certainly after A.D. 68 or 70 I should argue that Essene forms influenced the Church, and it is not to be ruled out that even before then the Church had already been influenced by its forms, although not captured by them.[4] And apart from Essene influences

---

[3] *According to the Scriptures* (Cambridge, Eng., 1953). Pertinent in this connection also is B. Gerhardsson, *Memory and Manuscript* (Uppsala, 1962); see my review in *Neotestamentica et Patristica*, ed. Van Unnik and Bo Reike (Leiden, 1962).

[4] See *The Setting of the Sermon on the Mount* (Cambridge, Eng., 1964).

there were other organizational patterns which could not but have influenced the Church from the beginning, those of the Synagogue especially. The recognition of this and of the cultic and liturgical existence of the primitive Church is challenging us to a new assessment of the strictly ecclesiastical factors, if I may so express it, in the early communities. I could illustrate this by a treatment of Matthew 18, for example, but I must desist.[5]

II

The second area where the Reformation issued in deep division was in the understanding of the relation between Gospel and Law. In its initial impulse, though not in all of its later manifestations, the Reformation may be regarded as the rediscovery of the Scriptures primarily in their Pauline emphases. But it tended to make Paul, understood in a particular way, the norm for the understanding of Christianity. Far be it from me to deplore a rediscovery of Paul! And, yet, has not the concentration on Paulinism, understood in terms of justification by faith alone, engendered a failure to do justice to other elements in the New Testament which are also integral to the Gospel? The latter is always a demand as well as a gift. To interpret the faith of the New Testament only, or even mainly, in terms of a rigid understanding of the Pauline antithesis of grace and law is precarious. It is to ignore three things: first, the tumultuous, tortuous nature of Paul himself, a fact which alone should make us chary of making his experience in any way normative; secondly, the exaggerations demanded by the circumstances of the historical controversy out of which that antithesis arose; and, thirdly, much evidence pointing to a law which remains in the new covenant of grace.

[5] The work of P. Carrington, G. D. Kilpatrick, Miss Guilding, and numerous other scholars deserves notice here, but the literature is already vast in this field.

Several factors have converged in recent scholarship to challenge us at this point. A deeper understanding of Judaism now makes it possible for us to deal with law more justly. On the other hand, a closer attention to the New Testament as a whole, and, indeed, to Paulinism itself as a whole, tends to the same result. We find in all strata of the New Testament, not a legal nihilism, but the affirmation of a messianic law. This is true of Paul himself. It is no longer possible to regard him as a solitary colossus, a firebrand apostle of a religion free from law, separated from the rest of the primitive community. He is "in the law of Christ" (*ennomos Christou*), urging the observance of the law of the Messiah. Matthew likewise confronts us with the Messianic Torah and the Fourth Gospel with its "new commandment." However much the New Dispensation differed from the Old, it retained a New Sinai in a New Covenant. We are being compelled to recognize that Gospel and Law are not in antithesis but conjoined. This fact I shall seek to illustrate, along with the next point to which I turn, in the discussion to follow on Paul and tradition.[6]

III

The third area where recent studies are issuing a challenge to us is in that of the relation of the New Testament to tradition. It is now a commonplace that the New Testament is a thoroughly ecclesiastical document, in the sense that it was produced by the Church, from the Church, for the Church. This has emerged from the work not only of form-critics but also of those scholars who have emphasized the role of the cult and liturgy in the emergence of the New Testament. At the risk of simplification, it is fair to say that Protestantism has usually opposed the Scriptures to

---

[6] I have sought to deal with this theme in *The Setting of the Sermon on the Mount.*

the Church, and it has been largely governed by the principle, *sola scriptura*. To a New Testament student such an opposition is increasingly difficult. The New Testament itself points us to the role of a tradition in the life of the Church: it is itself an expression or outcome of this tradition. This means that the New Testament cannot merely be set over against tradition, nor can its documents when they first emerge be set above the tradition because they themselves appeal to it. In short, the question of tradition is being reopened for us.[7]

At this point, on the principle that "an ounce of fact is worth a ton of theory," I shall indicate the kind of consideration which has led me to mention these areas of challenge. I do so by an examination of tradition in Paul, in illustration of the challenge being issued to us in the area of Gospel law and tradition. This is especially pertinent because Paul has often been regarded as the representative of freedom from tradition.[8] Of all the figures of the New Testament Paul perhaps is the best known, but he is none the less difficult to understand. And, in particular, it is hard to grasp how Paul understood the ethical or moral life of Christians in its relation to his theology. His own life he seems to have divided clearly into two parts: there was, first, his life under the law, when he was a Jew; and then, secondly, his life "in Christ." These two parts were distinctly separated by his experience on the road to Damascus. The act by which a

[7] I have been most helped at this point by the works of Professor Leenhardt of Geneva. See, for example, his article on "Sola Scriptura ou Ecriture et Tradition," in *Etudes Théologiques et Religieuses* 1:5–46 (1961), and the works referred to therein.

[8] I should state that from this point the material is extracted from a larger work entitled *The Setting of the Sermon on the Mount* (Cambridge, Eng.: Cambridge University Press, 1964), in which I am particularly concerned to examine the role of the words of Jesus in the primitive Church. I am indebted to the Cambridge University Press for permitting the republication of this section, without, however, the frequent use or reference to the original Greek as in the volume itself.

man acknowledged his faith and really began to live "in Christ" was equally distinct; it was baptism,[9] an act which symbolized for Paul a death to the old life under the Law, a death once and for all, and a rising to a newness of life "in Christ," or "in the Spirit." By baptism the Christian man through faith had died, had risen, had been justified; he was a new creation who had already passed from death to life, for whom the final judgment of God himself was past.

Was there room in such a man's life for anything more? Did he now need any law to guide him? Could he not now simply live, in spontaneous response to the Spirit that was in him, free from legal restraint of any kind? At first sight, at least, the contrast between the life before and the life after faith seems to be a contrast between a life under law and a life under grace, and it has often been stated that there is no room for "law" in the Christian life as Paul understood it: it was for him a life of freedom in the Spirit.[10] But, nevertheless, three factors complicated the new life "in Christ," as Paul recognized. First, although he was a new creation, the Christian man was still in the flesh and, therefore, still open to the attacks of sin. Secondly, because he was still in the flesh he was also still subject to the hostile supernatural forces which were arraigned against man; the prince of the power of the air, the elements of this world, these were still active, and had to be opposed. Saved and justified and even sanctified as he already was, the Christian was still living between the time of the first appearance of Christ and the End. Thus Paul was inevitably faced with the question of Christian behavior. How was a Christian to conduct himself "betwixt the times" in this

[9] Gal. 2:21; Rom. 6.
[10] The documentation for the above passages is familiar: see, for example, the excellent treatment in R. Schnackenburg, *Die Sittliche Botschaft des Neuen Testaments* (Munich, 1954), pp. 183–209, and my article in *The Interpreter's Dictionary of the Bible* (Nashville, 1963), on "Ethics in the New Testament."

world? Was Paul at all influenced by the ethical teaching of Jesus in answering this question?[11] There are many strands in his ethical exhortation which, while important, are not for our purpose of crucial significance,[12] but the two most characteristic emphases in the Epistles—namely, the rooting of the imperative in the indicative[13] and the concept

[11] This question is a corollary to a wider one, that of the relation between Paul and the "historical Jesus" and the early Church. See C. A. A. Scott, *Christianity According to St. Paul* (Cambridge, Eng., 1932), pp. 11ff; H. J. Schoeps, *Paulus* (Tübingen, 1959), pp. 48–51. He rejects any preoccupation of Paul with the historical Jesus, so also A. Schweitzer, *The Mysticism of Paul the Apostle* (New York, 1931), R. Bultmann, *Theologie des Neuen Testaments* (Tübingen, 1953), I, 185.

[12] For example, Paul appeals to "conscience," but only in a secondary way. See my article on "Conscience" in *The Interpreter's Dictionary* for bibliography. In a recent study, *Die Tugend- und Lasterkataloge im Neuen Testament* (Berlin, 1959), Siegfried Wibbing has dealt with Paul's use of lists of virtues and vices in his paraenesis. The closest parallels to these he finds in the Dead Sea Scrolls (e.g., 1QS iv. 9–11; iii. 13–iv. 26) where, as in Paul, the lists are set in a context of ethical dualism and of eschatology (see W. D. Davies, "Flesh and Spirit," in *The Scrolls and the New Testament*, ed. K. Stendahl [New York, 1957], pp. 169ff). Paul's use of such lists Wibbing explains in terms of the relation between the indicative and the imperative in his thought (pp. 117ff). Whereas the Dead Sea Scrolls connect the lists of vices and virtues with man's very creation by God, it is with baptism that Paul connects the virtues. Through this the Christian man has become a new creation. But he has to express this fact in deeds. These are enumerated in the lists of virtues, which, however, do not constitute a new law, their items being too generalized for this (p. 117). "Sie bieten Kasuistischen Gebots-order Verbotsreihen, um bestimmte Situationen des Lebens zu erfassen und zu regeln. Es sind zum grössen Teil abstrakte Begriffe, die hier nebeneinander gestellt werden" (p. 123). Wibbing may well be right in his understanding of Paul's use of the ethical lists, but his work prompts us to emphasize one point. That is, even though Paul does use generalized directions in the lists referred to, without formulating them into a law, where he uses the words of Jesus directly, he treats them as "law." The instances of these are few, but they are sufficient to establish that Christ for Paul was Lawgiver as well as Redeemer.

[13] The best statement of this problem known to me is a brief one by W. Joest, *Gesetz und Freiheit: Das Problem des tertius usus legis bei Luther und die neutestamentliche Parainese* (Göttingen, 1951), pp. 134ff. The German discussion can be traced in his footnotes. See especially Bultmann, *Theologie*, vol. I. M. Goguel, *L'Eglise Primitive* (Paris, 1947), pp. 441ff, contains a brilliant discussion of the problem.

of the good life as the fruit of the Spirit—present us with a
real problem in estimating the place of the words of Jesus
in Paul's thought. With these we must now deal.

(1) When Paul exhorts Christians to the good life, there
can be no question that he most commonly appeals to the
reality and character of the new life which they possess
"in Christ," with all that this implies. He urges them to live
in accordance with their calling, their sanctification, their
freedom, their sonship, their life "in Christ" or "in the
Spirit." To consider these realities makes sin intolerable.
As, for example, in 1 Thess. 2:10–12: "You are witnesses,
and God also, how holy and righteous and blameless was
our behavior to you believers; for you know how, like a
father with his children, we exhorted each one of you and
encouraged you and charged you to lead a life worthy of
God, who calls you into his own kingdom and glory." In
response to a call to participate in God's kingdom and glory
the Christian goes forward: the word of exhortation is at
the same time a word of encouragement.

Again in 1 Thess. 4:7–8 we read: "For God has not
called us for uncleanness, but in holiness. Therefore whoever disregards this, disregards not man but God, who
gives his Holy Spirit to you." The previous verses, also 4:3ff,
make it clear that God's call implies sanctification.[14] The
Christian is to accept the "lead" given to him by God's call,
maintained by God's spirit; he is "to live out" his new existence. I Cor. 6:15 is equally explicit. The "bodily" relation
of the Christian with his Lord makes relations with a prosti-
tute unthinkable. Similarly marriage with an unbeliever
is incompatible with the relationship of the Christian with
God: note 2 Cor. 6:15f, where again the metaphor of the
temple employed in 1 Cor. 6:15f emerges. In Rom. 7:4ff a

---

14 By this is meant that no sharp distinction is to be made, as in
later Reformation theology but not in Luther himself (see W. Joest,
Gesetz und Freiheit), between justification and sanctification.

new life is naturally regarded as the outcome of the new
relationship in which the Christian lives. Even where Paul
makes use of ethical commonplaces familiar to Hellenistic
Judaism he still appeals to the nature of the Christian man
in his exhortations. In this connection 1 Cor. 11:2ff is
instructive. In 1 Cor. 11:2–3 reference is made to the relation of men and women to Christ, but in 1 Cor. 11:13, 14
(cf. Eph. 5:32, 33) there is a reference to what is natural,
Paul making use possibly, though not certainly, of a Stoic
concept at this point. But as Dahl has pointed out: "This and
similar appeals to 'natural law' are not due to any lack of
consistency; they are in full harmony with the Apostle's
fundamental conviction, that what is realized in the Church,
the new creation, is in harmony with the original will of
God, the Creator. Sin corrupts creation; deification of the
creature in the end leads to unnaturalness (Rom. 1); but
in the Church all natural human virtues should be in high
esteem (Phil. 4:8)."[15]

In the passages to which we have referred Paul grounds
his imperative in an indicative: he urges Christians to become what they are. The following passages are also pertinent in illustration of this:

"Cleanse out the old leaven that you may be fresh dough,
as you really are unleavened" (1 Cor. 5:7).

"For freedom Christ has set us free; stand fast therefore,
and do not submit again to the yoke of slavery" (Gal. 5:1).

"If we live by the Spirit, let us also walk by the Spirit"
(Gal. 5:25).

"For you are all sons of light and sons of the day; we are
not of the night or of darkness. So then let us not sleep, as
others do, but let us keep awake and be sober" (1 Thess.
5:5–6: cf. Rom. 13:12–13; Eph. 5:8–10).

[15] N. A. Dahl in *The Background of the New Testament and its
Eschatology*, ed. W. D. Davies and D. Daube (Cambridge, Eng.,
1951), pp. 439f.

"Now as you excel in everything—in faith, in utterance, in knowledge, in all earnestness, and in your love for us—see that you excel in this gracious work also" (2 Cor. 8:7).

"How can we who died to sin still live in it? Do you not know that all of us who have been baptized into Christ Jesus were baptized into his death? We were buried therefore with him by baptism into death, so that as Christ was raised from the dead by the glory of the Father, we too might walk in newness of life" (Rom. 6:2–4).

"If then you have been raised with Christ, seek the things that are above, where Christ is, seated at the right hand of God" (Col. 3:1).

This rooting of the imperative in the indicative is found also in Matthew,[16] who is no stranger to the Pauline profundity at this point.

[16] See my *The Setting of the Sermon on the Mount*. It is not to be overlooked that the demand presented by Matthew in the "Sermon on the Mount" as elsewhere is the demand of Jesus, who came to the lost. For Matthew "Das Kommen Jesu zu den Verlorenen und Verworfenen ist doch mehr als ein vorläufiger Amnestieakt, der nur der Grundlage schafft für ein neues Gesetz. Es ist endgultige Gottestat. Die synoptische Gerichtsparainese, die auf den kommenden Gerichtstag, die noch ausstehende Entscheidung, die Gefahr des Versagens und Fallens hinweist, wird gegrenzt von der Verkundigung des in Jesus schon gegenwartiges Reiches und Sieges. Das Reich Gottes ist zu euch gekommen, der Starke ist gebunden von dem Starkerer (Matt. 12:28ff)": so W. Joest, *Gesetz und Freiheit*, p. 167. See also p. 157, "auch die synoptische Parainese ist indikativisch begründet in der Zuwendung Gottes zu dem Sünder, die in der Person und dem handeln Jesu leibhaftig wird." Joest (pp. 155ff) has attempted to show how Luther's understanding of Law (Gesetz) compares with those attitudes toward it which are found in the New Testament documents. Paul's understanding of Christ as the end of the Law, he asserts, affords a real parallel to Luther's doctrine of justification by faith, which he takes to be also the inbreaking of a "new aeon" for Paul and the indicative in which the Pauline imperative is grounded. But Joest is compelled to recognize that, as in Matthew and James, so in the Pauline epistles, particularly in the paraenetical sections, there is another attitude which is difficult to reconcile with that of Luther. Thus, Paul, as we indicate above, retains the concept of a future judgment in which man is judged according to his works, as do Matthew and James. There is no single Pauline understanding of the Christian life: justification by faith is only one aspect of it. It is possible not only to appeal

But the precise significance of this connection between the imperative and indicative in Paul is important. It has been claimed that the point of reference for Paul in the indicative is not the character or the life of the Jesus of history as such, and certainly not his moral teaching, but the pivotal elements in the kerygma, the facts of the incarnation as therein presented, namely, that Christ was born a Jew, under the Law (Gal. 4:4), of Davidic descent (Rom. 1:1), was betrayed (1 Cor. 11:23), was crucified (1 Cor. 2:2; Gal. 3:1; Phil. 2:6), was buried and rose again (1 Cor. 15:4; Rom. 6:4): these Paul refers to but not to the biographical details of Jesus' career. References to the character of Jesus do not serve Paul's central theological concepts but subserve his paraenetic purposes, that is, they are peripheral and not central. While the data given above reveal that the Apostle was concerned with Jesus as a historical and not a mythological figure, it is also clear that he does not call for any imitation of the life of Jesus, in its words and works, but only in its character as the act of God. The imperative of the Christian life is not attached to the deeds and teaching of Jesus but rather to the essential fact of his self-giving. On this view both the details of what Jesus did on earth and his teaching are largely irrelevant to Paul's understanding of the Christian faith.[17]

(2) The same conclusion would seem to follow from the second emphasis in Pauline ethical teaching, namely, on

---

from Matthew and James against Paul but from Paul against Paul. Just as Matthew ends his "Sermon" with a reference to the "End," in which obedience to the words of Jesus is the criterion for judgment, so too Paul looks forward to a judgment seat of Christ where, we may believe, the same criterion applies. For Paul and James, see the excellent study of J. Jeremias, *Expository Times* 66:368ff (1954–1955).

[17] J. Weiss, *Earliest Christianity*, Eng. trans. (New York, 1959), II, 555; Bultmann, *Theologie*, I, 185. See the discussion in G. S. Hendry, *The Gospel of the Incarnation* (Philadelphia, 1958), pp. 32–41, on "The Jesus of History," and H. J. Schoeps, *Paulus* (Tübingen, 1959), pp. 48ff.

the Christian life as the fruit of the Spirit. The passage in Gal. 5:16–24 is crucial: "But I say, walk by the Spirit, and do not gratify the desires of the flesh. For the desires of the flesh are against the Spirit, and the desires of the Spirit are against the flesh; for these are opposed to each other, to prevent you from doing what you would. But if you are led by the Spirit you are not under the law. Now the works of the flesh are plain: immorality, impurity, licentiousness, idolatry, sorcery, enmity, strife, jealousy, anger, selfishness, dissension, party spirit, envy, drunkenness, carousing, and the like. I warn you, as I warned you before, that those who do such things shall not inherit the kingdom of God. But the fruit of the Spirit is love, joy, peace, patience, kindness, goodness, faithfulness, gentleness, self-control; against such there is no law. And those who belong to Christ Jesus have crucified the flesh with its passions and desires."

A contrast is drawn between the *works* of the flesh, and the *fruit* of the Spirit, the implication being that the Christian life has the character of spontaneity. And in Gal. 5:18, 23 it is explicitly stated not to be bound by Law. Similarly in 1 Cor. 2:12–16 the Spirit apparently of itself assures to the Christian the possession of the mind of Christ, an illumination which is autonomous. Thus, again, the ethic of Paul in its concentration on the Spirit would seem to relegate the character of the teaching of Jesus to insignificance.

To judge, then, from the two most familiar emphases in Pauline ethics, as interpreted above, unlike Matthew, who combines with "the imperative rooted in the indicative" a very marked concentration on the words of Jesus, as the law of the Messiah, Paul would seem to have been, if not ignorant of, at least indifferent to the teaching of Jesus. Kümmel has expressed this with forceful clarity: "Paulus fühlt sich nicht als Schüler des geschichtlichen Jesus, sondern als Beauftragter des Auferstandenen. Und darum ist es nicht seine Aufgabe, weiterzugeben was er über den geschichtlichen Jesus und seine Worte gehört und überliefert erhalten hat, sondern Christus zu verkündigen."[18] But before accepting such an evaluation of Paul certain factors are to be considered.

And, before we proceed, two preliminary correctives to what we have written on the indicative-imperative and on the Spirit in Paul are necessary. There is, in the first place, an apparent contradiction, which may even amount to an antinomy, in Paul's treatment of the moral life. One side of this we have above indicated, namely, its rooting of the imperative in the indicative. But while this must be accorded its due prominence, another side emerges clearly, if not so persistently—what might be called the "vigilatory." Paul retains three concepts, the last of which amounts to an emphasis, which stand in uneasy juxtaposition with the claims he makes that the Christian has been saved, justified, sanctified, is now, in short, a new creation, who is merely called upon to be what he is. These are:

(a) The idea that, however much the justification which he has already experienced anticipates it or may be regarded as "final" in principle, the Christian still awaits a judgment yet to come, the last judgment.

(b) The idea that at this last judgment each will be rewarded, not according to his faith, but according to his works.

(c) The idea that in preparation for this final judgment obedience to the will of God is necessary, so that the Christian life turns out to be a training (*askesis*) and a call to vigilance.

All this means that for Paul Christianity is a "way" to be walked.

So, in the second place, while the spontaneity of the life

18 K. G. Kümmel, cited by H. J. Schoeps on p. 51.

in the Spirit is to be acknowledged, it has also to be recognized that Paul knows the Spirit as a kind of "law." The reader is referred to our treatment of the evidence[19] elsewhere. Suffice it here to add the words of Goguel: "Il faut maintenir que la justification, la possession de l'Esprit, l'appel au salut, la promesse de ce salut jouent dans la vie du Chrétien le rôle d'une loi, une loi, il est vrai, qui est intérieure."

For our purposes, the question how this "vigilatory" note in Paul and his understanding of the Spirit in terms of a law are to be reconciled with the "indicatives" of the Epistles or whether there is an antinomy to be recognized at the heart of Paulinism, need not be faced. Suffice it that the evidence reveals Paul as occupied with obedience and works. Our concern is to discover whether the words of his Lord provided him with a reservoir of ethical tradition and even with a "law" (a law not merely within as Goguel writes) upon which he drew for the moral education of his converts.

To begin with, neither "the indicative-imperative" emphasis nor that on the Spirit in Paul is to be divorced from the actualities of the life and teaching of Jesus. [The reasons for our insistence on this we have presented elsewhere: the reader is referred to *Paul and Rabbinic Judaism*, pp. 136ff, 195ff.] Here a general consideration is pertinent. To be convincing as kerygma the content of the life and teaching of Jesus must have been consistent with the nature of the kerygma: the appeal of Paul to the Incarnation was of necessity also an appeal to the life and teaching of Jesus which had exhibited the quality of the Incarnation in the actuality of history. There is no antithesis to be set up or implied between the idea of the Incarnation for Paul and

---

[19] W. D. Davies, *Paul and Rabbinic Judaism*, 2 ed. (London, 1955). The evidence for this is treated by my pupil N. Watson in a dissertation on "Justification by Faith and Eschatology" (Princeton University, 1959).

the facts of the life and teaching of Jesus as its actualization. To appeal to the kerygma was necessarily to appeal to the works and words of Jesus. Similarly the Spirit, whose fruit Paul describes in Gal. 5:16ff and elsewhere, is, if not identified with Jesus himself, at least closely related to him: it is the Spirit of Jesus which informs Paul about the nature of the good life. These considerations make it difficult to agree with those who would belittle, if not dismiss, the place of the Jesus of history, his deeds and words, from the mind of Paul.[20]

But these general, though very real, considerations apart, there are others which reinforce our insistence on the re-examination of the role of the words of Jesus in Paul's thought. These are roughly of two kinds. On the one hand, (a) there are those which arise from the general conceptual world of Paul or from categories which he seems often to have employed in clarifying the nature of the Christian Dispensation. On the other hand, (b) there are those which rest upon evidence which can be very precisely isolated in the Epistles themselves. Let us deal with each group in turn.

(a) There is much to indicate that a very significant part of the conceptual world in which Paul moved, *as a Christian*, was that of the Exodus. It is clear that, as for Matthew and other New Testament writers, so for Paul, there was a real correspondence between the Christian Dispensation and the Exodus of Israel from Egypt. The redemption of the Old Israel from Egypt was the prototype of the greater redemption from sin wrought by Christ for the New Israel.

---

[20] C. H. Dodd, in *The Evolution of Ethics* (Oxford, 1927) ed. W. Sneath, p. 301. This is, indeed, the focal point in much of the recent discussion on the "Quest of the Historical Jesus." See J. M. Robinson, *The New Quest for the Historical Jesus* (Naperville, Ill., 1959); R. Hepburn, *Christianity and Paradox* (New York, 1958); for a useful essay J. D. McCaughey in *The Reformed Theological Review* 20:1ff (1961).

This has been much recognized in recent scholarship.[21] 1 Cor. 10:1–10 reads as follows: "I want you to know, brethren, that our fathers were all under the cloud, and all passed through the sea, and all were baptized into Moses in the cloud and in the sea, and all ate the same supernatural food and drank the same supernatural drink. For they drank from the supernatural Rock which followed them, and the Rock was Christ. Nevertheless with most of them God was not pleased; for they were overthrown in the wilderness. Now these things are warnings for us, not to desire evil as they did. Do not be idolaters as some of them were; as it is written, 'The people sat down to eat and drink and rose up to dance.' We must not indulge in immorality as

---

[21] See, for example, *Moïse l'Homme de l'Alliance* (Paris, 1954); *Paul and Rabbinic Judaism;* J. Jeremias in *Theologisches Wörterbuch zum Neuen Testament,* ed. G. Kittel (Stuttgart, 1932–   ), vol. IV, article on Moses; E. Sahlin, on "The New Exodus of Salvation" in *The Root of the Vine,* ed. A. Fridrichsen (Westminster, 1953); C. F. Evans, "The Central Section of St. Luke's Gospel," in *Studies in the Gospels,* ed. D. E. Nineham (Oxford, 1955); Manek, on "The New Exodus and the Book of Luke," *Novum Testamentum* (January 1957), pp. 8ff; A. M. Farrer, *A Study in St. Mark* (Westminster, 1951); E. C. Hoskyns and N. Davey, *The Fourth Gospel* (Naperville, Ill., 1931), p. 147 *et al.;* H. M. Teeple, *The Mosaic Eschatological Prophet* (Philadelphia, 1957); F. L. Cross, *I Peter, A Paschal Liturgy* (London, 1954) [see review by C. F. D. Moule, *New Testament Studies* 2:56–58 (1955)]; P. Dabeck, in *Biblica* 23:175–189 (Rome, 1942), on "Siehe, es erschienen Moses und Elias, Matt. 17:3"; Chavasse, in *Theology* 54:289ff (August 1951), on "Jesus Christ and Moses"; H. J. Schoeps, *Theologie und Geschichte des Judenchristentums* (Tübingen, 1949), pp. 88ff; Goppelt, *Typos* (Gütersloh, 1954); J. Daniélou, *Sacramentum Futuri* (Paris, 1950), pp. 131ff on "La Typologie de l'Exode dans l'Ancien et le Nouveau Testament"; J. Guillet, "Le Thème de la marche au désert dans l'Ancien Testament," *Recherches de Science Religieuse* (1949), pp. 164ff; D. Daube, *The Exodus Pattern in the Bible* (London, 1963), *passim;* G. H. Williams, *Wilderness and Paradise in Christian Thought* (New York, 1962). For a criticism of the position advocated in the text, see Paul Neuenzeit, *Das Herrenmahl: Studien zur paulinischen Eucharistieauffassung* (Munich, 1960), pp. 148ff. He finds an overemphasis in *Paul and Rabbinic Judaism* on the New Exodus motif in Paul. Compare R. Schnackenburg, "Todes- und Lebensgemeinschaft mit Christus. Neue Studien zu Rom. VI. 1–11," *Theologische Zeitschrift* 6:32–53 (Munich, 1955).

some of them did, and twenty-three thousand fell in a single day. We must not put the Lord to the test, as some of them did and were destroyed by serpents; nor grumble, as some of them did and were destroyed by the Destroyer."

The interpretation of the Christian life as a counterpart of the Exodus is here made quite explicit; note especially that the experience of the New Exodus, like that of the first, demands the forsaking of immorality (1 Cor. 10:8); that is, the taking up of the yoke of Christ, although this is not expressly so stated. Again, Paul's understanding of the Eucharist is largely covenantal: it is for him the institution of the New Israel, the counterpart of the Old (1 Cor. 11:20–34).[22] This is reinforced in 1 Cor. 5:7, where Christ is referred to as a Passover lamb slain for Christians, and in 1 Cor. 15:20, where Christ is the first fruits. This last contains a side-glance at the ritual of the Passover; Christ is the first fruits of a new redemption. Out of the six passages noted above in illustration of Paul's rooting of the imperative in the indicative, two certainly, and a third possibly, are influenced by the thought of the Christian as having undergone a new Exodus. This is so as we saw in 1 Cor. 5:7 and the motif of freedom in Gal. 5:1[23] owes something to the motif. Moreover, if our argument elsewhere be accepted that the Pauline concept of dying and rising with Christ is to be understood in terms of a New Exodus,[24] then another passage, Rom. 6:2ff, from the six referred to, also contains this idea of the Christian Dispensation as a counterpart to the first Exodus. Among the metaphors used by Paul to expound his experience in Christ is that of "redemption," which, we cannot doubt, was intimately bound up in his mind with the thought of the emancipation of the Old Israel

[22] *Paul and Rabbinic Judaism*, pp. 250–254.

[23] On this, see D. Daube, *The New Testament and Rabbinic Judaism* (London, 1956), p. 282. The whole chapter on "Redemption" is illuminating.

[24] *Ibid.*, pp. 102ff.

from Egypt (Exod. 6:6; 15:13; Deut. 7:8; 15:15).[25] In
2 Cor. 6:16 the presence of God in the temple of the New
Israel, the Church, is expressly understood, we may assume,
as the realization of the promise made to Moses, as for
example in Exod. 25:8: "And let them make me a sanctuary
that I may dwell in their midst," or again in Exod. 29:43–5:
"There will I meet with the people of Israel, and it shall be
sanctified by my glory; I will consecrate the tent of meeting
and the altar . . . and I will dwell among the people of Israel, and will be their God." This is in agreement with the
view that in 2 Corinthians the thought of Paul is largely
governed by the understanding of the Christian life in terms
of a new covenant (2 Cor. 3:1–18) and of the sojourn in
the wilderness (2 Cor. 5:1ff). Moreover, the reference in
2 Cor. 6:14: "Or what fellowship has light with darkness?"[26]
reminds us that Christians for Paul are children of the day.
Thus, in Col. 1:12–13, we read ". . . giving thanks to the
Father who has qualified us to share in the inheritance of
the saints in the light. He has delivered us from the domination of darkness and transferred us to the kingdom of his
beloved Son, in whom we have redemption, the forgiveness
of sins." It is possible that here the Exodus motif is again
apparent in the use of the term "inheritance." In Deuteron-
omy this term is closely connected with the deliverance from
Egypt,[27] and it may be that for Paul it also suggests the
eschatological redemption, through the death and Resurrection of Christ, parallel to that wrought at the Exodus.
Certainly the motif of "light and darkness" which occurs in

---

[25] *Ibid.*, pp. 268–275.

[26] The use of the "darkness and light" motif in Paul can be connected perhaps also with the kind of dualism we find in the Dead Sea
Scrolls: see Wibbing, *Die Tugend- und Lasterkataloge im Neuen Testament*, pp. 61ff, *et passim*. On 2 Cor. 3:1–18, 5:1ff, see *Paul and
Rabbinic Judaism*.

[27] The Greek verb "to inherit" and its corresponding substantives
have a long association with the Exodus, the land of Canaan being the
"inheritance" of Israel, for example, Deut. 4:20, 21, etc.

the same passage suggests this. In 1 Pet. 2:9, 10 this motif occurs in a context which recalls the Exodus, and especially Exod. 19:4–6. In Mishnah Pesahim x.5 we read in the Passover service: "Therefore are we bound to give thanks, to praise, to glorify, to honor, to exalt, to extol, and to bless him who wrought all these wonders for our fathers and for us. He brought us out from bondage to freedom, from sorrow to gladness, and from mourning to a festival day, *and from darkness to great light* and from servitude to redemption; so let us say before him the *Hallelujah*" (italics mine). Specific references to darkness and light are clear in the Exodus story itself. In Exod. 10:21–23 we read: "Then the Lord said to Moses, 'Stretch out your hand toward heaven that there may be darkness over the land of Egypt, a darkness to be felt.' So Moses stretched out his hand toward heaven, and there was a thick darkness in all the land of Egypt three days; they did not see one another, nor did any rise from his place for three days; but all the people of Israel had light where they dwelt." The parallelism between Old and New Israel here may not be pressed, however, because the Old Israel did not strictly pass from darkness, although they were surrounded by it (Exod. 12:23). Nevertheless, the symbol of a passage from darkness to light was taken up by Deutero-Isaiah and employed to describe redemption (Isa. 42:16)—"I will turn the darkness before them into light, the rough places into level ground," a redemption which was a New Exodus. Paul in Col. 1:12, 13f may be governed by the same concept.

So far, however, we have only pointed to passages where the concept of the Exodus, as the type of Christian redemption, has been employed by Paul in a general sense. In many of the passages cited above as containing the New Exodus motif, while there is an appeal, implicit or explicit, to its consequences in good conduct, there is none to any specific commandment as such which characterizes the New

Exodus. Are we then to conclude that it was in the character of the Exodus, almost solely as deliverance, rather than as also imposing a demand, in the giving of the Law, that Paul found it pertinent for the interpretation of the Gospel? In other words, did anything in his understanding of the New Exodus "in Christ" correspond to those events in the total complex of the Exodus that transpired *particularly* at Sinai? It is our contention that there was, and that on grounds which may not be equally cogent but which are all worthy of attention. They constitute the second category of consideration which we mentioned above as specifically suggesting that the words of Jesus were important for Paul.

(b) We begin with the assertion that it has been insufficiently recognized how frequently the Epistles of Paul echo the Synoptic Gospels, even as it has been too readily assumed that the Apostle was indifferent to the Jesus of history, his works, and especially for our purpose, his words. Two factors are relevant: first, there is clearly traceable in the Epistles a process whereby reminiscences of the words of the Lord Jesus himself are interwoven with traditional material; and, secondly, there is strong evidence that there was a collection of sayings of Jesus to which Paul appealed as authoritative. In this connection 1 Cor. 7:25 is particularly instructive. The data we have provided in detail elsewhere; we here merely reiterate that the tables presented by Resch in his work *Der Paulinismus und die Logia Jesu* (1904) demand serious evaluation.[28]

With the echoes of the teaching of Jesus in his Epistles it must be assumed that Paul refers to a law of the Messiah.[29] This is not a mere overhang from a pre-Pauline Jewish-Christian legalism unrelated to the essentials of

[28] *Paul and Rabbinic Judaism*, pp. 136ff.
[29] 1 Cor. 9:21; Gal. 6:2. See *Paul and Rabbinic Judaism*, p. 142; C. H. Dodd in *Studia Paulina in honorem J. DeZwaan* (Haarlem, 1953), pp. 96–110.

Paul's thought. In addition to what we have noted in another work, the evidence seems to suggest that the interpretation of the teaching of Jesus as a New Law was not necessarily aboriginal in primitive Jewish-Christianity but only comes into prominence in later Jewish-Christianity after the fall of Jerusalem in A.D. 70.[30] Nor again is the phrase "the law of Christ" to be explained away as a vague equivalent to an immanent principle of life like the Stoic law of nature.[31] Moreover, though there are places where Paul seems to understand the law of the Messiah as fulfilled in the law of love, this last also does not exhaust the meaning of the phrase. Almost certainly it is a comprehensive expression for the totality of the ethical teaching of Jesus that had come down to Paul as authoritative. Paul's vocabulary at several points makes it clear that he regarded himself as the heir of a tradition of ethical, as of other, teaching, which he had received and which he had to transmit. He was the servant of one who had criticized the tradition of the fathers as obscuring the true will of God; he himself violently attacked the same tradition. Nevertheless, he turns out on examination to be the steward of a new tradition.[32]

[30] See M. Simon, *Verus Israel* (Paris, 1948), pp. 100ff, whose treatment, however, also shows that there were anticipations of the later interpretation of Christianity, as a New Law in the New Testament itself, for example, Jas. 1:25; Gal. 6:2; Heb. 7:12. The notion of a New Law is closely associated with that of a new people (p. 102f); J. Daniélou (*Théologie du Judeo-Christianisme* [Tournai, 1958], I, 216ff) notes how Christ became not only a New Law but the New Covenant.

[31] C. H. Dodd, *The Bible and the Greeks*, 2 ed. (Naperville, Ill., 1954), p. 37; the view is retracted in *Studia Paulina*.

[32] For what follows, see these pivotal works: O. Cullmann on *The Tradition*, now published in English in *The Early Church*, ed. A. J. B. Higgins (London, 1956), pp. 59–104; L. Cerfaux, in *Recueil Lucien Cerfaux*, 2 ed. (Gembloux, 1954), pp. 253–282, on "La Tradition selon Saint Paul"; and H. Riesenfeld, *The Gospel Tradition and its Beginnings* (London, 1957). See also P. Neuenzeit, *Das Herrenmahl*, pp. 77–88; J. Waggenmann, *Die Stellung des Apostels Paulus neben den Zwölf* (Giessen, 1926), pp. 44ff, *et passim*; Bultmann, *Theologie des Neuen Testaments* (Tübingen, 1953), pp. 464–473.

The *content* of this tradition can be broadly divided into two groups:

(1) That which deals with Christian preaching where the tradition is identified with the Gospel or the apostolic message itself. The chief passages (italics mine) are:

"And we also thank God constantly for this, that when you *received* the word of God which you heard from us, you *accepted* it not as the word of men but as what it really is, the word of God, which is at work in you believers" (I Thess. 2:13).

"For I *delivered* to you as of first importance what I also *received,* that Christ died for our sins in accordance with the scriptures, that he was buried, that he was raised on the third day in accordance with the scriptures, and that he appeared to Cephas, then to the twelve. Then he appeared to more than five hundred brethren at one time, most of whom are still alive, though some have fallen asleep. Then he appeared to James, then to all the apostles. Last of all, as to one untimely born, he appeared also to me. For I am the least of the apostles, unfit to be called an apostle, because I persecuted the church of God. But by the grace of God I am what I am, and his grace toward me was not in vain. On the contrary, I worked harder than any of them, though it was not I, but the grace of God which is with me. Whether then it was I or they, so we preach and so you believed" (1 Cor. 15:3–11).

"For I would have you know, brethren, that the gospel which was preached by me is not man's gospel. For I did not *receive* it from man, nor was I taught it, but it came through a revelation of Jesus Christ" (Gal. 1:11–12).

"As therefore you *received* Christ Jesus the Lord, so live in him, rooted and built up in him and established in the faith, just as you were taught, abounding in thanksgiving. See to it that no one makes a prey of you by philosophy and empty deceit, according to human *tradition,* according to the elemental spirits of the universe, and not according to Christ" (Col. 2:6–8).

(2) Tradition concerned strictly with rules or orders for the Christian life, as in 1 Cor. 11:2: "I commend you because you remember me in everything and maintain the *traditions* even as I have *delivered* them to you." 2 Thess. 2:15: "So, then, brethren, stand firm and hold to the *traditions* which you were taught by us, either by word of mouth or by letter." See also 1 Cor. 7:10, 12, 40; 11:14; 1 Thess. 4:15.

The *forms* of the terminology employed to describe the reception and transmission of all forms of the traditions in both (1) and (2), while they appear in Hellenistic sources,[33] almost certainly have their origin for Paul in a Jewish milieu. Note the following: "hold to the tradition" (1 Cor. 11:2; 15:2; compare Mark 7:18); "stand in the Gospel which you have received" (1 Cor. 15:1; in the traditions, 2 Thess. 2:15). Most striking, however, is the use of "receive" and "deliver" (1 Cor. 11:2, 23; 15:3; I Thess. 2:13; 2 Thess. 2:15; 3:6; Gal. 1:9, 12; Phil. 4:9; Col. 2:6, 8), which translate the Hebrew *qibbel min* and *masar le* respectively.

Thus, the *terminology* used by Paul was customary in Judaism. Are we to conclude from this that he regarded the Christian tradition as similar in its nature to that handed down in Judaism, or was there an essential difference between them? In other words, is there a "rabbinic" element in the Pauline understanding of tradition, that is, the conception of a tradition of a prescribed way of life transmitted from "authority" to "authority"? The question revolves around Paul's understanding of the source of the Christian tradition with which he was concerned. And in the first group of materials, mentioned above, the tradition is explicitly stated to have been derived, not from men,

[33] J. Dupont, *Gnosis* (Bruges, 1949), pp. 59f.

but directly from God. In I Thess. 2:13 it constitutes the
message *of God*; and while in I Cor. 15:1–11 its exact
source is not described, both in Gal. 1:11–12 and Col.
2:6–8 the tradition is deliberately, and very forcefully, set
over against the tradition of men. Thus, so far as the content of his Gospel as such is concerned, that is, if we may
so express it, as kerygma, Paul insists that it was given of
God himself, who was its sole source. However, while in
I Cor. 15:1–11 Paul does not describe the source of the
tradition, he clearly presents it in non-Pauline terms,[34] in
a form molded by the Church probably at Jerusalem, so
that in one sense he can be claimed to have received it
from men. But this is true for him only of the form; the
substance of the tradition was God, as his call was from
God. While Paul could not but be aware of human agencies who had been at work in the precise formulation of
the tradition containing his Gospel, his emphasis was not on
this aspect of the matter, which was entirely secondary.
What intermediaries there were in themselves were not
significant. Paul's emphasis was on the Gospel as born of
the divine initiative in Christ. As far, then, as what we may
call the primary content of the kerygma was concerned,
the tradition was not understood by Paul in a rabbinic manner. This is as true of I Cor. 15:1–11, as of Gal. 1:11–12.
Even though in I Cor. 15:1–11 he might seem at first sight
to be quoting authorities, as does Pirqe Aboth 1.1–2, this
is, in fact, not the case. The authorities in I Cor. 15:1–11
are not teachers transmitting an interpretation of a primary
deposit, the one to another, but witnesses severally of a
primary event. In Aboth 1.1–2 we find a chain of successive authorities; in I Cor. 15:1–11 a series of "original"
witnesses. The chronological sequence in Aboth denotes
authorities increasingly removed from contact with the

---

[34] J. Jeremias, *The Eucharistic Words of Jesus*, Eng. trans. (Oxford,
1955), pp. 128ff.

original deposit, and increasingly dependent on the preceding secondary authorities, but the chronological sequence in 1 Cor. 15:1–11 is intended merely to describe the order in which the "immediacy" of the event was experienced by each witness; that is, it is not a rabbinic sequence. The source of Paul's Gospel is God himself, who took the initiative in revealing himself in Jesus Christ, and, through his Resurrection, created witnesses to Jesus Christ in the world. Thus Jesus Christ is not strictly the source of the kerygmatic tradition but its content: Jesus of Nazareth, crucified, buried, and risen is the primary deposit of the Christian tradition, given by God himself. In 2 Corinthians Paul contrasts the Christian ministry with that of the Old Covenant, and it is of the highest significance that it is Paul himself, not Jesus, who is set in parallelism with Moses: Jesus is rather parallel to the Law, that is, the revelation granted to Moses. Jesus is not the first link in a chain of teachers, no new Moses, but rather a new "Law."[35]

As far, then, as those passages which deal with the kerygma as a tradition are concerned, Paul does not think of himself as a Christian rabbi dependent upon teachers, the first of whom was Jesus. But what of those in the second group, isolated above, concerned with a tradition of teaching? Is here another emphasis in which Jesus is thought of as a New Moses? In 1 Cor. 10 the implication is unmistakable that Jesus is such: incorporation into Christ, the Rock, who is distinguished from the first Moses, is, nevertheless, parallel to that into Moses, and here the moral reference of the incorporation is made clear. The passages in which Paul cites the words of the Lord as authoritative would seem to support this implication. But here there is a complication. Paul in 1 Cor. 10:1ff uses the term, not Jesus, but Christ: elsewhere he speaks neither of a law nor of a word "of Jesus," but "of Christ" and "of

[35] *Paul and Rabbinic Judaism*, pp. 148ff.

the Lord." Is this significant? Cullmann thinks that it is. While recognizing that there were words *of Jesus* in the tradition, by concentrating his attention on a passage which we omitted from our classifications above, because it demands separate treatment, Cullmann comes to a striking conclusion. The passage concerned is the following in 1 Cor. 11:23-24: "For I received from the Lord what I also delivered to you, that the Lord Jesus on the night when he was betrayed took bread, and when he had given thanks, he broke it, and said, 'This is my body which is for you. Do this in remembrance of me.' "

Here the source of a particular tradition—not an ethical one, however—is declared to be "the Lord," which refers, so Cullmann maintains, neither to God, the ultimate source of the kerygma, nor to the Jesus of history, but to the Risen Lord. This can only be reconciled with the fact that we have previously noted, that Paul had received tradition from others, by claiming that the Lord, the exalted Christ, was himself the transmitter of his own words and deeds. Thus in 1 Cor. 7:10, "Unto the married I command, yet not I but the Lord," *"it is the exalted Lord who now proclaims to the Corinthians, through the tradition, what he had taught his disciples during his incarnation on earth."*[36] Elsewhere in Col. 2:6 the Lord is the content of the tradition. The Lord is, therefore, both author and content of the tradition; the genitive in the phrase "the Gospel of Christ," in Rom. 15:19 and elsewhere, is a subjective genitive: "the exalted Christ is Himself originator of the Gospel of which He is also the object."[37] While, as we noted above, the tradition is connected with the Jesus of history, Cullmann insists that we owe the tradition really to the exalted Lord. On 1 Cor. 11:23 he writes: "The designation Kyrios not only points to the historical Jesus as the chrono-

---

[36] O. Cullmann, *The Early Church*, p. 68. His italics.
[37] *Ibid.*, p. 69.

logical beginning of the chain of tradition as the first member of it, but accepts the exalted Lord as the real author of the whole tradition developing itself in the apostolic Church. Thus the apostolic *paradosis* can be set directly on a level with the exalted Kyrios."[38] The use of the aorist in I Cor. 11:14 indicates how the exalted Lord who *now* commands in I Cor. 7:10 and probably in I Thess. 4:15 is the same as the Jesus who walked on earth. "The exalted One Himself after His resurrection delivers the words which He has spoken." In this way, although Cullmann does not ignore the historical Jesus in this matter, he virtually relegates him to the background and elevates the *Kyrios* to supreme significance. It agrees with this that it is necessary for the exalted Lord to repeat what he had declared on earth. Moreover, Cullmann is thus able to connect the tradition with the activity of the Spirit, because the Kyrios is closely related to, if not identified with, the Spirit in Paul.[39] The conclusion is that tradition in Paul is opposed to the rabbinic principle of tradition in Judaism in two ways: "Firstly, that the mediator of the tradition is not the teacher but the *Apostle* as the direct witness; secondly, the principle of succession does not operate mechanically as with the rabbis, but is bound to the Holy Spirit."[40] Cullmann refuses to treat the two groups of material distinguished above as different kinds of tradition: they are both to be understood as derived, as an undifferentiated whole, from the Lord, so that not only the kerygmatic tradition that Paul received and transmitted, but also the didactic is to some extent removed from the historical Jesus, and any analogy between Christian and Jewish tradition is obviated. Jesus as teacher, or Jesus as counterpart of Moses, has little significance for the tradition, but only Jesus as Lord. The

[38] *Ibid.*, p. 62.
[39] *Ibid.*, pp. 7off; see *Paul and Rabbinic Judaism*, pp. 182, 196.
[40] O. Cullmann, *The Early Church*.

Christ of Paul is not easily recognizable as the Jesus of the Mount, as Matthew understood him.

But is Paul so to be interpreted? Is the sharp distinction between the exalted Lord and the Jesus of history which Cullmann finds really present in Paul? Certain considerations are pertinent.

(a) The exegesis of certain texts suggested by Cullmann is questionable. Thus in 1 Cor. 7:10, 12, is it correct to interpret the verse to mean that the exalted Lord is now commanding (verse 10) or refusing to command (verse 12)? In 1 Cor. 9:14 the past tense is used of a command of the Lord and it is probable that the reference in the former two passages is also to a commandment given by Jesus in the past, which is in force in the present. When Shakespeare wrote of the pound of flesh, he did not mean Shylock to imply that the particular law referred to was there and then enacted, although he used the present tense. So too Paul in 1 Cor. 7:10, 12 merely claims that a past commandment of Jesus is still in force.

Again the very passage on which Cullmann leans most, 1 Cor. 11:23–6, points not to a distinction between Jesus and "the Lord," but to their identity. In 11:26 we read: "For as often as you eat this bread and drink the cup, you proclaim the Lord's death until he comes."[41] Clearly the "Lord's" death can only refer to the death of the historical Jesus, which probably takes the place in the "Christian Passover" or Eucharist of the historical event of the Exodus in the Haggadah of the Passover. The Jesus remembered and proclaimed is also the present Lord and the Lord to come. Past, present, and future meet in the name "Lord,"

---

[41] The force of "proclaim" here is "to make haggadah of it"—as was the Exodus "proclaimed" in the Passover Haggadah. See *Paul and Rabbinic Judaism*, pp. 252–253; G. Buchanan Gray, *Sacrifice in the Old Testament* (Oxford, 1925), p. 395; and for another approach, P. Neuenzeit, *Das Herrenmahl*, pp. 128ff.

because "the Lord" is "Jesus." That very Holy Spirit to which Cullmann appeals in support of his position testifies to this very truth. While "no one speaking by the Spirit of God ever says 'Jesus be cursed!' " it is equally true that "no one can say 'Jesus is Lord,' except by the Holy Spirit" (1 Cor. 12:3).

(b) It has been claimed that Paul never refers to a word of Jesus as a commandment. This, however, is debatable.[42] In any case, the claim might be countered by the statement that nowhere does Paul regard the Spirit, the connection of which with "the Lord" Cullmann rightly emphasizes, as the source of ethical commandments, although it is that of moral power. The term "law" in Rom. 8:2 ("For the law of the Spirit of life in Christ Jesus has set me free from the law of sin and death") denotes not so much commandments as "principle."

(c) A factor which is not clear in Cullmann's discussion is the exact meaning which he ascribes to the term "Lord." Does he mean the "Risen Lord" and the "Exalted Lord" to refer to the same phenomenon? He uses the two terms apparently interchangeably and rather sharply separates both the Risen Lord and the Exalted Lord, whom he seems not to distinguish, from the historical Jesus. The improbability that this separation should be accepted appears when we set Paul's understanding of the didactic role of the Lord, as Cullmann understands it, over against the data in the rest of the New Testament. Mark's conception of the activity of the Risen Lord we cannot certainly determine, either because the end of his Gospel has been lost, or, if he did finish it at 16:8, because he does not tell us anything about this activity. If we follow R. H. Lightfoot and others, and find in Mark 16:8 the expectation of an almost immediate

[42] For detail see the full edition of this article, in *The Setting of the Sermon on the Mount*.

Parousia to be enacted in Galilee, then no didactic activity of the Risen Lord can have been contemplated by Mark.[43] Clearly Mark cannot help us in our quest into the functions of the Risen Lord. Matthew, however, is rich in significance just at this point. It is probable that for Matthew the Resurrection is coincident with the glorification of Jesus as Lord. "All authority in heaven and on earth *has* been given to Him": the aorist tense in 28:18 is to be taken seriously. Jesus as Risen is in heaven, that is, glorified. But the ethical instructions which he issues are identified with those which he had given to his own while on earth, and, we may assume, particularly those recorded in Matthew's "Sermon on the Mount."[44] The Jesus of history had initiated an ethical paradosis which the glorified Christ reaffirms; the latter neither initiates the Christian paradosis nor repeats what, as the historical Jesus, he had previously delivered on earth: he needs merely to refer to the tradition of the latter. When we turn to Luke there is a significant change. The Risen Christ instructs his own (Luke 24:27, 44ff; Acts 1:6ff), although no explicit reference is made to any moral teaching he may have given. After forty days, however, the Risen Christ ascended into heaven, where he was glorified. Contact with him, of a direct kind such as had been theirs hitherto, is now denied his disciples until he comes again "in the same way as you saw him go unto heaven" (Acts 1:11ff). The Risen Christ taught the things concerning himself (Luke 24:44ff) and gave commands (Acts 1:2ff) and spoke of the Kingdom of God (Acts 1:3)—all of which possibly[45] *implies* ethical instruction—with a reference to what he had taught on earth. But the impression given is

---

[43] *Locality and Doctrine in the Gospels* (London, 1938), pp. 1–48.

[44] *Ibid.*, pp. 66ff, on 28:16–20. He does not do justice to the didactic factor in the passage.

[45] The exact content of the teaching in Acts 1:2–3 is difficult to assess. It is too precarious to claim on this basis that the Risen Lord gave ethical instructions. But this does not invalidate the distinction we make in the text between the Risen and the Glorified Lord in Acts.

that the *glorified* Christ did not teach. This is the emphasis in Acts 2:32–6; 3:13–21, which reflect perhaps the earliest Christian preaching, and, by implication possibly, in Acts 13:30–31. On the other hand, in Acts 10:40–41 the Resurrection alone is to the fore, there being no emphasis on any Ascension. A didactic function is ascribed to the Risen Christ. Luke would seem to confine teaching whether ethical or other to the latter. The Lord of Glory is not directly available for such.[46] In the Fourth Gospel there is a reference to the Ascension implied in 20:17, but emphasis is laid most on the Risen Christ. Moreover, for John the real glorification of Jesus had already occurred in the crucifixion.[47] It follows that there is nothing in the Fourth Gospel comparable to Matt. 28:16–20 because, essentially, the Resurrection could add nothing to the glory of the crucifixion. For John it is neither the Risen Jesus nor the Exalted Lord who exercises the task of teaching in the Church, but the Holy Spirit, to which this function is not thus directly applied in Paul. The content of the teaching of the Spirit, however, is rooted in teaching already given by the historical Jesus. "But the counsellor, the Holy Spirit," so we read, "whom the Father will send in my name, he will teach you all things, and bring to your remembrance all that I have said to you" (John 14:26).

For our purpose what is significant in all the above is that, however the relation between the Risen Christ and the glorified or exalted Lord be conceived in the rest of the New Testament, whether in terms of Ascension or not, the teaching ascribed to both figures always has reference to the teaching of the historical Jesus, both in ethical and other matters. The presumption, therefore, is that Paul also, unless he was quite removed from the main currents of the Church, intended the same reference. This is particularly

[46] In Matthew there is no statement on the Ascension as such.
[47] John 17:1.

reinforced by the fact that Paul's understanding of the Risen Christ seems to be closest to that of Matthew. He does not mention any Ascension, but only appearances of the Risen Christ, who becomes the object of worship of the Church. The Resurrection would appear to be for him the glorification.[48] That the glorified one was the Risen Jesus would therefore have been central to Paul. That he called him the Lord does not mean that he was removed from the Jesus of history, with whom he is indeed identical.

(d) This last leads us to what should never have been questioned, namely, that the term "Lord" stands in Paul for the historical Jesus in 1 Cor. 11:23. The last phrase, "you proclaim the Lord's death until he comes," in 1 Cor. 11:26 *must* refer to the historical Jesus and any distinction between "the Lord" and "the Lord Jesus" in 1 Cor. 11:23 is unlikely. In Acts 9:5, 13, 17, 27; 22:8, 19; 26:15 the Risen Lord is made to refer to himself as Jesus, and "Lord" is used of Jesus 80, 18, 103, 52 times respectively in Matthew, Mark, Luke, John. Early Christianity thought of the historical Jesus as "Lord," and so did Paul.[49]

Paul then inherited and transmitted a tradition which has two elements, a kerygmatic and a didactic. How are these elements related in his thought? Were they sharply differentiated, as Cerfaux holds, one being conceived as from God and the other having its *point de départ* in the historical Jesus, so that there are two sources for the tradition? Or is Cullmann[50] justified in claiming that both ele-

---

[48] It agrees with this that the Resurrection of Christ is the inauguration of the New Age, not of an age preliminary to this; see *Paul and Rabbinic Judaism*, pp. 285ff.

[49] For a balanced statement, see L. Cerfaux, *Christ in the Theology of St. Paul*, Eng. trans. (New York, 1959), pp. 179–189, especially pp. 187f.

[50] On Cullmann's understanding of "the Lord," see *The Christology of the New Testament*, Eng. trans. (1959), pp. 195ff. Surprisingly he does not develop his understanding of the Lord as a designation of "the tradition" in this volume.

ments issue from the Risen or Exalted Lord, who took the place of all Jewish paradosis? Cullmann makes too sharp a distinction between the Lord as the source of all paradosis, and the historical Jesus as, at least, the source of the didactic paradosis. Cerfaux makes too rigid a distinction between the two kinds of paradosis. But he does greater justice to the texts by giving due place to the historical Jesus as an initiator of one aspect of the tradition. Jesus as Lord and Jesus as teacher were both one for Paul. He may have dwelt more in his epistles on the former, but this is not because he did not recognize the significance of the teaching of Jesus, which to him was authoritative.

And this brings us to the final point, the possibility that for Paul the Person and the Words of Jesus had assumed the significance of a New Torah. In addition to the evidence for this supplied above, we refer to our treatment elsewhere.[51] The objections to this view have been many. But too much weight should not be accorded to the claim that, since Paul was indifferent to the life of Jesus, he was also indifferent to his moral teaching. Nor need the absence of an explicit claim that Jesus is the New Torah be taken as decisive.[52] The same motives which may have led Paul to avoid the use of the term *Logos,* the fear of being misunderstood by Hellenists, may have led him to avoid the description of Christ as the New Torah, which might have been misleading, in discussions with Jewish-Christian and Jewish opponents. Most serious is the objection that the concept of Christ as the New Torah contradicts Paul's radical criticism of the Law and his insistence on salvation as a free gift of grace in the epistles. The Law is there conceived of as a preliminary, provisional discipline, whose term the

[51] See *Paul and Rabbinic Judaism,* pp. 147–176.
[52] Contrast at this point L. Cerfaux, *Christ in the Theology of St. Paul,* p. 274n36; and W. Manson, *Scottish Journal of Theology,* September 1948, pp. 218–219.

coming of Christ has closed.[53] Indeed does not the Law for Paul come to fulfill functions ascribed by Judaism to Satan himself?[54] Thus, that Paul thought of Christ in terms of the Law is unlikely; more likely was he to view the Law in terms of Christ.

Full force must be given to these objections. But while, in ascribing to Paul the concept of Christ as the New Torah we are going outside Paul's *explicit* words or formulae, we are hardly going beyond his implicit intention, if we can judge this from his use of Jesus' words and life in his ethical exhortations and from his application to Jesus of those categories that Judaism had reserved for its highest treasure, namely, the Torah, that is, preexistence, agency in creation, wisdom. To be "in Christ" was for Paul to have died and risen with him in a New Exodus, and this in turn meant that he was to be subject to the authority of the words and Person of Christ as a pattern. The historical circumstances of Paul's ministry, set as it was in a conflict against Judaizers, has given to this aspect of his interpretation of the Christian Dispensation a secondary place, a fact further accentuated by the violence of Paul's personal engagement with the Law in Judaism not strictly as "Law" in the sense of moral demand only but as a whole cultural or social system which had the effect of cutting him off from the fascinating Gentile world.[55] But, though Paul attacked Judaizers and avoids referring to himself or to Christians as "disciples," at no point is he free from the constraint of Christ's example: he has as a Christian "learnt Christ,"[56] and this we

---

[53] I have summarized this in an article in *The Interpreter's Dictionary*, on "Law in the New Testament."

[54] G. B. Caird, *Principalities and Powers* (Oxford, 1956), p. 41.

[55] See C. H. Dodd, *New Testament Studies* (Manchester, 1953), p. 721. That Luther's struggle over Law and Gospel was also sociologically conditioned is noted by W. Joest, *Gesetz und Freiheit*, p. 135, and E. Benz, *Zeitschrift für Religions- und Geistgeschichte* 4:289ff (1951), on "Das Paulus-Verständnis . . ."

[56] On the expression to "learn Christ" (Eph. 4:21), see W. Manson, *Jesus the Messiah* (Naperville, Ill., 1943), p. 54.

may understand in a twofold way. He has learnt his words as formerly he did those of the Torah,[57] and he has become an imitator of Christ,[58] as formerly he had doubtless been an imitator of Gamaliel. The process of learning in Judaism had a twofold aspect—the learning of teaching and the imitation of a life, that of the rabbi. The concept of the rabbi as living Torah and, therefore, as the object of imitation would be familiar to Paul, as it would have been to Philo,[59] who regards the Patriarchs as living the Law before it was given. When Paul refers to himself as an imitator of Christ he is doubtless thinking of Jesus as the Torah he has to copy—both in his words and deeds. A passage in Romans 6:15-17 suggests the formative power of the teaching of Jesus in Paul's conception of the Christian life, and reveals his understanding of this teaching in relation to grace. It reads: "What then? Are we to sin because we are not under law but under grace? By no means! Do you not know that if you yield yourselves to any one as obedient slaves, you are slaves of the one whom you obey, either of sin, which leads to death, or of obedience, which leads to righteousness? But thanks be to God, that you who were once slaves of sin *have become obedient from the heart to the standard of teaching to which you were committed,* and, having been set free from sin, have become slaves of righteousness" (my italics).

The precise meaning of the words "have become obedient from the heart to the standard of teaching to which you were committed . . ." in Rom. 6:17 has been disputed.

---

[57] This is implied in his use of the citations to which we have already referred.

[58] I Cor. 11:1; I Thess. 1:6; Phil. 2:5.

[59] See my volume, *Torah in the Messianic Age and/or The Age to Come* (monograph series, Society of Biblical Literature and Exegesis, vol. VII, Philadelphia, 1952). It is not irrelevant to restate the fact that the Law itself has a "personal" character for Philo: see J. Daniélou, *Théologie du Judeo-Christianisme,* p. 217. For Judaism, see my "Law in First Century Judaism," in *The Interpreter's Dictionary.*

F. W. Beare's comment, however, is to be treated seriously. He finds Paul to be claiming that "the Christian Didache, when it is followed with a wholehearted obedience, imparts to our lives a specific character and pattern, moulding them into the likeness of Christ. St. Paul speaks more often, it is true, of the power of the Spirit as the transforming influence in the Christian life; but it is quite wrong to imagine that he thinks of the leadings of the Spirit as a succession of formless impulses or vagrant illuminations. Here, in correlation with the call for obedience, he thinks naturally enough of the specific moral instruction in which the guiding of the Spirit is given concrete expression (Phil. 4:8–9). For all his faith in the Spirit, the Apostle thinks of the Christian life as disciplined and ordered in keeping with clear and concrete instruction given by precept and example. Such teaching is here conceived as the die or pattern which shapes the whole of the life which yields to it, in conformity with the will of God. No antithesis with the Law or with other (non-Pauline) "forms" is implied or suggested. He is thinking simply of the Didache which belongs to the Gospel, the teaching concerning the way of life which is worthy of the Gospel of Christ, considered as a mould which gives to the new life its appropriate shape or pattern."[60] The Christian life as Paul understood it was lived within a formative ethical tradition. This tradition is not an isolated deposit, however, but part and parcel of what Paul understands by the Christian Dispensation, and, therefore, seen, not in opposition to grace, but as a concomitant of it. At no point is Paul without law (*anomos*); he is always within law (*ennomos*). To this extent Paul is at one with Matthew who also places the law of Christ in a context of

---

[60] *New Testament Studies* 5:206ff (April 1959), "On the interpretation of Rom. 6:17." We should emphasize, as Beare does not, the role of the words of Jesus in the tradition. Beare refers to the other interpretations that have been suggested. We find his the most plausible, with the qualifications mentioned.

the grace of Christ. This is nowhere clearer than in a section which is usually quoted in proof of the succor of Christ, but which also contains within itself the demand of Christ. "Come to me, all who labor and are heavy-laden, and I will give you rest. Take my yoke upon you, and learn from me; for I am gentle and lowly in heart, and you will find rest for your souls. For my yoke is easy and my burden is light" (Mt. 11:28–30). The "yoke of Christ" stands over against the yoke of the Law. The upshot of all this is that Paul, who is usually set in antithesis to Matthew, would probably not have found the Matthaean emphasis on the "law of Christ" either strange or uncongenial. He, too, knew of the same law, although the circumstances of his ministry demanded from him greater concentration on other aspects of the Gospel.[61]

We may now sum up. In the light of the above, it can be urged that Paul had access to a tradition of the words of Jesus. This he had "received" and this he "transmitted"; to this, whenever necessary and possible, he appealed as authoritative, so that this tradition constituted for him part of the "law of Christ." Caution is, however, necessary in making this claim. Out of the epistles as a whole, the passages where this emerges are few and the use that the Apostle made of a catechesis derived possibly from a non-Christian Hellenistic-Jewish tradition, into which he introduced few, if any, express words of Jesus, makes it doubly clear that he did not formulate a "Christian-rabbinic" casuistry on the basis of the words of Jesus that he had received. Whether the reason for the paucity of evidence in this matter is due to the historical fact that Paul during his ministry had to contend with "judaizing" tendencies, as was suggested above, is uncertain. Nevertheless, it is not going too far to claim that part of the being "in Christ" for Paul was standing under the words of Jesus. Paul, like Matthew,

[61] Compare O. Cullmann, *The Early Church.*

appealed to these as authoritative. As for Matthew, so for Paul, there was a real correspondence between the Christian Dispensation and the events of the Exodus. The redemption of Israel from Egypt was the prototype of the greater redemption from sin wrought by Christ. Thus Christ for Paul also had the lineaments of a new and greater Moses. He shared with Matthew a common understanding of Christ and his words. Like Matthew, Paul too can speak of a law of Christ, partly, at least, composed of Jesus' words; he was governed by a tradition.[62]

CONCLUSION

In the first part of the above treatment I generalized boldly; in my discussion of Paul and tradition I have dealt with details. The relevance of this latter discussion for the dialogue between Protestantism and Catholicism is clear. The Reformation appealed to a Paul dominated by the conception of justification by faith, and understood its own struggle with Rome in terms of Paul's struggle with Pharisaism. The Reformation saw in Paul's insistence on faith alone a justification for its own rejection of the "pharisaic" tradition of Rome. But now it appears that the Paul to which it appealed was himself bound to a tradition, that "justification by faith" paradoxically coexisted in Paul's mind with loyalty to a tradition. It is in this context that, it seems to me, Pauline studies are compelling us to a reexamination of the ground of our divisions.

I am fully aware that in any discussion of such themes it is history, and not simply origins, with which we have to cope: it is, indeed, history that is in the saddle and riding us, not origins. The issues that separate us today are fraught, not only with the initial impulses that called them into

---

[62] I deeply regret that J. R. Geiselmann's essay on "Die Tradition," in *Fragen der Theologie Heute*, ed. by J. Feiner, et al. (Zurich, 1957), pp. 69–108, reached me too late for use in the above.

being, but with the developments of centuries. But it is not, therefore, irrelevant to turn to origins, and to do so is to recognize that the New Testament, which is, in a sense, the record of all our beginnings, provides us all with a new, reconciling impulse for our present tasks.[63]

---

[63] On the problem of the relation between history of origins and dogma in Catholicism, from a Protestant point of view, see the trenchant remarks of J. S. Whale, *The Protestant Tradition* (Cambridge, Eng., 1955), pp. 251ff. He cites Cardinal Manning's famous words that "the dogma must overcome history." But it is to be recognized that much recent Protestant theology has ignored or repressed questions of origins in the interests of dogma. Above we point out an instance where history can mitigate Protestant and Catholic "dogmatic" differences.

WORD AND SACRAMENT
IN PROTESTANT WORSHIP

CYRIL C. RICHARDSON

OWING to the wide diversity of Protestantism it is not possible to give as clear and comprehensive a survey of its worship as is possible in the case of Roman Catholicism. While the Latin rite is, of course, not the only one in Roman Catholicism and there are a number of Uniat rites in different languages, nonetheless, there is a basic uniformity which characterizes the vast majority of Roman Catholic liturgical observances. With the churches of the Reformation it is different. Yet there are fundamental leading themes characteristic of all Protestant services and these we shall survey. We must, however, always bear in mind that the wide range of Protestant services is such that different emphases have tended to characterize the various denominations, and throughout Protestant history there has been no fundamental pattern universally observed.

Before treating the basic concerns of Protestant worship, it is well for us to bear in mind the large dependence of Reformation liturgy upon the forms of worship in the later Middle Ages. Originally Protestant services were revisions of the Roman Mass and of the medieval vernacular service of Prone, which was inserted in the Mass before or after the sermon. Furthermore, a type of devotional piety centered in subjective meditations characterized the Lay Folk's Mass Books which were widely used in the Late Middle Ages. Not a little of the Protestant attitude toward the Holy Communion ultimately derives from these layman's handbooks.

It is thus important to note that in the realm of worship the Reformation represented a continuity with the medieval past as well as a revolution. In the general structure of the service, in the quality of devotion, in the emphasis on the passion of Christ in the celebration of the Lord's Supper, and finally in the continuing idea that the congregation should basically remain passive, there is a clear connection with the Mass of the later Middle Ages. On the other hand, the Reformation stands as a revolution in introducing a fundamental emphasis upon the Word of God, upon the need for corporate worship and for greater intelligibility as well as simplicity. It is noteworthy that many of the features in the schema of the present Vatican Council have a direct parallel in the concerns of the Reformers. In consequence it is likely that the Catholic services will become more like Protestant ones just as, under the impetus of the current liturgical revival, Protestant services are recovering something of their Catholic past and becoming more like Roman ones. This presages well for an eventual unity of the spirit among Christians in so far as they appreciate the many diverse facets of worship and grow closer together in their common concern for the life in Christ.

BASIC CONCERNS OF
PROTESTANT WORSHIP

Let us now look at some of the basic concerns which have dominated Protestant worship throughout its history. While these concerns have been given varying emphases among the differing denominations, nonetheless they may be said to be characteristics in general of Protestant liturgy.

The first one is this: That the *Word* may prevail. By the Word of God the Reformers meant first and foremost God's disclosure of himself in Jesus Christ. This revelation of God in his freedom is given in the words of Scripture as well as in the sacramental acts of the Church. Fundamentally, however, it means the declaration of God's forgiveness and the condescension of the divine love in our redemption. It was this aspect particularly which Luther stressed in his liturgies where the warmth of piety centering in the grateful recognition of the divine love is dominant. For Calvin, on the other hand, the Word means primarily the declaration of the *gloria Dei.* This is, of course, not without the note of the divine love, but it gives peculiar prominence to God's transcendence. There is a word of Calvin that very well expresses the whole character of his services: "We are born first of all for God and not for ourselves."

Because the Word is something that is spoken directly to man's understanding in God's self-disclosure, the importance of the sermon and the reading of the Scripture in the vernacular are primary concerns of the Reformers. Luther, for instance, in his *Formula Missae* writes, "But the important thing is this, that everything be done so that the Word prevails and does not become a clamor or a whine and rattled off mechanically as it has been heretofore." Or again, "Where God's word is not preached, it is better that one neither sing nor read or even come together." Hence, it has been characteristic of Lutheran worship that even at sacramental services a sermon is regarded as essential. Unless man is given the opportunity of hearing the Word of God and of intelligently grasping the character of the divine revelation, worship descends to superstition. Calvin equally is concerned with this importance of the presentation of God's revelation by sermon and Scripture. He writes in the *Institutes,* "The principal object of the sacrament, therefore, is not to present us the body of Christ simply . . . we never rightly and advantageously feed on Christ except as crucified and when we have a lively apprehension of the efficacy of his death." It is this "lively apprehension" that is the fundamental point of worship. Sacramental forms can so easily fall into superstition, the intoning of prayers in a foreign tongue can become so unintelligible, that the full significance of participating in the disclosure of the divine glory and love in Jesus Christ becomes obscured.

It is for this reason that the reading of Scripture itself becomes sacramental. In the place of the snippets from the Epistles and Gospels, which the English reformers used to refer to as "pisteling and gospeling," the Reformation stressed the need for much longer passages of Scripture and full and adequate expositions of them in the sermon. The sermon characteristically took on the quality of instruction, and indeed the use of the scholar's gown became indicative of the relation of the minister to the congregation. In some ways the educational and instructional character of worship was overemphasized and its more prophetic meaning along with its more mystical elements tended to be obscured. However, the large emphasis given to Scripture and its exposition was basically an attempt to speak directly to the worshiper about the divine condescension in Jesus Christ.

As a result of the emphasis upon the Word, there was a consequent decline of sacramental worship. While all the reformers except Zwingli wished that the celebration of the Lord's Supper should be the normal form of Sunday worship, nonetheless the tendency for there to be only a preaching service quickly asserted itself. There were many reasons for this. There were, on the one hand, political reasons, as in Geneva, where the town councils refused Calvin's insistence upon weekly celebrations of the Lord's Supper, because they feared riots and the opposition of the people who might imagine the Roman Mass was being restored. Another reason had to do with the infrequency of communicating in the later Middle Ages. The rule which had been laid down by the Fourth Lateran Council of communicating once a year at Easter was widely followed and attendance at Mass was generally not for the purpose of receiving the elements. Consequently, when the Reformers stressed the corporate character of worship and insisted that the Lord's Supper should only be celebrated when all communicated, celebrations became infrequent, since the people were disinclined to break their medieval habit. The service of the sacrament could not be celebrated with no one or only a handful to participate. Thus, the Protestant service really became a *missa sicca,* in which the service of the Word, derived from the Synagogue, stood alone without reaching its consummation in the sacrament.

Yet a deeper reason for the decline of the sacrament must be observed in the theological understanding of the Lord's Supper which dominated the thinking of the Reformers. They tended to view the Holy Communion as a reduplication of the Word. Thus, if the Word had already been preached and the Scripture read and expounded, what was done in the Lord's Supper was merely a repetition of the same thing. It expressed in more tangible and visible form what had already been accomplished in words. We shall revert again to this point, but it is perhaps the deepest reason why the celebration of the Holy Communion became monthly or quarterly as a consequence of the Reformation.

The second fundamental concern of Protestant worship was that superstition should be made impossible. There should be no "hocus-pocus," which actual phrase is a corruption of the Latin words of consecration "hoc est corpus meum." The white walls and the streaming daylight from the large windows of New England churches are symbolic of this desire to have everything clear and in the open without any possibility of reverting to magical tendencies. A number of features of Protestant worship directly come from this concern. Intelligibility was stressed above the sense of mystery. Everything was to be done aloud and spoken in the vernacular, so that there could be no misunderstanding.

The feeling which had developed from the fourth century that the consecration prayer should be said in a subdued voice because of the character of the liturgical mystery, was something quite alien to the Reformation spirit. Then, again, simplicity was a dominant concern. Cranmer's objections to what he calls "dumb ceremonies" indicate a typical spirit of the reformer. Elaborate worship was now superseded by the most simple forms which were regarded as having less danger in them and as being more directly intelligible to the congregation. Finally, the sense of corporate worship was emphasized over against priestcraft. In the revisions of the Roman Mass which the Reformers undertook, a number of the ancient prayers in which the priest addressed God in the first person singular, were converted into the first person plural, in order to indicate that the minister is the leader of the congregation rather than one who mediates between the congregation and God. Furthermore, the emphasis upon Psalm singing in the simple Genevan tunes gave point to this feeling for corporate worship, just as the requirement that the Lord's Supper should only be celebrated when the people were willing to communicate, equally emphasized the communal character of worship. All these concerns were directed against any identification of the religious symbol with the reality to which it points. Superstition, which did to some measure characterize the late Middle Ages, was to be offset by a type of worship in which the congregation could participate with understanding and without the dangers of magic. This, of course, posed very serious problems for Protestant worship, in that there was always a tendency for the symbols to be divorced from the realities to which they pointed, and the rational forms to be so emphasized that the sense of mystery in worship was overcome.

A third dominant concern of Protestant worship was that the free Spirit of God should be given opportunity. This was particularly developed in the left-wing Reformation among

Independents, Congregationalists, and Baptists. Here the emphasis fell first upon extemporaneous prayer. The immediate, direct experience of conversation with God was to supersede written and traditional forms of prayer. Even the Lord's Prayer was regarded as inadequate for public worship because it could be rattled off mechanically and did not have that immediate and spontaneous freshness which the more left-wing reformers felt to be the note of true worship. John Cotton, for instance, in 1642 could write, "Nor will it stand well with the holy gesture of prayer, which is to lift up our eyes to heaven, if we cast our eyes down upon a book." This is a typical Puritan attitude to the Anglican *Book of Common Prayer*. Barrow could ask, "May such old, written, rotten stuff be called prayer? May reading be said to be praying?" Or, again, John Owen could write, "All liturgies are false worship (and not the English only), used to defeat Christ's promises of gifts and God's Spirit." There was a consequent opposition to written sermons as well as written prayers. Worship was to be conducted in such a way that one would be open to the immediate and direct influence of God's Spirit and not bound by traditional forms.

This implied giving emphasis to intimacy in worship. In the small congregation of devoted believers, fellowship with God was looked upon from the point of view of a direct and immediate relation in which the worshiper gave personal utterance to that which the Spirit of God evoked in his heart. Not only the minister but the layman prayed aloud, prophesied, and exhorted. Certain of the extreme forms of such worship in speaking with tongues, religious dancing, and so forth, were developed in the more radical of these groups.

Finally, it must be observed that a certain tension between form and freedom has been characteristic of Protestant worship precisely because of this desire to stress the free Spirit of God. Only in the Anglican communion has there been an attempt to enforce uniformity. In general, classical

Protestantism has tried to relate form to freedom by providing model services and model prayers, but allowing the minister a good deal of latitude in their use and composition. Calvin himself was not averse to a set form of worship. He even urged its usefulness, contending that it was "to help the unskillfulness and simplicity of some . . . that the consent of the churches with one another may appear . . . that the capricious giddiness and levity of such as effect innovations may be prevented." Yet the forms he provided for Geneva were models rather than forms which had to be followed in detail by the minister. His attitude, as that of Luther, was the same which had characterized the ancient church. Hippolytus had provided his liturgy in the *Apostolic Tradition* as a guide to Zephyrinus, the Bishop of Rome, whom Hippolytus as a learned scholar seems to have felt was in need of some guidance. In the general Protestant scene today some measure of form and freedom is to be observed in practically all denominations, and indeed the 11 o'clock Sunday service is rather similar in the large Protestant bodies.

The final basic concern of Protestant worship has been the revival of the liturgy of the ancient Church. It was the desire of the Reformers to recover the way of worship in the New Testament and the early period. This was the Reformation counterpart of the Renaissance concern to return to the sources. The motto was *ad fontes.* Hence Calvin could subtitle one of his liturgies, "Selon la Coustume de l'Eglise ancienne." It is for this reason that the Reformers felt that Word and sacrament belonged together; and indeed Calvin himself regarded their separation as "a vicious custom," and annual communion as a veritable "invention of the devil." We have already indicated some reasons why the sacrament tended to decline in importance, but it must be stated that the early Reformers, while they did not have the scholarly resources we have today for understanding New Testament and early Church worship, nonetheless were vitally concerned that there should be a return to the original forms of worship in the Christian Church.

The modes of worship that characterize the Protestant denominations today are beginning to betray an increasing uniformity. There is a general Sunday morning service in the Presbyterian, Methodist, Lutheran, and Congregationalist traditions which, while there are differences in detail, nonetheless has assumed a basic pattern. It opens with a choral procession and with a sentence from Scripture, which is followed by a confession of sins and absolution. Then there is a responsive reading from the Psalter followed by hymnody or a chant. After this there comes the morning lesson and then the pastoral prayer, which may be a single long prayer or divided into shorter collects. The service tends to reach its climax in the sermon, which is followed or preceded by an anthem, the collection of alms, and a hymn. The service concludes with a benediction and a recessional.

This structure in essence is, of course, the first part of the mass. There have been many changes but the main outline of intercessory prayer, psalmody, and sermon goes back to the Synagogue service that the early Christians inherited from Judaism.

While a good deal of variety is introduced into the service of the Word, in the celebration of the Lord's Supper the specific forms of the different denominations tend to be more closely observed. These differ in the various churches, but there are now emerging "ecumenical" liturgies that attempt to recover a good deal of the Catholic past while still preserving fundamental Protestant points of view. Perhaps the most notable of the ecumenical liturgies has been the Anglican, for Cranmer attempted to weave together many diverse sources in his book. In the Holy Communion the basic structure and a good deal of the material comes directly from the Sarum Use, but this has been modified both by Protestant concerns and also by materials derived from Lutheran and other liturgies. In the middle of the nineteenth century in this country the Mercersburg liturgies appeared. They were a notable contribution since the leaders of that movement of the Reformed Church in America, namely Nevin and Schaff, had a concern for recovering the Catholic heritage. One might also note the liturgy of the United Church of Canada: the uniting Methodists, Presbyterians, and Congregationalists made use of their diverse liturgical heritages, weaving them together in a common service. The more recent revision of Lutheran liturgies both in Sweden and the United States has recovered the traditional pattern of the consecration prayer in the place of the *verba* of the typical Lutheran liturgy. In the Congregational Church in this country the *Book of Worship for Free Churches* indicates the extent to which the liturgical revival has affected that communion. A similar revision of the *Westminster Directory* is now being undertaken and will doubtless issue in an equal concern for recovering the Catholic elements of the past. Perhaps the most notable ecumenical liturgy of the modern day is that of the Church of South India, which has united Catholic and Protestant elements with rare skill and success. Equally interesting though less influential is the Taizé liturgy of the French Reformed community, which is dedicated to Church unity and of which Max Thurian is the distinguished leader.

The characteristics of these ecumenical liturgies are— first, the attempt to recover traditional structures; secondly, the preference for biblical language in the central prayers where there have been the keenest thological divisions; and, finally, the introduction of responses that heighten the congregation's participation in public prayer. The responses inserted in the consecration prayer of the Church of South India are particularly significant in this connection.

There are a number of other factors that make for ecumenical liturgy among Protestants. One of these is hymnody. Increasingly Protestant churches sing hymns from every period of the Church's development, and indeed one might say that in the realm of hymnody there is the most notable ecumenical spirit. Again, the recovery of the Church year among Protestant groups who formally disavowed it has been important. Nowadays not only Easter and Christmas, but Epiphany, Lent, Advent, and a number of holy days such as All Saints are observed. Then, too, the introduction of silence into worship has been a sign of learning from other denominations. This has not grown extensively, but the impact of Quakerism on Protestant worship is not to be underestimated. Finally, the architecture of churches in which there has appeared the "divided chancel" with the altar in the center and the pulpit at the side, has indicated a desire among Protestants to return to a type of architecture which did not give undue prominence to the pulpit and which followed the norm developed in the early basilica and the Gothic church. In all these ways there has been a movement toward a recovery of the Catholic heritage without compromising the basic concerns of the Reformation.

MEANINGS AND ANTITHESES

The point at which there has been the greatest division in the tradition of Protestantism concerns the understanding of the Lord's Supper. Here the issue of the meaning of religious symbols has been acutely debated and no resolution of the matter is yet in sight. However, in a number of ways to which we shall return later, some advance appears to be possible today; and even a measure of reconciliation with basic patterns of Catholic thought is not out of the question.

The early Protestants took sharpest exception to the Roman Catholic doctrine of transubstantiation. Here a number of issues were involved. In the first place, most of the Protestants approached the doctrine of the Lord's Supper from the point of view of a nominalist philosophy in the structure of which transubstantiation was either meaningless or superstitious. What was affirmed by all parties was that after the consecration the bread remains bread and there is no conversion of its inner substance into the Body of Christ. Furthermore, the majority of Protestants laid emphasis upon the element of subjectivity in sacramental religion. They felt that the Roman Catholic doctrine unduly stressed the objectivity of the sacrament; and while in many ways they attempted to preserve the sense of objectivity, they wished to correlate it more deeply than Roman Catholic theology had, with the subjective dispositions of the recipients. Basically one can say that the general viewpoint from which the Protestant doctrine was worked out, was that which had been characteristic of sacramentals in the Roman tradition. The doctrine of *ex opere operato* was denied, and in its place emphasis was put on *ex opere operantis.* That is to say, the significance of the sacraments did not lie only in the objective act of God and of the priest, but rather in the action of God that was apprehended by the act of faith. One other point is of some importance, namely, that baptism was regarded as a pattern to which the doctrine of the Lord's Supper should conform. In Catholic theology a sharp distinction between these two sacraments was made, and the *res sacramenti* was regarded as present in the consecrated elements in a way that it was not in the rite of baptism. It is this approach to the Lord's Supper from the doctrine of baptism that gives point to the Protestant concern for *ex opere operantis.*

The three basic doctrines that were devised were those of Zwingli, Luther, and Calvin. We may briefly characterize them in this way. Zwingli regarded the elements of the Lord's Supper as picturing the past event for faith. In him there is a fundamental split between spirit and nature, so that the things of nature do not participate in the divine but rather give a symbolic expression to that which is grasped by faith alone. The significant action of the Lord's Supper falls in the realm of spirit, mind, and consciousness. Faith, to be sure, is regarded as a gift of God. Zwingli even refers to it as a *res*. Nonetheless, the transaction of the Lord's Supper is one in which faith is fortified by God and the outward elements are merely picturesque ways of reminding the believer of God's act in Jesus Christ. The fundamental emphasis, furthermore, falls upon the deep gratitude of the believer for what is done in Christ, and therefore the leading theme of the Supper is *eucharistia* (thanksgiving) for a benefit already received. Zwingli does not, of course, deny the presence of Christ in the Supper. Rather does he say that he is present by his divine nature, and that all talk about participating in the Body of Christ is metaphorical for the reception by faith of the benefits brought by the Passion. The Body of Christ, in any literal sense, is inaccessible because in heaven, and irrelevant to the action of the Supper. Religion has to do with mind and spirit, not with matter. This clear-cut distinction fitted the type of mathematical thinking that was developing; and the general position has been furthered by the spirit of our technological age in which the autonomy of nature, separated from the world of spirit, has been given undue weight.

In Luther a quite different doctrine emerges, and one which is marked by some originality. For Luther, the action of the Lord's Supper is much more integrally connected with the world of nature, so that the divine is mediated through material forms. Luther emphatically denies transubstantiation partly because he is a nominalist, but also because he regards transubstantiation as an act of *man* which seeks to win God's favor, and hence is indicative of work-righteousness. Rather does Luther see the Supper as the gift of *God* for man who can do nothing on his own to win salvation. It is not possible for the Christian minister to convert the substance of the bread into that of the body of Christ by means of the consecration. Rather is something done by God for *us* in the consecration. What this is, is the manifestation of the hidden ground of existence. By means of the *verba* of consecration the body of Christ, which is ubiquitous and everywhere, is made accessible so that it can be grasped by faith. This is what Luther means by the *esse repletive*, a category that he adds to the modes of Christ's presence, which had been worked out by Occam. For Luther the Body of Christ is the hidden mystery in, with, and under all things. The Body of Christ cannot be looked upon as an object seated on a golden throne in a transcendent heaven. He vehemently attacks Zwingli's view as involving a childish view of God. The "Body of Christ" is an expression in Luther for the basic religious reality underlying all creation. Thus, when the *verba* are said, that which is present in "every loaf of bread on the table, in every leaf on the tree," is made manifest and accessible. The ordinary loaf on the table contains the Body of Christ no less than the loaf on the altar. The point, however, is that in the loaf on the ordinary table the Body of Christ is hidden and inaccessible, whereas on the altar it is revealed and made available. God appoints a word in terms of which the mystery of his being behind all existence is *greifbar*—made accessible to the believer. While in Lutheran dogmatics the full implications of Luther's own position were not always accepted, nonetheless the sharp distinction between Lutherans and other Protestants has been on this question of the objective presence of Christ in the sacramental elements.

Calvin attempted to steer a middle course between that of Zwingli and Luther. He worked out with great clarity what had been begun by Melanchthon and by Bucer. This view can be expressed in terms of the complementarity of physical action and spirit. While the bread is not regarded as in any way changed by virtue of the consecration, or as participating in the divine, nonetheless, the physical action is viewed as having attached to it the promise of God in such a way that when the Lord's Supper is celebrated a spiritual transaction between God and the believer takes place. The locus of this transaction is the realm of spirit, mind, and consciousness. Calvin tends to explain it in two ways. Either by the virtue of God's Spirit, the Body of Christ in heaven is brought to the believer so that he "participates in some measure in Christ's immortality," or, on the other hand, the spirit of man is raised by God to the heavenly realm, there to partake of the Body of Christ. The objectivity of the action is greatly stressed. It lies in God's promise that when the physical actions are performed a corresponding but not integrally related action between God and man's spirit occurs. In the *Consensus Tiguriensis* (The Zurich Consensus) the Calvinist and Zwinglian positions were brought close together. This has by and large been the doctrine of the Reformed Church.

On the question of the sacrifice in the Lord's Supper, the Protestant position gave the emphasis to three things. In the first place (as is made clear in a recent book by Aulén) the once-for-all-ness of the Cross is given the great stress. In no way can the Lord's Supper repeat it, nor can the action of the Supper participate in the Cross as if the latter were a transcendent and timeless reality. Rather is the emphasis placed upon the uniqueness and the *Einmaligkeit* of the Passion. Thus, the Catholic doctrine in connection with the sacrifice of the Mass is excluded. In its place the Protestant liturgy expresses the themes of the sacrifice of ourselves, our souls and bodies, and also the sacrifice of praise and thanksgiving. Many texts from the early Church which deal with the latter type of sacrifice are quoted; and insofar as the early Fathers attacked the literal sacrifices of pagan and Jewish religion, there is a close connection between the Protestant mind and that of the early Church. However, it must be observed that the full implications of the early doctrine were not grasped by the Reformers.

From these basic ways of looking at the Lord's Supper a fundamental antithesis between the Protestant and the Catholic viewpoint arose. There was a contrast for one thing between table and altar. For the Protestant the table of the Lord's Supper was the table around which the faithful gathered to receive that which God promised, but in no way to participate in an actual sacrifice. Then again there was a contrast of prophet and priest. Protestants stressed the prophetic element of the Word, whereby the declaration of God's forgivenesses was made, over against the action of the priest in converting the substance of the bread into that of the Body of Christ. Finally, we may observe the contrast between the surplice and gown, on the one hand, which were the vestments of Protestants, and the chasuble and alb on the other, which were the traditional eucharistic vestments. The surplice was a medieval development for the choir offices. The gown was either the scholar's gown as Luther had used it to preach in, or else the gown of the upper bourgeoisie which Zwingli had adopted in the Zurich services and which was similarly taken over in Geneva. These vestments symbolized the service of the Word as a choir office, or the educational significance of the exposition of Scripture. The chasuble and alb, on the other hand, while they had their origins in the normal wear of the upper classes in the later Roman Empire, had taken on a sacrificial significance. This occurred in the ninth century when a Judaizing movement overtook the Church in the early Middle Ages. When dress had sufficiently changed for the alb and chasuble to seem somewhat esoteric, they were given the meanings attaching to the priestly vestments in Leviticus. In consequence they came to signalize the garb of the sacrificing priest.

NEW EMPHASES TO
OVERCOME THE ANTITHESES

It is clear from what we have already said that the basic antitheses of the sixteenth century are still with us. Reconciliation between Catholic and Protestant positions appears impossible if we continue to think along the lines which led to the sixteenth-century separation. It presages well, however, for some possible ecumenical theology, which will gather together both Catholic and Protestant insights, that the stark divisions of the Reformation are coming to be viewed rather as overemphases on both sides than as truly expressive of the meaning of the Lord's Supper and other sacramental forms. It is patent, for instance, that the concepts of table and altar cannot be separated. If, on the one hand, the significance of the Lord's Supper leads to the Communion as the corporate act of the fellowship of Christ, then, on the other hand, sacrificial ideas cannot be excluded from the Lord's Supper. It is a sacramental act whose significance lies in its relation to the total sacrifice of Christ, and in consequence the altar is not a concept which can be excluded as if it was irreconcilable with the idea of table. In actual fact, table and altar in their Hebrew as well as in their Greek equivalents are words which interchange. An altar is a place on which an offering is made, and this very place is itself a table, for every offering culminates in a communal feast. Similarly the contrast between prophet and priest cannot be held to be one of mutual exclusion. The Word is not something which cancels the priestly act of the sacrament, but rather Word and sacrament belong together in a mutual fulfillment.

Perhaps the most fundamental point at which to begin some reconsideration by means of which these antitheses can be overcome is the notion of worship itself. We are all familiar with the commonplace that worship in its linguistic origin is connected with the word "worth," and worship gives expression to that which man prizes most highly. This, however, while it may be satisfactory for a theology based on the idea of value (as Ritschlianism, for instance), is not fully satisfactory. The underlying notion in worship is that of *being*, the word "worth" itself coming from the Anglo-Saxon *weorthan*, which means "to be." Worship is the act in which man recovers his being in relation to God. He overcomes the split between himself and his ultimate ground. All worship, therefore, must be looked upon not merely as the expression of what man values, but rather as the means by which man discovers the true meaning of his existence and realizes the basic nature and the destiny for which God intended him. In this light, we have a much larger concept in terms of which we can look at different aspects of the act of worship.

A second helpful approach is that of realizing that the concept of sacrifice cannot be limited to that of death. In this regard all Western theology, whether it is Roman Catholic or Protestant, has tended to lay undue weight on the notion of sacrifice in connection with the passion of Christ. Sacrifice actually is a much broader term. It means to "make holy"—*sacer* and *facere*. The process of making holy or recovering one's "wholeness" in relation to God involves much more than the concept of death. At least four fundamental notions are implied, and all of these should find expression both in the actual liturgy as well as in the understanding of the Lord's Supper. These four moments of the sacrificial act are offering, dying, rising, and finally participating in the eschatological banquet. The significance of the Lord's Supper is that it presents the total sacrifice of Christ in such a way that the believer can participate in it and reenact it in his own being. There is first offering, that is to say, the abandonment of the self to God. There is then dying, the actual experience whereby the ego-centered na-

ture is crucified. But that leads to resurrection. We rise with
Christ, and this finds its fulfillment in the communal banquet that gives expression to the End. This banquet is both
a present realization of the heavenly sphere and also an
anticipation of the final fulfillment. Here both future eschatology and realized eschatology are united. In this larger
concept, then, of sacrifice we see worship as the total act
in which there is presented the whole work of Christ in
such a way that we are able to live through it ourselves and
participate in that which he has accomplished in terms of
human nature. This further leads us to a consideration of
the way in which the sacrificial action of the service so
presents Christ that his perpetual relation to the Father is
made manifest and made accessible. It is necessary at this
point to go beyond the idea of the once-for-allness of the
Cross, to appreciate its significance as the historic expression of the eternal reality of the Divine Nature. It is because
the Divine Nature is love that the sacrifice of Christ is an
eternal act and is thus able to be made present in worship
here and now.

A third important consideration in our rethinking of sacramental forms is the notion of participation. In the act of
worship we "re-call," "re-present" that which has already
been done but whose significance lies beyond the historical
moment in which it was done. There is an actualization of
Christ in and among us, and not merely a remembering of
what was done in the first century A.D. Here it is important
that due weight be given both to the objective and subjective
aspects of sacramental worship. It lacks reality if the subjective experience of faith is played down. But it lacks power
if there is an insufficient appreciation of the way in which
the act of Christ is objectively present. The outward forms
are not merely reminders of something that was once done,
but are themselves the vehicles through which the eternal
significance of what was done is made available. Hence

there may be a way of speaking about the sacrifice of the Mass in such a manner that elements of superstition can be eradicated, and all talk about repeating the cross (which certainly is not genuine Catholic talk) can be avoided.

The mystery theology of Odo Casel is perhaps of some help in this connection. It may indeed be said that he derived his material too much from Hellenistic religions and not sufficiently from the biblical notion of *anamnesis.* It would perhaps be better to take such a celebration as that of the Passover fully to bring out the significance of biblical "remembering." In the biblical notion, the community is able to relive the events of the past and make them genuinely their own, because of the corporate personality of the group. The Jew in celebrating the Passover does not think of the crossing of the Red Sea as something which happened to people long ago. Rather is he bidden to think of *himself* as one who was rescued from Egypt, because he is a participator in the heritage of the people of Israel. In the same way, the Church understands that the crucifixion occurred not only in the first century but occurs in some sense in connection with us here and now. We are the inheritors of a tradition. We are the heirs of the early disciples. And thus in the act of worship there is made present, in a way in which we can grasp it and be grasped by it, the eternal significance of what was once done in Palestine. These events are present events as well as past events, and the whole significance of the act of worship is to make present the past in such a way that we are able to relive it in ourselves and thus recover our true being and destiny. It is along lines such as these that perhaps we shall be able to overcome the false antitheses that were posed in the sixteenth century, and achieve some vital reconciliation between Catholic and Protestant understandings.

"REFORMATIO"

GERHART B. LADNER

IN THE EARLY Christian age the Pauline message that man, who was created in the image of God, must be reformed to that image, was an ideal postulate for the individual Christian; as such it maintained itself as a living reality in the Church, and quite especially in the monastic sphere.

I shall speak today of the continued life of this early Christian idea of reform in the Western Middle Ages, to be more exact, of two of its principal phases and aspects. One of these is the Hildebrandian or Gregorian Church reform of the late eleventh century, the other, the Franciscan movement of the early thirteenth. Taken together they encompass, I think, much of the essence of medieval *Reformatio*.

Before the Hildebrandian age reform had, to repeat it, been primarily individual or personal, and monastic. There was no full realization that the Church as a whole might be in need of reform. Of course, as always in history, there were anticipations. So, for instance, the ever repeated renewal of the enactments of councils goes back to Christian antiquity and constituted a point of reference for the reformers of the eleventh century. It must also be remembered that certain heretical or schismatic groups—most prominently the Donatists—had asserted that the whole Church was corrupt and had to be renewed from top to bottom. Yet such movements had never been able to rise above a sectarian status; they had not been able to gain even gradual approval through the consensus of the Church.

It was quite different with the Church reform of the

eleventh century. In the incredibly short span of two generations this reform very thoroughly transformed the ecclesiastical structure of the West and its relation to the political order; and in spite of powerful and lasting resistance in imperial and royalist quarters this transformation was rather generally accepted. The emergence of a strong and successful urge for general reform in that period was due to increasing awareness of a vast discrepancy which existed between the form of life of the contemporary Church of the eleventh century and that of the Apostles, martyrs and early Church Fathers. It was widely felt that in several important respects this discrepancy entailed great dangers for the spiritual substance of Christianity. It is hardly necessary to discuss here the well-known early medieval combination of theocratic kingship and of proprietary rights of laymen over Church offices as well as Church goods. This combination lay at the root of all difficulties. Neither is it necessary to give a detailed picture of the abuses which resulted from it, among which simony, that is to say, the selling and buying of ecclesiastical offices, and clerical concubinage were the most obvious and widespread. The critics of the situation saw it chiefly in moral terms and were unable to perceive clearly that—leaving abuses aside—it was largely a product of the great changes which had occurred in consequence of the disappearance of the Roman Empire and of the Germanization and feudalization of Western Christian society. And yet the most consistent among the reformers, above all Gregory VII himself, recognized one essential point very clearly. The time-honored antidote to worldliness, namely, monastic conversion, was in the eleventh century no longer sufficient by itself—if for no other reason, for the quite decisive one that by and large monasticism itself had become greatly affected by the prevalent fusion of theocratic royal government and lay ownership of ecclesiastical institutions. Concretely, more often than not abbots were not canonically, that is to say, freely, elected by monastic communities but were nominated by rulers or great nobles who had founded or enriched the monasteries and felt justified in expecting economic and political support from them.

At this point Cluny and the so-called Cluniac reform movement will immediately come to mind. Did not the Cluniacs initiate the great Church reform of the Hilde-brandian age? Was the Gregorian reform not simply a con-tinuation and extension of the Cluniac monastic reform? This question has in fact been among the problems most debated by medieval historians for the last thirty years, and I think that thanks to the efforts of many scholars one can now see the solution fairly clearly.

To put it succinctly—the novelty and greatness of Cluny lies much more in its spirituality, of which the liturgy was the center, than in its institutions.

Though Cluny itself was absolutely free in its abbatial elections and constituted an independent entity within the feudal order, the great Cluniac abbots and their monks did not any more than other monastic reformers of pre-Gre-gorian times object on principle to theocratic lay govern-ment and to the proprietary Church system. And yet, it remains true that the almost total exemption of Cluny itself from extraneous, that is to say, nonmonastic, influences en-abled it to concentrate in a new manner upon the innermost core of the religious life, on public and private prayer, on the liturgical and individual worship of God. Thus, it came about that Cluny and the monasteries reformed by it, through the splendor of their liturgy and of the literature and art which flowed from it, spiritually illumined Western Christian society of the tenth and eleventh centuries. It is also true that the monastic renewal was not limited to Cluny and its dependencies and that the spiritual dynamism which emanated from it radiated into the clerical and lay world at large, affecting, for instance, French knightly society and some of the great rulers of the time, such as the Emperor Henry III, and, last but not least, the reform circles in Rome—especially from the time of Leo IX, that is to say, from 1049 onward. There can be little doubt that the reforming fervor of a Humbert of Silva Candida, of a Hildebrand himself owed something to the spiritual forces which Cluny had set in motion, but there can be no doubt at all that the Gregorian reformers directed their fervor toward aims which were both more universal and more specific than those of Cluny and of other monastic centers of the time: more universal because directly concerning the Church as a whole, more specific because legal-institutional and explicitly Rome-centered.

The principal characteristics of the Gregorian Church reform were in fact two: canonistic foundation and papal guidance. Its central ideas were *veritas* and *iustitia*, to be vindicated against ill-founded and unjust *consuetudo*; its practical instrument was reassertion and extension of papal primacy, which had been formulated in Christian antiquity, most impressively perhaps by Leo the Great, but which after the time of Gregory the Great, with the exception of the pontificate of Nicholas I, had lain more or less dormant.

Already around 1050, two decades before Hildebrand became Pope, we find a lively new interest in the law of the Church, and this interest is closely linked to papal prerogative. It was Hildebrand himself who about that time asked another of the early reformers, Peter Damian, to collect canonistic texts relative to papal primacy, and a steady sequence of systematic collections of canon law, reflecting the spirit of the reform, does actually begin about that time.

In this connection the rather generally accepted and ingenious theory of Fr. G. B. Borino, that the famous *Dictatus Papae* of Gregory VII—long considered as his personal program of papal world domination—is in reality a list of chapter headings of a lost canonistic collection concerning papal primacy, is especially noteworthy.

The *Dictatus Papae* is inserted in the original register of the letters of Gregory VII, which is still preserved in the Vatican Archives. These letters, as well as others by Gregory and his immediate successors, allow us to see clearly how the reform popes asserted papal authority based on canon law, with the avowed intention of keeping to the right norm between custom on the one hand and innovation on the other.

I think a letter fragment of Gregory VII or his second successor, Urban II, is most revealing in this respect: "If anyone allege custom he should realize that the Lord said: 'I am the way and the truth and the life' (John 14:6). He did not say: I am the custom, but he said: I am the truth." This terse formula goes back directly to St. Augustine and indirectly to St. Cyprian and Tertullian; in the Gregorian and post-Gregorian age it was to enter the codification of canon law through Ivo of Chartres and Gratian. The principle that truth is superior to custom was of the greatest importance for the Gregorian reform movement; but so was the rejection of untraditional innovation enunciated against Cyprian by Pope Stephen I in the baptismal controversy of the third century, and never forgotten since: *Nihil innovetur nisi quod traditum est*, "Let nothing be innovated except that which is part of tradition." These two principles are like the obverse and the reverse of a single coin. As Cyprian had already asserted and Augustine had formulated more clearly, they are not essentially opposed to each other. The question is rather whether or not a custom is in conformity with the truth and its truthful tradition. If it is not, it must be reformed. Such reform is not an innovation which would violate tradition; it is rather the undoing of such innovations in favor of customs which are in accordance with truth and tradition. To build a bridge from the old truth to acceptable

customs of the present, across half a millennium of inveter-
ate "bad customs," this was, in fact, the problem and aim of
the Gregorian reform.

Notwithstanding his assertion that the pope may issue
new laws whenever necessary, Gregory VII never tired of
repeating that he was not an untraditional "innovator," that
he had not come to set up new customs in the Church, but
only to renew the old and true ones. He claimed both law-
ful and necessary renewal and avoidance of rash innovation.

The aims of the Gregorian reformers were not limited to
the abolition of simony and clerical concubinage, or even
clerical marriage, nor was lay investiture at first a central
problem for them, though the soon ensuing conflict between
the papacy and the kingdoms, especially the Holy Roman
Empire, is known as the Investiture Struggle. What Hildebrand and the other reformers of his generation considered
as absolutely essential was to make sure that henceforward
the *sacerdotium*, from the pope down to the last priest and
cleric, would be motivated by spiritual and not by temporal
interests. Only thus could the whole Church, the whole
Christian world, be reformed. This spiritualization could
be attained only if elections, first of all to the papal office
and then to all ecclesiastical offices, were carried out in such
a way that the Holy Spirit could operate freely in them.
Ecclesiastical elections must be under the control of that
element in the Church which had been ordained primarily
for a spiritual purpose, that is to say, the priesthood. Since,
however, in the actually existing conditions of the Gregorian
age the priests and bishops themselves were so largely involved in nonspiritual concerns—beginning with their own
familial interests and ending with the economic aggrandize-
ment of their churches and the political tasks allotted to them
by emperors and kings—ultimate sacerdotal control de-
volved quite naturally upon the papacy, once it had freed
itself from lay control. Thus, in 1080, Gregory VII for-

mulated the beginnings of a new law of devolution according to which, later on, any uncanonical election could be supplanted or remedied by the pope himself.

It would seem, then, that Gregory VII's centralization of the Universal Church in the Roman Church and the papacy, which was to have such great and lasting consequences, was necessitated by conditions that demanded reform and was the only means by which this reform could be brought about. His exaltation of the Roman Church was hardly conceived of as a maximum program of world domination or even world conversion, but rather as a guarantee of the preservation of the Church's spiritual essence which he saw incorporated in the sacerdotal office to which liturgy and doctrine were entrusted.

It is very clear—and has been stressed strongly in several recent studies of the Gregorian Church reform by Catholic as well as Protestant scholars—that this reform led to an unprecedented assertion of the hierarchical principle in general and to a concentration and absorption of all particular hierarchical functions in the papacy. The old claim of Petrine primacy in the Church and of Petrine continuity in the Roman see was now put forward with a fervor that had definitely mystical overtones and with a vigor which, it can hardly be denied, was at times not exempt from fanaticism.

It has always been recognized that the assertion of Petrine jurisdictional primacy in its specifically Gregorian form constituted a turning point of Church history and became a source of strength as well as a cause for opposition.

All the more important is it for the historian to understand and to point out how closely in the mind of Gregory VII the Petrine claim is connected with his conceptions not only of justice but also of love and unity.

Let me first consider his conception of *iustitia*, which to him was literally and tremendously alive, since it was divine.

In a more personal way than for the other reformers justice was for Gregory the living core of the renewal of canon law.

It is well known that on his deathbed Gregory VII said: "I have loved justice and hated iniquity, therefore I die as an exile." These words are often interpreted as an expression of self-righteousness combined with bitterness, but this does not sufficiently explain them. It is abundantly clear from the pope's numerous letters that he really loved justice and was at the same time convinced that justice will and must suffer in a world which, before its final judgment, is only in part a godly world and perhaps mostly a world of the devil. He also knew that nobody can be just without the grace of God and that under ordinary circumstances it was by no means certain that actions which seemed to be just were really so. Yet, there was for him an ultimate criterion of justice and that was conformity with the faith of St. Peter and his successors, for Christ had prayed for Peter that his faith would not fail and that once converted he would confirm his brethren (Luke 22:32).

Petrine and papal justice was thus the measure and guarantee for the justice of the whole Church and adherence to it was necessary for each individual Christian. But not only justice was involved: Peter's justice was based on his love for Christ, and love for Peter and for the Petrine Church of Rome was in the eyes of Gregory the indispensable concretization of true love for Christ. It was above all through Gregory—though Humbert of Silva Candida and others had prepared the way—that love for the Roman Church as *caput et cardo,* as *mater et magistra,* assumed mystical connotations which it had never before possessed to the same degree. Ever since Gregory VII the Roman Church has been invested with a charismatic character, which to be sure it had never lacked but which this pope greatly enhanced, making it a very living thing after a lapse of many centuries. Whatever else he achieved or failed to achieve, it cannot be denied that he was able to inculcate into the Church a growing and often ardent desire to be in union with Rome, to be obedient to the pope.

It is essential to realize fully that for Gregory VII love for the Roman Church, justice under the Roman Church, unity with the Roman Church ultimately were only meant to bring about the Christian world's love for Christ. All Gregory's Petrine mysticism is rooted in and oriented toward his theocentric, Christocentric view of the world which was exceedingly well presented in a remarkable study by the German Protestant historian August Nitschke, published in volume five of *Studi Gregoriani* (1956).

It is, however, very important to realize also that certain aspects of Gregory VII's Roman centralism have not been permanently accepted by the Roman Catholic Church. This is rather obvious today when in connection with the Second Vatican Council the relation between papal primacy and the apostolic authority of the bishops is being discussed so thoroughly; I need only refer to the well-known book of Fr. Hans Küng, *The Council, Reform and Reunion*, and to recent studies by the Dominican Fr. Yves Congar and the Jesuit Fr. Karl Rahner. But already the First Vatican Council, following intimations of the Council of Trent, had safeguarded the divine ordination of the episcopal office better than it had been done by Gregory VII and the Gregorians, whose single-minded concern for the centralization of the Church in the papal office had made the pope not only the supreme judge in all spiritual matters but also had derived all authority in the Church from him as from its supposed origin. Chapter 3 of the Constitution *De ecclesia* of the First Vatican Council on the contrary states clearly that the primatial power of the supreme pontiff does not oppose or obstruct the ordinary or immediate jurisdictional power through which the bishops, who were put by the Holy Spirit in the place and succession of the Apostles, tend and rule their flocks; this episcopal power is rather to be maintained, strengthened and vindicated by the supreme and universal pastor. According to the words of St. Gregory the Great: "the honor of the universal Church is my honor. The solid strength of my brethren is my honor. Then am I truly honored when to every single one [of them] due honor is not denied."

Before we leave the age of Gregory VII, I might make a brief remark about the concept of papal "plenitude of power" in Church-state relations, which developed out of the Gregorian reform. It has, I believe, been proved in recent years, especially by the works of Fr. Friedrich Kempf of the Society of Jesus, Professor at the Gregorian University in Rome, that the principles of Gregory VII did not necessarily or always lead to those hierocratic views which were held by some popes and theologians of the later Middle Ages and which are often unduly generalized. It has been shown that on the contrary the so-called Gelasian two-power doctrine was never obliterated and that it over and over again emerged as the *communis opinio* of the Church. Papal *plenitudo potestatis* was, and should be, considered an essentially spiritual concept, though it could in certain historical situations extend far into the temporal sphere for spiritual reasons.

Protected in principle by the Gregorian monarchical concretization of the doctrine of Petrine primacy, the hierarchical Church between 1100 and 1300 could attempt to exercise spiritual leadership and control over the whole of Christian society. Looking at the great achievements of twelfth- and thirteenth-century Christian culture, the least, I think, one can say is that this attempt met with a fair measure of success.

Nevertheless, there were not a few deficiencies and faults in the great structure, and Gregory VII, whose spirituality was more eschatological than it was incarnational, would have been the last to be surprised. Perhaps Bernard of Clairvaux, who was both true heir of the Gregorian age and true forerunner of the age of Francis of Assisi—perhaps St. Bernard, who called himself not without reason the chimera of his century, is the greatest symbolic protagonist of a necessary transition to a new kind of *Reformatio*, which is ministerial rather than authoritarian, and at once more personal rather than institutional. In his memorandum, addressed to his pupil, the Cistercian Pope Eugene III, and entitled *On Consideration*, Bernard very clearly outlined the new dangers which arose from the centralization of Church government and from the unavoidable ecclesiastical bureaucraticism and fiscalism which went along with it. On the one hand, the Great Abbot of Clairvaux in true Gregorian fashion extolled the powers of the papacy—it was he, it seems, who first applied the term *plenitudo potestatis* to papal government—on the other hand, he was hardly less outspoken in his criticism of the Roman Curia than those satirists of the time who wrote that the Church of Rome now lived according to the gospel of the silver mark rather than of St. Mark.

In the latter half of the twelfth century and at the beginning of the thirteenth it was indeed a great question whether the intellectual, political, economic, and cultural advances, brought about in part by the general freeing and quickening of the human spirit which had been one of the results of the Gregorian reform movement, could be absorbed by, or harmonized with, the evangelical inspiration which was itself awakening to new forms of life.

It was in this situation that, to use the words of Pope Gregory IX, which are found also in one of the oldest Franciscan legends, there appeared Francis of Assisi as the morning star or even the rising sun of spring that kindles new life. Thomas of Celano in his great praises of the new and *mirabilis religio* of the saint of Assisi describes the world of his time as old and slack, as far removed from the fervor of the Apostles. In the midst of conditions in which, as he says, the perfection of the primitive Church was buried, there burst forth the new man, the *homo novus Franciscus*, who finally was found worthy of a new and stupendous miracle, of the conformation of his own body to that of the crucified Lord through the stigmata. This unheard-of event, Thomas of Celano says, was only the ultimate seal set upon Francis' long-standing special relationship to Christ on the cross. In the beginnings of Francis' conversion the Lord from the cross had spoken to him those fateful words which showed him the task of reform which he must accomplish: *Repara domum meam que ut cernis tota destruitur,* "Repair my house, which, as you see, is being wholly destroyed."

It is hardly necessary to recall how St. Francis at first took this command literally and rebuilt several churches with his own hands, divesting himself for this purpose literally of all property. In a truly memorable and symbolic scene Francis even shed the clothes which were part of his paternal heritage and stood naked before his, no doubt able and honest, but irate and uncharitable, earthly father Bernardone, who represents the successful merchant-aristocracy of the flourishing Italian pre-Renaissance civilization; he was then sheltered by the Church, represented as it were by the cloak which the Bishop of Assisi threw around him. From that moment onward the following of Christ, the preaching of Christ by word and by example, in absolute poverty, in consequent freedom from worldly cares, and in joyful peace of mind, emerged as the special way in which St. Francis was to repair the house of God, was to attempt a reform of Christian society.

At this point it must, however, be made clear that, notwithstanding the incomparable personality of St. Francis, what he did was by no means altogether novel. His way of life had been anticipated by all those groups which, since the very age of the Gregorian Church reform, had attempted to imitate the life of Christ and the Apostles, and had striven for the *vita apostolica*. This term occurs since the late eleventh century to designate the ideals of such itinerant preachers as Robert of Arbrissel or Norbert of Xanten. It would seem that their preaching was largely a call to penance, in the sense of a change of heart. Such, as we shall see presently, will be the case also in the penitential confraternities of about 1200, Franciscan and otherwise. The name by which the itinerant preachers of the twelfth century wanted to be known was highly significant, too: *pauperes Christi*. Earlier this name had meant either the destitute and beggars or the scriptural poor in spirit, among whom could be counted the monks because of their individual poverty and their renunciation of the world. Now a new and more radical conception of *paupertas* was linked to a renewal of the *vita apostolica*. *Nudus nudum Christum in cruce sequi, nudam crucem nudus sequi,* "denuded must we follow Christ, naked on the cross; denuded must we follow the bare cross"—these sayings, attributed to St. Robert of Arbrissel and to St. Norbert, though probably derived from St. Jerome, were really programmatic for the *pauperes Christi* of the early twelfth century, whose purpose did not differ in this respect from one of the most central aspects of Franciscan spirituality. Nevertheless, the old monastic ideal was then still so strong that the apostolic movement, in so far as it did not become heretical, issued into new monastic or quasi-monastic orders, such as the Premonstratensians of St. Norbert or Robert of Arbrissel's Congregation of Fontevrault.

Why did it take another one hundred years before *vita apostolica* and *paupertas Christi* could make another and more lasting breakthrough in the Mendicant Orders, and especially in the Franciscan movement? Or to put the question differently, why was the early twelfth-century *élan* for these ideals carried on for most of the remaining century chiefly by heretics? These questions are all the more justified as there can be little doubt that the whole apostolic movement, which had arisen at the turn from the eleventh to the twelfth century, had been born out of the spiritual exaltation of the Gregorian reform and had at first been actively supported by the reformed papacy itself. This is true even of one of the most revolutionary manifestations of this kind, the famous Milanese Pataria movement of the second half of the eleventh century, whose leaders, whether clerics or laymen, had preached against the simoniac and otherwise corrupt clergy.

Why, then, did the Church, and especially the papacy, between the age of St. Bernard, c. 1140, and that of Innocent III and St. Francis, c. 1200, find it impossible to guide the spiritual enthusiasm for the *vita apostolica* into orthodox channels?

If we leave aside the more radically unorthodox Cathari, whose derivation from the eastern Manichaeans seems now to be definitely established, the answer to such questions seems to lie in two directions. There was, on the one hand, the fact that the apostolic impetus could and did easily lead to integral anti-clericalism. On the other hand, the clerical hierarchy was perhaps somewhat unprepared to cope in a constructive and really understanding manner with movements which seemed to jeopardize in a new way the positions won by the Gregorian reform through hierarchicalization and centralization of the Church. The historian can up to a point appreciate both points of view. He can see that it was difficult for those who wanted to return to, or lead toward, a purer Christian life to accept the sacraments from a clergy which, in too many of its representatives, was still deeply enmeshed in the world. He can also see that it was one of the great achievements of the Gregorian reformers and their continuators to have clarified after considerable oscillation those principles of sacramental theology according to which the validity of the sacraments is independent of the personal worthiness of those who administer them, while at the same time insisting that faithful adherence to a canonically elected hierarchy culminating in the papacy is a safeguard and norm for the maintenance of the substance of the Christian religion.

The new crisis which arose in Western Christendom at the end of the twelfth century was quite different then from that which had confronted the Gregorian reformers a century earlier. For, more often than not, the evangelical or apostolic spirit stood in contradiction to what we may perhaps call the Catholic spirit, if we mean by the latter a deep concern for the unity of the Universal Church. In a historian's hindsight it is perhaps obvious that this contrast was itself contrary to the nature of the Church. It would seem that it was the tragedy of Peter Waldes and of other heretics of the same type that they did not see it so. I say, "it would seem" deliberately, because I think that in some of the relevant cases, and especially in that of Peter Waldes, it is still not clear whether before falling into heresy they were given the charitable and favorable hearing by Catholic authority which St. Francis, St. Dominic, Durandus of Huesca, and others later received.

However this may be, it was quite definitely one of the most essential traits of Francis' call to a new life that he over and over again exhorted his followers not to be separated under any circumstances from the sacraments, especially the eucharistic sacrament—in which alone, he says, the Son of God can be corporeally seen in this world—and therefore likewise not to be separated from the hierarchical order of the Church, which reaches from the lowest priest to the pope. In his own words, "We must assist the priests" and "We want to live according to the form of the Roman Church."

At the same time his own way of life and that of his companions were emphatically unhierarchical. This is why the Rule of 1221 calls all Franciscan superiors ministers and servants of the other brethren (*ministri et servi*) and in a general way states that Franciscans, wherever they are, must behave as *minores et subditi*, whence the name *Fratres Minores*, Friars Minor.

Francis, who was not himself a priest, brought about a most far-reaching spiritual renewal in the midst of the turbulent and complex society of his time, and he did so without ever using the negative means of recrimination or revolt against the hierarchical order of the Christian World. He must have known of the Waldensians and other harsh critics of the contemporary Church, but in this respect he did not follow them. It is very characteristic of him that in imitating the life of Christ and the Apostles more perfectly perhaps than any man before or after him, he did not stress any one aspect of this life—even be it poverty—at the expense of its other aspects. The literal and contentious interpretation of evangelical and apostolic poverty which was later so tragically to disrupt the Franciscan Order was not his, even though he did suffer cruelly from the necessity of making concessions with regard to the early Franciscan community's ideals of poverty and simplicity. These concessions, which, because of the extraordinary expansion of the Order, had become unavoidable, were incorporated into the Rules of 1221 and 1223, still in his lifetime.

In his Testament St. Francis did attempt once more an almost integral reassertion of his ideals, but here, too, humility and obedience to the hierarchical Church were imposed with equal force.

Since two generations of scholars have largely cleared up the extremely complicated source problems of early Franciscan history, we need not and must not be misled by the great temptation to which the Franciscan Spirituals succumbed when they reduced Francis' intention all too exclusively to the observance of poverty.

If we glance at the basic texts in which his purpose is defined, such as the Testament, the First Life by Thomas of Celano, and also the Rule of 1221, we find above all a most striking identity of Francis' message with that of the Gospel, and this in a way which is most closely related to *Reformatio*. I am referring to Francis' call to penance, *penitentia*.

This was not merely a call to mortification of the body, though this, too, was important to him, but above all to a truly new beginning of life in preparation for the Kingdom of God, penance in the sense in which the Baptist and Jesus himself had preached it. The Latin term *penitentia* is here rather misleading. The Greek Gospel term *metanoia*, change of mind or of heart, suggests better what Francis' intention was.

As the saint says in his Testament: "The Lord granted me to begin penance by being merciful to lepers." It was his first decisive change of heart. According to the First Life by Thomas of Celano this was followed soon by the evangelical call in the Portiuncula Church, where a priest explained to him the *vita apostolica* and the *paupertas Christi* as corollaries of the preaching of the Kingdom of God and of penance. It was his preaching of penance and the example of a changed heart which drew large numbers of people of all classes, laymen and clerics, men and women, toward Francis, so that, as the First Life written by Celano expresses it, the Church of Christ was renewed (*renovatur*) in a three-fold manner, meaning the Friars Minor, the Poor Clares, and the Third Order of St. Francis.

It is of interest that the Friars Minor at first called themselves the Penitent Men of Assisi and that later on the members of the Third Order, who could not go as far as St. Francis and his companions in renunciation of the world, but still would change their lives for the better, were called *Fratres et sorores de penitentia*. The crucial role of *penitentia* in the Franciscan movement is documented also in chapter 21 of the 1221 Rule for the Friars Minor, which is a sample sermon to be used by all brethren if they so choose; in it penance in the sense of change of heart is the keynote: "Do penance (Matthew 3:2), Bring forth fruit worthy of penance (Matthew 3:8) . . . Blessed those who die in penance because they will be in the Kingdom of God."

There is no doubt a connection between the Franciscan concept of penance and that of older penitential brotherhoods, especially those of the twelfth century, just as there were pre-Franciscan forms of the *vita apostolica* in general. Yet, Francis' personality was so exceptional that old ideas received through him all the fullness of their original life. He was a radiant bringer of peace out of spiritual freedom and joyfulness. He was the closest imitator of Christ the world has ever known. This was the essence of his *Reformatio*. When Cardinal Giovanni Colonna introduced him to Pope Innocent III as "a very perfect man who wanted to . . . observe evangelical perfection in all things . . . and would reform the faith of the Holy Church . . ." he spoke only the truth.

Comprehensive and yet specific investigations, which would ascertain to what extent exactly the Franciscan movement actually did bring about concrete reforms in late medieval society, are still far from being complete or exhaustive, though there are some promising beginnings. Many such studies would, I think, be needed and would probably be rewarding. One thing at any rate is certain: through his example St. Francis of Assisi invited all men to a new and more personal form of Christian religiousness.

St. Francis' *Reformatio* was indeed eminently personal and in a sense the Franciscan movement was a return to the personal conception of reform which had dominated the patristic and early medieval periods.

Yet, it was a return with a new background and within a new framework. The background was a Western-Christian civilization of its own, which had finally replaced the remnants of ancient civilization. The framework was the reformed Church of Gregory VII and Innocent III with both its greatness and its flaws. We do not know how Francis would have fared had he lived before the Gregorian Church reform. We must not forget that the centuries which were shaped by a St. Benedict, a Venerable Bede, a Charlemagne, an Odo of Cluny were Christian centuries, too. Yet, hardly could St. Francis have then loved the Roman Church as much as he did or have accepted her guidance so wholeheartedly. Conversely, there would have been neither the same urgent need nor a really adequate place for the Franciscan movement in pre-Gregorian Christianity even apart from the differences in economic-social conditions. Thus one is justified, I believe, in seeing in Gregory VII and Francis of Assisi the two greatest, complementary figures of medieval *Reformatio*.

If it is true that the scriptural and patristic reform idea, after having lived for centuries in its personal and monastic realizations, finally issued into the general Church reform of the Gregorian age, then it may perhaps also prove true that the *Reformatio* of the poor man of Assisi still has a great role to play in the never-ceasing renewal of the entire Church.

WHO REFORMS THE CHURCH?

MARTIN A. SCHMIDT

T HE REFORM of the Church is the work of God himself, who works through "spiritual men," that is, through such members of the Body of Christ as are quickened by his spirit and therefore are able to contribute to the quickening of the whole body. But who are these "spiritual men"? When we enter the epoch of Occam, of the conciliarist movement, and of Wyclifism, we see how the need for ecclesiastical reform was felt in such a way that there was no longer agreement about the way in which God would take care of this need. While the cry for reform increased in power, the problem inherent in any concept of reform was increasingly felt. Serious advocates of reform disagreed on the best method because divergent concepts of "God reforming his Church" developed.

With William Occam joining the ranks of the Franciscans who protested against Pope John XXII in behalf of "evangelical poverty" there rose much more than simply a new advocate of reform and another critic of hierarchical power and wealth. The possibility that a pope could fall into heresy had been discussed by canonists for a long time.[1] But for Occam the very ground of the Avignonese pope's "heresies" was that he had assumed rights in the ecclesiastical body which did not belong to him. And this misunderstanding of a man's power in the Church for him was grounded in a misunderstanding of the ways in which God's own power works. The question how powers and privileges are dis-

[1] B. Tierney, *The Foundations of the Conciliar Theory* (Cambridge, Eng., 1955), pp. 8f, 60–67, 214f.

tributed in the Church was traced back to the author and distributor of all powers and privileges.

Occam entered the debates about Church and society as a man who saw man's being an image of his Creator in ways characteristically different from the ways of the older schools of scholasticism. To him man does not bear that quality of inner similarity with the primary cause (according to the general rule that the closer an effect is related to its cause the more similarity with the cause it has). To Occam the relation of causality does not imply an inner proportion of being.[2] Even God himself does not know his creatures in another form of being than in that which he has given them, that is, in the ways of contingent existence, *quia illud esse creaturae est ipsa creatura* (because "being of the creature" is nothing else than the creature itself).[3] This man's being does not make him into the symbol of or into the participant of another, higher, more general form of being. The epitome of his being is that he is who he is (a *res positiva*),[4] in the same way that God, in his being, is who *he* is.

But this radical freedom and self-sufficiency of man is relative insofar as it is not preserved without order. God expresses his *potentia absoluta* not in the way of unstructured arbitrariness but in the form of his *potentia ordinata* (ordained power), and this means for man that a relation is established in which his freedom is not annihilated but preserved and protected. Insofar as God has revealed and

---

[2] G. de Lagarde, *La naissance de l'esprit laique au déclin du moyen âge*, vol. V: *L'individualisme ockhamiste: Bases de départ* (Paris, 1946), pp. 169–171; L. Baudry, *Lexique philosophique de Guillaume d'Ockham* (Paris, 1958), pp. 40ff; Ph. Boehner, "Ockham's Theory of Signification," in *Collected Articles on Ockham*, E. M. Buytaert, ed. (St. Bonaventure, N.Y., 1958), pp. 201–232, particularly pp. 203–209.

[3] Occam, I *Sent.* d 36 X. Cf. Lagarde, V, 119.

[4] Lagarde, V. 171f; P. Vignaux, *Nominalisme au XIVe siècle* (Montreal, 1948), pp. 73–96.

commanded this and not that, he is our God, the God of positive revelation and order. Men may enjoy their own existence as long as they do not destroy their God-given freedom in unruly conflicts but rather use the possibilities of preserving it, by acquiring property for example, or by appointing rulers who keep the individual interests from clashing against each other.[5] In this way of taking care of their "common interest" (not by setting forth a "supreme good" which is not man's own good),[6] men may be said to be "God's men."[7] Any human law or power which opposes itself to God's primary law and power disturbs the divinely ordered balance of freedom and order. Man may enjoy that freedom which is his. But he may not put himself in the place of God by claiming a power of a more absolute character.[8] The pope, then, cannot claim for himself *plenitudo potestatis* (fullness of power) in both spiritual and secular matters because, according to God's ordination, he is the "vicar of Christ" only as far as Christ's *human* nature is concerned.[9] This shows how Occam does not consider things of the Church in terms of ontological participation. If "vicar of Christ" meant someone who participates (as symbol or as instrumental cause) in Christ's rul-

[5] Lagarde, vol. VI: *L'individualisme ockhamiste: La morale et le droit* (Paris, 1946), pp. 177–185; Lagarde, vol. IV: *Guillaume d'Ockham: Défense de l'empire*, nouvelle édition refondue et complétée (Louvain and Paris, 1962), pp. 193–234.

[6] Lagarde, VI, 48–81, 186–192; IV, 223–234.

[7] Lagarde, VI, 124–163; particularly p. 155n34. Both the "divine" and the "natural" law Occam understands as expressions of God's *potentia ordinata*. Although he does not identify these two forms of law, "tout au long de son oeuvre politique il met presque toujours sur le même pied 'droit naturel' et 'loi divine' " (*ibid.*, VI, 134).

[8] See M. A. Schmidt, "Kirche und Staat bei Wilhelm von Ockham," *Theologische Zeitschrift* 7:265–284 (1951).

[9] R. Scholz, *Wilhelm von Ockham als politischer Denker und sein Breviloquium de principatu tyrannico*, Monumenta Germaniae historica, VIII (Stuttgart, 1944), p. 69f (*Brevil.* II:9). All subsequent references to the *Breviloquium* of Occam are to this edition, which notes many parallels from other political writings of Occam, particularly from his *Dialogus*.

ing his Church, then it would be impossible to make such a distinction between Christ's human and divine natures. The way in which the pope is considered as a "vicar" is understood in terms of commission or delegation.[10] In the same way that for Occam, the logician, a concept of a thing "stands for" (*supponit pro*) the thing, the pope, considered as *vicarius,* is not a secondary "head" of the Church, by duplicating, in a derived way, Christ's headship but rather sets forth, by not assuming human power, the example of Christ according to his humility. He is not to derive any other privilege from Christ than that of representing, in his actions, the saving action of Jesus Christ. In this way he does not "rule" the Church (instrumentally, participating in Christ's power) but "stands for" a certain use of power which is essential for every member of the Church and in which every member does as his own work what Christ has shown us in his work: "The kings of the nations exercise lordship over them; and those in authority over them are called benefactors. But not so with you; rather let the greatest among you become as the youngest, and the leader as one who himself serves" (Luke 22:25).[11] Therefore, the pope has a *principatus* indeed. But it is a *principatus ministrationis* (ministrative leadership), not a *principatus dominativus* (dominative leadership).[12] A servant does not serve as instrument of another servant. (That other servant, in such a case, would no longer be a servant but a ruler.) Rather each servant does at his place what service requires; and in this way the service of one servant "stands for" the service of another servant, if we want to know what service is.

[10] "Si ergo Christus talem plenitudinem potestatis pro tempore, quo venit ministrare, non ministrari, voluit abdicare, sequitur, quod papae, vicario suo, talem plenitudinem potestatis non concessit." *Brevil.* II:9.

[11] C. K. Brampton, ed., *The De Imperatorum et Pontificum Potestate of William of Ockham* (Oxford, 1927), 7:2 (p. 14f). Hereafter abbreviated as *De imp.*

[12] *Ibid.,* 6; 7:2, 4, 7; 26:2 (pp. 12f, 14f, 16, 17, 45).

Service as basic character of the Church is more than merely a correct concept. It has the power of a law. Christ gave to the Church the *lex evangelicae libertatis*. Occam ascribes to it a "more negative" character insofar as it forbids the use of the Gospel for the increasing of slavery among men by adding new yokes and loads. No one should become a slave of another man on account of *this* "law."[13]

But where does dominative authority have its place, if it is ruled out in Christ's foundation? A prince who has secular power (and this includes the pope insofar as secular power was granted to him *ab hominibus*[14]) ultimately has his power from God. But he does not have it as a participation in God's power, rather as his own power granted to him according to the will of God. His use of power does not "stand for" the use God makes of his power; for the power which a king has over his subjects came about in such a way that men delegated their own individual privileges to a common ruler. The way of delegation, therefore, does not directly go from God to a prince but goes from God to men and then from men to such rulers as they have chosen to be their rulers.[15] Occam says that a powerful one has his power "from God" neither as God's direct delegate (like Moses) nor as a sacramental representative of God. There is a third way of transfer of power: *a Deo et hominibus* concurrently.[16] Such a power as one may have belongs to the general world government of God, not to the Church (whose negative power structure has been described). External power, however, may be used *for* the Church. As far as the

---

[13] *Brevil.* II:3, 4 (pp. 56–59). Occam invokes this *lex* frequently. For the problem of its more negative expression in *Brevil., De imp.,* and other minor political writings, see Lagarde, IV, 61f. For seeing Occam's ecclesiology in its more positive contours, a full use of his great *Dialogus* is indispensable. For this presentation I was not able to embark upon such a vast and difficult study.

[14] *Brevil.* I:10 (p. 51).

[15] See Lagarde, VI, 199–209; IV, 219–234.

[16] *Brevil.* IV:5, 6 (pp. 149–151).

visible Church is a part of this world, she also has a part in
the check-and-balance system which is everywhere in the
world. A prince who, on account of his external power, is
able to check the illegitimate claims of a clergy that strives
for power instead of setting forth the example of Christ—
such a prince serves the Church. But this is a service of an
indirect, external character.[17] (Even a pope can render this
kind of service if external power was granted to him and he
uses it in order to protect the Church against tyranny of
princes.[18]) In itself it is a power *respectu servorum* (with
respect to slaves), not *respectu liberorum* (with respect to
freemen).[19] Only the service in the name of Christ—
secundum humilitatem (according to humility)—is the essential, inalienable duty of Christians. The service which
external power may render has to do with the preservation
of the external conditions which are not indifferent for the
way in which evangelical liberty unfolds.[20] One could say:
The "ministrative service" (service *per se*) has to do with
the *esse* of the Church. The "dominative service" (a certain
use of dominative power) may have to do with the *bene
esse* of the Church. But Occam does not express it in this
way. He relates the latter service to the *tota Christianitas*
(entire Christendom).[21] The first service, however, is related
to Christ himself, and that Church which is engaged in this
kind of essential service seems to be the same body as that
which Occam calls the "infallible Church."

17 Cf. *De imp.* 1:1 (p. 4), 7:1 (p. 13f).
18 *Ibid.*, 10:3 (p. 23). Limits of this emergency power, *ibid.*, 23:4
(p. 40f). In *Brevil.* VI:2 (pp. 197–201), Occam is much more cir-
cumstantial and cautious.
19 *De imp.* 7:2 (p. 15), 13 (p. 27).
20 See above, note 17.
21 Cf. *Brevil.*, prol. (p. 39), where the term *universitas* is used. In
De imp. the concern for the (*tota*) *Christianitas* is frequently expressed
(see index, p. 102). The *bonum commune* or the *utile* for the Christian
society is at stake. See, for example, *De. imp.* 7:11 (p. 13); *Dialogus*
I:vi:85 (ed. M. Goldast, in *Monarchia S. Romani Imperii*, II (Frank-
fort, 1614), 603f.

Tota Christianitas is a societal phenomenon in which powers may be delegated to rulers from individuals in whose behalf now the rulers act. This happens in all forms of society. Thus it happens also among Christians. He who acts in behalf of this Christian society may also act for the well-being of the Church. But, if our analysis is correct, it does not seem to follow that such a powerful one acts in behalf of that true Church which has the truth of evangelical life inalienably. As instrument and representative of the Christian society he may render a service of external protection to the Church. But he does not "stand for" her. The true Church is only represented by those who, by the same token, are representatives of *Christ,* who "stand for" the truth of Christ. Occam was not a *spiritualis.* When he spoke about those in whom the Church is ultimately and truly found, he was not illuminated by Joachimistic visions. Yet the "democratic" conception of Marsilius of Padua was far from him when he wrote, for example (in his letter to the chapter general of the Franciscans): "Rather than conceding that these errors (that is, those of Pope John XXII) are compatible with the faith, I should believe that the whole Church of God could be saved in a few, yea even in one person."[22] This is the Church whose justification is not in the fact that it includes persons who represent a majority or universality of Christians. Its kind of catholicity Occam has, more than once, indicated with the words: "If God is for us, who is against us?" (Rom. 8:31). I am not intending to say that Occam has no further suggestions about the ways in which we may see the interrelations between *tota Christianitas* and the "true Church." However, two concepts of the Church have now become distinguishable in such a way that there is a Church which is so truly Church

---

[22] *Epistola ad Fratres Minores,* p. 15, in *Guillelmi de Ockham opera politica,* ed. H. S. Offler, III (Manchester, 1946), 1–17. Cf. *De imp.,* prol. (pp. 1–4).

that it could not be said of her, it "needs reform," and there
is a Church whose societal structure puts her in the sphere
of the checking and balancing of powers. While the Church
according to the first concept has no power of herself but
"stands for" the power of God's truth, the Church according to the second concept includes powerful ones, whose
powers, however, are of a basically secular character, powers of which one may hope that they are used for the best
of the Church, but of which one could hardly say that they
are used *by* the Church *qua* Church. According to the first
concept God himself would be the only "reformator" of his
Church. But how he does it remains his sovereign secret.
(His only promise is that he is with his Church even if she
be reduced to one person.) According to the second concept,
the Church has possibilities of improving her situation. But
how these possibilities may be actualized in a true renewal
of the Church is not a question for which we may expect a
clear answer from Occam.

But this is not the dilemma of Occam alone. To those
who, both during and after his time, considered the situation of the contemporary church—who often were much
more involved in concrete programs of reform—the same
dilemma presented itself in ever new variations.

Could we claim that the curialists of the fourteenth and
fifteenth centuries were happily free from this dilemma?
Here the pope was understood as the secondary head of
the Church with the full power of instrumentality. The primary cause of the unity of the Church, Jesus Christ, is also
the primary cause of its renewal. From this generally believed truth the curialists would deduce that the same is
true of the secondary cause through which Christ governs
his Church. It was also possible that a curialist saw in the
power of the papacy as well the guarantee and earthly
origin of all reform, but also, at the same time, its most
important target and object. This was the case, for example,

in such an energetic call to reform as the *De planctu Ecclesiae* of Alvaro Pelayo.[23] *In tempestate prasesentis diluvii, aquarum multarum tribulationum ad Christi vicarium et eius ecclesiam approximabo* ("in the present stormy flood and in the waters of many tribulations I shall cling to the vicar of Christ and to his Church"). It is understandable that in such a situation of taking refuge things are said about the papacy which allow for little functional distinction between the role of Christ and that of the pope . . . *ut qui videt eum oculo contemplationis et fideli, videat et Christum. Sententia igitur papae et sententia Dei una sententia est* (". . . so that he who sees him with a contemplative and faithful eye sees also Christ. Therefore the judgment of the pope and the judgment of God are one judgment"). The same papacy, however, becomes the primary target of Alvaro's complaint: *Heu, Domine, quia ipsi sunt in persecutione tua primi, qui videntur in Ecclesia tua primatum diligere et regere principatum* ("Woe, Lord, that those are first in the persecution of thee who are seen to like the primacy in thy Church and to rule the first see"). This appeal from the failing persons of the leaders to their unfailing office, this firm resolution to combine faithfulness to the institution with the most bitter criticism of its abuses —is this a way of avoiding the dilemma between that Church which needs no reform and that Church which seems unable to reform herself? It must be observed that here the discussion of the government of the Church (of its *status*) and of its needs (the *planctus*) become almost unrelated to one another. According to the first view, the ultimate appeal would be that God will act through his vicar: He in whom the Church is visibly united must also be the visible instrument of its reform. But, according to the

---

[23] Complete title: *De statu et planctu Ecclesiae.* Editions: Ulm, 1474; Lyons, 1517; Venice, 1560. The quotations are taken from I:68, I:29, and II:6.

second view, only a pope will play this role whom God
himself has reformed. Alvaro, as far as I see, emphasizes
only the second point. Concerning the first point, he dis-
cusses more the privilege of the curia than the way in which
this privilege is used. But then he does not simply say that
the pope must be what he is supposed to be according to the
dignity of his office. He appeals to the spirit of Francis of
Assisi. This last appeal is not derived from the governing
power which goes from Jesus Christ through the pope, but
rather from the example of Christ's humility as followed
by Francis. One would like to see how these two aspects
belong together. But can they be brought together in such
a way that one is the *conditio sine qua non* of the other?

The advocates of conciliarism had a very remarkable
understanding of the double role which "a head" plays with
respect to its body. As vicar of Christ, the pope was, for
Gerson, he *ad quem* the Church finds her unity.[24] And
overwhelmingly the lack of unity during the Great Schism
was felt as an ecclesiastical monstrosity. But in this very
emergency the Church was called to "procure its own
union"[25] with the pope not as instrumental subject but as
object. In this respect, the "secondary head" was rather a
result of the action of the body than a medium of Christ's
primary headship. But in which way was the pope still
understood as a "head" at all? Two very different understandings of "head of the Church" were combined in conciliarism. According to B. Tierney, Western conciliarism
had its roots in the understanding of a Church as a corpora-

---

[24] See Gerson's *Tractatus de unitate Ecclesiae,* in *Gersoni opera
omnia,* ed. E. du Pin, vol. II (Antwerp, 1706), pp. 113–118; also in
The Library of Christian Classics, vol. XIV: *Advocates of Reform,* ed.
M. Spinka (Philadelphia and London, 1953), pp. 140–148, hereafter
abbreviated as *LCC.* Here most of the twelve considerations begin with
the words: "Unitas Ecclesiae ad unum certum Christi vicarium . . ."
In with the ablative case is not used in connection with the pope but
only in connection with Christ.

[25] *Ibid.,* consideratio II (*LCC,* XIV, 142).

tion. This concept had been developed by canonists of the
thirteenth century. In this approach it became possible to
understand any human "head" of a Church, including the
pope, as the representative of a corporate authority which
originally belonged to "all members." This had little to do
with the traditional concept of the *corpus mysticum,* in
which the pope did not represent the members but represented Christ, the invisible head, to his members (a function of representation which was not derived at all from
the members). The leading thinkers of conciliarism had
moments of keen awareness of the tension between those
two different conceptions of the Church. But their ever
repeated claim that a council had a priority in being assisted
by the Holy Spirit and in interpreting God's law did not
make up for the preponderance of juristic arguments (sometimes of considerations of more expediency) for their various
and always shifting assessments of the pope's role in the
Church. Their theological consideration of Christ as the
primary head of the Church put both council and pope on
a secondary level of representation. But when it came to
demonstrating that the council was a "superior" form of
representation, then, on the one hand, it was said that the
Universal Church needed a representation as "universal" as
possible (the pope being only the "administrator" of this
unity, or only the "head" of the particular Roman Church)
and so, in this strict sense, more a member than a head of the
Universal Church. On the other hand, it was said again
and again that the Holy Spirit, who is always with the
congregation of the believers, would be with this truest
representation of the congregation.[26]

Is it true, however, that God is always with the greater

[26] Tierney, pp. 132ff. See also G. Heinz-Mohr, *Unitas Christiana:
Studien zur Gesellschaftslehre des Nikolaus von Kues* (Trier, 1958),
and Ray C. Petry, "Unitive Reform Principles of the Late Medieval
Conciliarists," *Church History* 31:164–181 (1962).

quantity of representation? Henry of Langenstein[27] raised exactly this question, and his answer, based on Occam's discussion of the "infallible Church," including the quotation of Rom. 8:31, said, interestingly enough, that the council as a representative body was not infallible by reason of the number of representatives but by reason of the Holy Spirit. If the Holy Spirit is only with one person (as Henry envisions as an ultimate possibility) and of this one it is still said that he "puts his trust in this most holy procedure," then apparently this means that the Holy Spirit is not with the council as such but that the council provides only an opportunity to listen to the Holy Spirit. The Spirit may speak to *one,* before, through this one, he convinces the many. Dietrich of Niem speaks of the same "infallible Church," the Church of the elect, when he asks: "But why should we labor for the Union of the Universal Church, if that Church is, and always has been, undivided, one, and has never suffered schism?" And the answer: "I do not say that the Universal Church can be reunited since she cannot be divided by schism, because she can even be preserved in one individual. But I say that we must labor for her unity, that is, for the harmony and pacification of her members . . . Hence in this Church we, the faithful, have been born not for ourselves alone, nor ought our acts of justice and peace to illumine merely ourselves, but also our brothers and other Christians . . . Furthermore, we must labor for the unity of the Universal Church, as we are wont to say, because the exercise of her power and authority, which is in the Apostolic Church, is greatly impeded by those contending for the papacy and by schisms."[28]

When we take those two words of Henry of Langenstein

[27] *Epistola concilii pacis* (du Pin, II, 809–840; LCC, XIV, 106–139), cap. 15.

[28] *De modis uniendi ac reformandi Ecclesiam,* in H. Heimpel, ed., *Dietrich von Niem; Dialog über Union und Reform der Kirche, 1410* (Leipzig and Berlin, 1933); LCC, XIV, 149–174.

and of Dietrich of Niem together, how can we understand the function of the council? The council is not a representative body with which the Holy Spirit is present in the same way that He is present with the elect. But the council is that assembly where the Holy Spirit speaks, through the elect, as fully as possible to the whole Church because here the whole Church is as fully as possible represented. The council as such, then, is the best way for the self-reform of the Church. Among various possible human ways of reform, it is the best "way open to man," and in this human fashion it is "the way of the Spirit."[29]

Does all this now really mean that an ecumenical council is the "only way of God"? For all the meaningfulness of the conciliarist statements, we feel that, after all, God, as far as he reforms the Church, through the elect, may use a council but may also have other ways. Briefly, the necessity of the conciliar way is not shown on a theological level. The curialists had a firmer understanding of the indispensability of the pope than the conciliarists had of the indispensability of a council. It is all too well understandable that as soon as a council tried to carry on the reform without any longer representing the undivided and undisputed unity of the Universal Church, the great days of conciliarism were over. The theological justification of conciliarism was not strong enough to survive the rebellion of the Council of Basel against the pope.[30]

It seems that Wyclifism here provides us with a basic clarification. If "office does not make a man holy"[31] but everyone who is moved by the Holy Spirit is called to act

[29] Henry of Langenstein (above, note 27), cap. 14, 15; LCC, XIV, 124f, 128.

[30] See above, note 26. Cf. M. A. Schmidt, "The Problem of Papal Primacy at the Council of Florence," *Church History* 30:35–49 (1961), particularly p. 36f.

[31] John Hus, *On Simony* (LCC, XIV, 196–278). For editions of the original Czech text see LCC, XIV, 194, ch. 4 (p. 212).

in behalf of the Church, in the manner of Matthew 18:15–20[32]—is this not the end of all worries about delegations, representations, and privileges? The only office in the Church is the preaching of the Word of God, administering the sacraments and prayer.[33] Whoever lives "according to Christ's will" becomes a reformer automatically. "For seeing his neighbor drowning in a damning sin, and possessing the God-given power to help him (as a member of the same body), how can such a man be justified if he does not use the power?"[34] But if offers of help and admonition are not accepted, the member-to-be-helped becomes a member-to-be-cut-off.[35] In this way, the true Christian does God's reforming work in the most direct way. The Church of the elect and the societal Church are no longer in a problematic dilemma. In the actions, choices and judgments of those who follow the commandments of the Lord, the Holy Spirit himself is continuously either realizing and expanding the true Church in the organized Church or cutting off the ostensible Church from the true Church. But in which case realizing and expanding—in which cutting off? The predestination of God ultimately remains a mystery. And if to follow God's command in a visible and assessable way means to do it "humbly," what are the chances of overcoming those "fellow-members," particularly priests, whose pride ought to be reformed before anything else can be reformed? "O Christ!" exclaims Hus, "it will take a long time before the proud priests will become so humble as to

---

[32] *Ibid.*, ch. 7 (pp. 251f).

[33] *Ibid.*, ch. 4 (p. 214).

[34] *Ibid.*, ch. 9 (p. 265).

[35] *Ibid.*, ch. 10 (p. 276). Wyclif's *Tractatus de officio pastorali*, ed. G. V. Lechler (Leipzig, 1863); LCC, XIV, 32–60, begins as follows: "The office of a Christian, to which the faithful should diligently attend, ought to be twofold: to purge the Church Militant of false shoots not bedded in the Highest Pastor, who is the vine of the entire Church; and to dispose its branches that they may better bear fruit for the blessing of the Church."

subject themselves to the Church for sin, as thou, being innocent, hast subjected thyself."[36] Again, and now in a very
direct, legalistic form, the identification or harmonization
of two reforms was attempted: that reform whose subject
is God through Jesus Christ in the Holy Spirit, and that
reform which is a work of men, a self-reform of the Church.
The differences among the Hussites themselves suggest
that man's judgments about "how should the reform be
carried through by men in the name of God" are always
conflicting. A simple biblical precept like Matthew 18:15–20
cannot bring men on the *one* way which then would be
God's way.

Luther[37] did not try to see the human and the divine aspects of "reformation" in a causal or any other structured
relationship. He used the word very reluctantly. Mostly he
saw it as a work which, at a given time, a man with ecclesiastical responsibility would try to undertake, and, in most
cases, was not able to carry through because this very Church
was not willing to be reformed. Positively, he envisioned a
reform of the universities. But in his time and in his life,
he saw something at work which he did not call "reformation" but rather the work ("the running," "outpouring,"
"judging," etc.) "of the Word of God." Thinking in terms
of Isaiah 55:10f, "reformation" to Luther would not be
the "rain" of the Word itself but rather all that which is
happening to the soil, in vain labor, in rewarded labor, in
the growing of the fruits. There is no "privilege" of reforming (the *ius reformandi* of the princes was neither of
Luther's nor of Melanchton's terminology). There is a gen-

---

[36] Hus, *LCC*, XIV, 274.
[37] For this paragraph, see H. Frhr. v. Campenhausen, "Reformatorisches Selbstbewusstsein und reformatorisches Geschichtsbewusst-
sein bei Luther 1517–1522," in *Tradition und Leben* (Tübingen,
1960), pp. 318–342, particularly 337ff; and W. Maurer, "Reformation," in *Die Religion in Geschichte und Gegenwart*, 3 ed., V
(Tübingen, 1961), 858–873, particularly pp. 861–865.

eral call to reform. But Luther's "Address to the German Nobility" does not use the word "reform" for that general and manifold action for which it calls. The word used there is "improvement of the Christian estate," and this seems to mean, on the one hand, more than the reforming measure that may be expected from this or that dignitary, and, on the other hand, less than that reformation of total character which is God's own work. In the Resolution to Thesis 89[38] Luther makes his most comprehensive statement with respect to the term *reformatio: Ecclesia indiget reformatione, quod non est unius hominis Pontificis nec multorum Cardinalium officium, sicut probavit utrumque novissimum concilium, sed totius orbis immo solius Dei. Tempus autem huius reformationis novit solus ille qui condidit tempora.* "The Church is in need of a reform—which is not the duty of one man, the pontiff, or of many cardinals (as the most recent council has proven both points), but of the whole world, even of God alone. But the time of this reform is known to him alone who has founded the times." It seems to me that Luther has not restricted the problem of a "reform" to the Middle Ages and to his own time. There is no glorification of an *ecclesia reformata* (or *reformanda in nostris temporibus*). One easily says too little or too much by using such standard terminology. The term "reform" takes on a meaning which encompasses every time and directs it toward God's own time.

[38] *D. Martin Luthers Werke: Kritische Gesamtausgabe,* I (Weimar, 1883), 627.

CONSCIENCE IN A PLURALISTIC SOCIETY: THEOLOGICAL AND SOCIOLOGICAL ISSUES

JOHN L. THOMAS, S.J.

IN SPITE of their obvious significance the ethical and moral implications of pluralism have aroused only sporadic concern in our society. A number of plausible hypotheses to explain this surprising neglect come readily to mind. The majority of Americans like to regard themselves as morally responsible, sincerely religious people. As Supreme Court Justice William O. Douglas stated it when speaking for the Court in the Zorach case, "We are a religious people whose institutions presuppose a Supreme Being." An optimistic, pragmatic outlook, alien to concern with "dogmatic subtleties or philosophical abstractions," as well as to the peculiar *Angst* experienced by some contemporary Europeans, has long characterized the national mind. Thus, at the turn of the century, William James pointed out what he considered to be the triumph of the "healthy-mindedness" of liberal Christianity over the "morbidness" traditionally associated with the "old hell-fire theology." He predicted the continued growth of a "new sort of religion of Nature," based on the contemporary idea of universal evolution. He felt that this lent itself so well to a theory of general meliorism and progress that it seemed tailored to the religious needs of the healthy-minded.

Following a similar line of thought, several contemporary observers maintain that the major faiths have become so thoroughly secularized that they no longer stand outside of and above society, but have become a subordinate, integral part of the total social system, historically well adapted to serve its purposes and promote its interests. Thus, discussions of doctrinal differences among not only the various denominations but also the major historical faiths can have a merely academic interest, for religion in practice has become the handmaid of democracy, and the major faiths constitute "parallel shoots on a common stock."

This would mean that the traditional creeds have ceased to furnish the faithful with distinctive transcendental criteria for evaluating their world, inasmuch as the standards of value promoted by the churches are no longer derived from religious dogma but from secular society itself. Religion remains popular because modern man, experiencing a loss of identity within his society, and facing a challenge to survival from without, is turning to religious organizations in search of secular security, rather than to religion itself for transcendental significance. Our present purpose does not call for an evaluation of this hypothesis, yet its current popular acceptance may throw considerable light on the neglect we have mentioned.

Perhaps equally relevant in this regard has been the longstanding reluctance of many social scientists to acknowledge the pertinence of values in their analyses. Alva Myrdal called attention to this trait in the opening chapter of her *Nation and Family*: "An established tendency to drive values underground, to make the analysis appear scientific by omitting certain basic assumptions from the discussion, has too often emasculated the social sciences as agencies for rationality in social and political life." She goes on to remind her fellow scientists that "to be truly rational, a social program, like a practical judgment, is a conclusion based upon premises of values as well as upon facts." Writing in *Commentary* a few years ago, sociologist Reinhard Bendix was even more critical: "Modern social science teaches us to regard man as a creature of his drives, habits, and social roles, in whose behavior reason and choice play no decisive part . . . men are regarded as unable to achieve objective knowledge or to be guided by it." Fortunately, many social scientists are beginning to show a marked interest in the study of values, though past neglect has left the subject of the present Colloquium somewhat undeveloped scientifically.

Considering that the study of conscience in a pluralist society may be approached from a number of different starting points and at several different levels, the aim of the present paper, as I conceive it, is to furnish a more or less general theoretical backdrop for the discussion of specific issues to follow. Hence, after an introductory observation on the Gospel message and a brief definition of terms, I shall describe the essential elements of ethical and religious systems and show how much systems may be interrelated.

The salient features of the traditional Roman Catholic approach to the ethical process will then be presented, and in the light of these more or less theoretical considerations, I shall try to identify some of the major implications of pluralism for both society and the individual minority group.

INTRODUCTORY OBSERVATIONS

Judging from the high esteem in which they hold religion, and the religious training of their children in particular, it appears that most Americans take it for granted that religious beliefs necessarily exert a direct, relatively obvious influence on the moral outlook and conduct of the faithful. A glance at the history of the Christian churches suggests that this common sense assumption may be highly questionable. There is little evidence of such direct relation during the industrial revolution, for example, while a comparison of Latin American, Continental, and American Catholicism, indicates that even groups cherishing apparently similar religious beliefs may develop considerably different ethical viewpoints and patterns of moral conduct.

A consideration of the religious and ethical aspects of the Gospel message proves enlightening in this connection. Jesus appears at one and the same time as the Saviour who came to redeem, the divine Son who manifests the love of the Father for us and through whom we come to the Father, and the Teacher who proclaims and exemplifies the laws of the Kingdom. Thus, the religious and ethical aspects of his message are closely related, for he is both wise man and Saviour. Although his teaching grows out of the Old Testament and constantly refers back to it, so that it takes for granted the imperatives of the Decalogue proclaiming respect for the utter sovereignty of God and right order in human relations, nevertheless, he reacted strongly to several elements in the contemporary religious tradition. In opposition to the minutely detailed code of ethics and casuistry of the Pharisees, he stressed the positive command to love, based on a moral attitude characterized by purity of heart, God-centered orientation of life, and readiness to serve God in the Kingdom.

Hence, Jesus did not present a detailed code of ethics and none will be found in the Gospels. The ethical ideas of purity of heart, dedication, and service have a rational aspect and are consequently open to further development, but the essential dynamic of the Gospel message which was to work as a leavening force throughout the world was the command to love—God and neighbor—two precepts but one love, as a great Church Father reminds us. As the early Christian communities, although somewhat eschatologically inhibited in the beginning, gradually fashioned their distinctive modalities of creed, cult, and code, their varied cultural predispositions toward developing different doctrinal and ethical emphases became apparent. Thus the Christian communities of the East came to differ from the West, while ethical thought tended to develop along two distinct though related lines, in terms of what might be termed a "wisdom" morality reserved for a religious elite and a "code" morality for the majority.

In this sense, we may take it as a general principle that the ethical outlooks and moral patterns stemming from a religion will depend not only on the inherent logic of its doctrinal principles but also upon the cultural setting within which they are developed. The consciences of American Christians will necessarily reflect the influence of American society, together with the varied statuses held by different Christian groups within that society. The relation between a religion and society is a two-way street. We might add that the American experience is so interesting because it represents the point in Western history when traditional Christian thought was most completely exposed to the influences of modern democratic institutions. Under these circumstances, Christian thinkers were forced to re-examine traditional concepts, as well as long-accepted definitions of the social situation, since their positions as voluntary minority organizations did not permit them to attempt to put new wine into old bottles under the aegis of secular power.

DEFINITIONS

For the purposes of the present discussion the term *pluralistic society* will be taken to signify an ongoing society within which several relatively distinct, organized, and sizable religious faiths or denominations function as identifiable subcultures. The significance of pluralism in this context stems from two assumptions: that these separate communities of believers are more or less organized and consequently possess social power, and that the distinctive conceptions of man and society that they foster are relevant to their ethical outlooks and moral conduct.

In this respect contemporary American society appears to reveal all the characteristics of pluralism. In the practical order our cultural "designs for living," as Linton would say, lack unity and consistency; our "blueprints for behavior" are confused and contradictory. In other words, to borrow a phrase from sociologist Robin Williams, the current culture offers no "relatively standardized prescriptions as to what must be done, should be done, may be done, and must not be done." Members of society are presented with socially acceptable alternatives in each of these categories, and it is presumed that they will make their choices of ends and means in terms of the varied conceptions of man and society that they cherish.

It should be noted, however, that in spite of the obvious complexity and pluralism in our society, the admittedly vague conception of the traditional "American Way" still exerts an operative, unifying influence on our political, economic, and social institutions. Although the conception is difficult to define, we think of it in terms of respect for the individual, personal freedom and responsibility, initiative, equality of opportunity, and the right to strive for happiness and fulfillment at the physical, intellectual, and spiritual levels of our being. These are positive, "middle range" values, not easily measured or given precision, but nevertheless real and highly prized in our culture. At least in their genesis and early development they stemmed from a shared conception of man and society based on Western cultural traditions, and if there is a sound basis for the frequently asserted contention that modern man is experiencing "alienation," "anomie," "schism of the soul," and "lack of identification," it may be that rapid and extensive social change has led to the discovery that the "American Way" is no longer based on a shared image of man.

In the present context the term *conscience* denotes moral conscience. Broadly defined, this signifies the aptitude of man to pass judgments of moral value on an action, whether this action be considered in the abstract or the concrete, in regard to a general or particular case, and objectively or subjectively. Defined more strictly, conscience is the knowledge or awareness that each individual has of his own action insofar as this is morally good or bad. In other words, it is an essentially subjective judgment of moral value passed by the individual on his own action as he himself sees it. The term is used in this strict sense when we say, for example, that a man must follow his conscience or that conscience should not be coerced.

Although the distinction between conscience and moral law or moral science should be maintained, for these latter deal with general principles, I feel that for the purpose of the present Colloquium we may find it useful to widen the scope of our concern to include considerations relating to what might be called the total ethical process. This less restrictive approach will give us greater freedom in working toward a clarification of the ethical dimensions of thought and action as we tend to perceive them.

Because most systems of moral values institutionalized in known societies, together with the concepts that give them cognitive meaning, are commonly presumed to be either directly of religious origin or more or less closely related to religious beliefs, there is a tendency to identify religion and ethics, or, at least, to assume a necessary relation between them. Nevertheless, in the practical order, judgments of values may not be directly related to religious beliefs; while in the speculative order, ethical systems have been developed without explicit religious referents. To be sure, no societies known to us are found to be morally indifferent, yet unless religion is so broadly defined as to be indistinguishable from some kind of ultimate concern, it is not clear that religious beliefs fulfill a creative function in the formulation of ethical outlooks among all human groups. Hence, although our immediate aim is to discuss the ethical approach of one specific religious group, it may prove helpful at the outset to offer a few observations concerning the form and function of ethical and religious systems in general. These considerations should enable us to understand the interrelatedness of ethics and religion in a given case, as well as to identify some of the problems that may arise under conditions of pluralism.

SYSTEMS OF ETHICS

Considered as a philosophical discipline, ethics is usually defined as the practical science of moral good and evil in human acts. Thus, moral philosophers seek to discover general moral principles and to deduce from these the norms that should guide human action in particular cases. The phenomenon of moral consciousness is a matter of universal human experience. All men display some awareness of the difference between the "is" and the "ought" in human conduct, and among all human groups we find that obligations, commitments, and judgments of what is good and evil are clearly recognized. Hence, all schools of ethics accept the fact of moral consciousness in man, though they may explain its nature and origin in various ways.

For present purposes, we may define a system of ethics as a more or less integrated, hierarchically arranged set of general moral principles, together with the complex of related codes and norms representing the culturally defined application of these principles to the specific categories of human action routinely encountered by the group. A developed ethical system defines both the morally acceptable ends of human activity and the means by which they are licitly to be achieved. Although it is conceded that human groups universally distinguish between the "is" and the "ought," the specific contents of the "ought" tend to be culturally articulated and consequently are normally learned during the socializing process by means of which new members are integrated or identify with the group. Indeed, the maintenance of an adequate socializing process must be regarded as one of the major functional requisites of an enduring free society, since only if new members internalize at least the basic value orientations of the group can the solidarity required for shared activity be retained.

In the final analysis, every ethical system implies a conception or image of man, the human agent. Considered in its broadest sense, this image involves a set of beliefs concerning man's origin, his relation to space and time, the essential qualities of his nature and consequently his orientation toward his fellowmen, society, and the world of nature, and finally, his life purpose or destiny, that is, the desirable terminus of his development or fulfillment in the cosmic order as he defines it. In other words, although all men recognize the quality of oughtness in human conduct, the specific contents of this oughtness are necessarily related, in the final analysis, to the distinctive image of man people cherish. This does not imply that significant social symbols, endowed with ethical qualities, may not persist as cultural residues in any ongoing social system. However, to the extent that these residues are not related to the prevailing image of man, they gradually cease to be operative or may summarily be rejected in situations of crisis. Moreover, in an ethically pluralistic society like our own, individuals or groups may retain traditional norms although they no longer accept the image of man to which these norms were logically related and without which challenges from opposing value systems cannot be answered adequately.

The persistence of an ethical system depends on its creativity, that is, on its capacity to define the content of oughtness in human conduct under constantly changing circumstances and in new situations. Moreover, under these conditions, an ethical system will remain integrated and can retain its identity only to the extent that its creativity is rooted in the image of man that it originally embodies. This observation merely calls attention to the fact that practical judgments of ethical relevance are conclusions based upon the application of premises of values to sets of social facts; and these premises of values, in turn, are related to an image of man. This fact is frequently overlooked because pertinent value premises are seldom stated explicitly when ethical judgments in the practical order are expressed.

How does an ethical system relate to society? First, it affects the structure of the social system that men establish to answer their essential needs. Second, it affects the synthesis by which man harmonizes his inner and outer worlds. These functions call for some explanation. In regard to the first, the manner in which an ethical system affects the social structure can be seen from an analysis of any integrated social or cultural system. Such analysis reveals several elements of primary importance. First, we find a basic, underlying set of values or ideals constituting the culture's ultimate goals. These goals are defined in terms of the elemental beliefs concerning the origin, nature, and purpose of man shared by the group. Hence, at least in their original formulation, these goals imply a shared image of man, the human agent.

Second, further analysis reveals various sets of derivative values and purposes. These represent specific institutional objectives or, in other words, the culturally devised applications of the group's ultimate goals to concrete social institutions such as the economic system, the state, the family, and so on. They answer the speculative question concerning what normative values should guide the fulfillment of such essential human needs as food, shelter, clothing, sex, cooperation, power, religion, and so forth.

Third, there are the concrete social means or patterned relations by means of which these derivative institutional goals are to be realized in concrete circumstances. These represent the morally acceptable social procedures through which people interact and secure the fulfillment of their varied needs within a specific social system.

The second way in which an ethical system affects society is by supplying the normative elements for that necessary synthesis through which harmony between man's inner world and the world of his social activity is achieved. By offering man an explanation of the significance and purpose of life, the system provides him with an intelligible frame of reference within which his persistent pursuit of happiness can be meaningfully defined. Normless striving, or the pursuit of happiness without pertinent value referents, becomes a frustrating process not long to be tolerated. When there is no inner vision, no concept of the good life, no clearly defined aspirational goals and ideals, man's social striving in his outer world loses its real significance. It is reduced to a process lacking a purpose that can be related to the wholeness of life.

One final observation relating to the development and continuity of an ethical system seems relevant. Inasmuch as the maintenance and continued elaboration of a given system of ethics involve a more or less clearly defined, distinctive conception of man, an abiding awareness of the assumed relation between this image and general moral principles, and an ability not only to apply general principles to specific categories of action but also to recognize what principles are pertinent to the situation, we may conclude that what may be termed the total ethical process will be the concern of only a minority in any given society. Except for brief, often critical, interludes, the majority do not reflect on the moral standards and norms they observe or the logical coherence of their accepted codes of conduct with more general moral principles. Preoccupation with the immediate tasks at hand, together with the unquestioning acceptance of prevailing concrete moral norms, tends to preponderate in their conduct.

On the other hand, there have appeared in all historical societies known to us some persons displaying unusual sensitivity and reflectiveness concerning ultimate moral principles and the foundations of ethical codes. This minority appear not only as innovators, but they function as conservatives, preserving continuity with the group's traditional moral ultimates. Contrary to the majority who take their moral standards and norms for granted, they scrutinize, refine, and seek to improve them. In this sense they are bearers of what students of civilization have variously named the great tradition as opposed to the little tradition, of high culture vs. low, of classic vs. folk culture, of hierarchic vs. lay culture, of the learned vs. the popular tradition. As Redfield puts it: "In a civilization there is a great tradition of the reflective few, and there is a little tradition of the largely unreflective many." Obviously, in ethical systems as in cultures, these two traditions are interdependent, but the point we wish to stress is that the continuity and integrated development of cultural and ethical systems alike depend primarily on the efforts of a creative, reflective minority.

To recapitulate briefly, since an integrated ethical system involves an image of man, together with the general moral principles related to this image and their culturally defined applications to various categories of human action, it fulfills the dual function of supplying an answer to man's perennial quest for order in his universe and of specifying the contents of the oughtness that he universally recognizes as a quality of his conscious human acts. In the on-going social process the values of an ethical system are concretized or expressed in the normative qualities of the essential institutional objectives men formulate in satisfying their basic needs, as well as in the standards and norms regulating their conduct in pursuit of these objectives. Hence, individual members of society become aware of the pertinent applications of an ethical system both through the broad value orientations and codes of conduct they normally internalize during the socialization process. Since the majority of persons tend to be primarily concerned with only immediately pertinent, concrete norms, the persistence of an ethical system will depend upon a reflective minority who recognize its essential elements and consequently can guarantee its continuity and creativity in the face of change.

RELIGIOUS SYSTEMS

As we use the term here, a religious system represents the complex of creed, cult, and code constituting a group's total conception of their relations to the transcendent and of the practical consequences that stem from these relations. Whether we are discussing religion among the so-called primitives or in the higher civilizations, it is well to note that manifestations of the sacred do not appear as segmented, relatively isolated phenomena. Rather, they are part of a more extensive system, including the various religious experiences of the group, together with a set of traditional theories frequently embodied in rituals, symbols, and myths, explaining the origin of man and the world, the major characteristics of the human situation, and the speculative basis of approved moral norms.

Hence the primary elements of a religious system include a set of concepts or beliefs concerning the transcendent, viewed either as an entity or entities having a significant relation of supremacy over man and the human condition.

The content of this creed is expressed in dogmas, myths, and symbols, while religious festivals, ceremonies, and rites guarantee its purity and continuity in the group. Moreover, in addition to the distinctively religious acts prescribed by creed and cult, a religious system tends to furnish the basic principles underlying the group's major value-orientations and moral codes of conduct.

This latter point is highly pertinent to the present discussion, for it indicates the relation between religion and ethics. In discussing the nature of this relation, it is well to note that it manifests many modalities. In archaic cultures, for example, religion furnishes the paradigmatic solution for every existential crisis, since religious myths define the exemplar models not only of all ritual and cult, but of all significant human activities. Among the major religious systems of civilized societies, the relation tends to become somewhat more complex.

Perhaps we can express this relation more clearly by stating that, in addition to the formally prescribed and proscribed activities associated with creed and cult, each religious system affects ethical practices to the extent that it defines the conception of man held by the group. We have already pointed out the paramount importance of the conception of man in the formation of ethical systems. Hence, to the extent that a given religious system supplies the essential elements of the group's definition of the origin, nature, and destiny of the human agent, it furnishes the indispensable ideological foundation for the system of ultimate goals and premises of values lying at the core of their ethical system. Although this function of a religious system should be obvious, it is frequently overlooked because, as we have indicated, moral judgments in the practical order are frequently expressed without explicit reference to the ultimate moral principles upon which they are necessarily premised.

In other words, a religious system tends to determine the

individual's status or position in the cosmic order by defining his essential relation to space and time (both sacred and profane), to nature, and to his fellow men (in terms of age, sex, in-group, and out-group), and to the transcendental (the sacred, the holy, the supernatural, the divine, conceived as a being, or beings, and/or the manifestation of their force and power in nature). Although the degree and extent to which different religious systems define these relations may vary considerably, it is worth noting that explicit definitions of the "sacred" involve implicit definitions of the "profane," so that the group's attitudes toward the "secular" are necessarily conditioned by their religious beliefs and practices. At the same time, since religious systems do not function in a social vacuum, they are necessarily affected by the historical situation and cultural form within which they operate. This adds up to saying that the relations between the sacred and profane, or the religious and the secular, are reciprocal. Explicit beliefs and attitudes in one area necessarily condition beliefs and attitudes in the other, with the result that we cannot adequately understand one without some understanding of the other.

Furthermore, inasmuch as a religious system becomes socially concretized or crystalized in a distinctive creed, cult, and code of conduct, like a system of ethics, it may affect individual members of society in a variety of ways. First, through the normal process of indoctrination and training, or through conversions, new members identify with the system and become participating members. From the viewpoint of the individual, this process may imply little more than the routine acquisition of the group's religious beliefs, attitudes, and practices, or it may be accompanied by those personal experiences of the holy that Rudolf Otto characterized as numinous, that is, experiences induced by the revelation of an aspect of divine power.

Second, since a religious system tends to become institutionalized, that is, to involve not only an in-group of the faithful, a moral community, but also a visible system of symbols, objects, acts, offices, functions, organizations, and so forth, all members of the society within which a religious system operates are more or less aware of it and consequently are affected by it. The resulting interaction, often unconscious and unperceived, may produce the greater sensitivity of all to the moral values and norms promoted by the religious system; or conversely a hostile reaction to them, leading to added emphasis on opposing goals and practices.

Finally, to the extent that a religious system affects cultural institutions either by determining their structure, by defining institutional goals and the acceptable means to achieve them, or by supplying the value referents to the social symbols operative in society, it necessarily influences the ethical orientations of all the participants of the culture. This explains why some members of a society who have never been directly associated with a religious system nevertheless may cherish value-orientations and moral ideals representing the finest ethical development of this system and having no rational foundation apart from it. Once the beliefs and attitudes of a religious system have become thus "institutionalized" they continue to influence the ethical practices of people long after the religious system itself has ceased to attract their active adherence.

Like a system of ethics, a religious system must remain creative if it is to endure. This implies that it must continue to supply a relatively consistent, orderly, meaningful interpretation of the total, evolving human situation experienced by its adherents, thus enabling them to "make sense" of their world, and by offering them an explanation of the significance and purpose of life, providing them with an intelligible frame of reference within which their perennial pursuit of happiness can be defined. Although a religious system that fails to remain creative in this regard may survive either as a cultural residue, or because it still serves as a convenient vehicle for the promotion of cherished social customs and in-group solidarity, it is, in reality, no longer significant as a religious system, and men must look elsewhere for their interpretations of life.

It follows that a religious system, like a system of ethics, will depend upon an elite for its development and promotion. Many religious systems make explicit or implicit provisions for special statuses and functions in this regard, while those systems that avowedly make no such distinctions among their membership nevertheless rely upon a dedicated, well-informed, and specially concerned minority to conserve and promote continuity of creed and cult. In the long run, the progress and development of a religious system will be closely related to the quality of this minority. At the same time, in any on-going religious group there will exist some differences in the beliefs, attitudes, and practices of the majority and those of the minority. Because they tend to be primarily preoccupied with the more secular demands of daily existence, the former take the system for granted, concentrating on custom, required ritual observance, and personally pertinent practical applications.

On the basis of these brief observations concerning some aspects of the form and functioning of ethical and religious systems we may conclude that men develop their definitions of what is right or wrong in the practical order within a broader framework of value referents, organized into fairly consistent schemes or general patterns, and related to their conception of the nature of man and of the world in which he lives. It follows that religious systems affect ethical judgments primarily to the extent that they influence man's conception of human nature and the world. Since every religious system attempts to define more or less clearly the status or position of man in the cosmic order, it is clear that whenever a religious system is accepted it will necessarily affect the ethical judgments of its followers.

Furthermore, as we have indicated, because man is a creator, bearer, and to a limited extent, a product of his culture, that is, of the organized systems of artifacts and symbols by which he modifies his environment and lends it symbolic meaning, a religious system will affect the ethical judgments of a group to the extent that it influences their culture, particularly in its functions of supplying a set of beliefs answering man's questions about himself and his world, and a set of standards for evaluating moral conduct. This influence may persist unperceived, since, short of periods of crisis, the majority of men do not question the foundations of their culturally learned beliefs or the ultimate premises underlying their standards of conduct. At the same time, however, in a rapidly changing, complex society, some members of a religious group may adopt behavioral patterns based on unrecognized premises of values that conflict with their own. As we have suggested, it is the function of the elite in both ethical and religious systems to assure the continuity and creativity of these systems by clarifying the relations between approved practices and accepted principles, as well as to indicate logical applications of pertinent premises of values to changing situations.

Finally, as a practical science, ethics has for its object human conduct or the right ordering of man's individual and social life, and consequently its method must consist in the logical application of its general principles to the varied situations of human conduct. Hence, the study of the relation between a specific religious system and ethical practices implies some understanding of how participants of the religious system envisage the ethical process. It should be obvious that a general religious imperative such as the command to love one's neighbor as oneself acquires ethical significance in the practical order primarily when it is applied to a specific human relationship in a concrete situation. There are several possible ways of regarding the relation between general principles and judgments of moral value.

In archaic cultures, for example, primitive religious man simply regulated his activities in accordance with the ideal image revealed to him in his myths, for he believed that his religious myths offered the exemplar models not only of ritual but of all significant human acts. In some religious systems, ethical solutions to new situations tend to be sought not by selecting and applying pertinent principles but, following the method of code ethics and casuistry, by seeking for precedents in traditional religious documents regarded either as revealed or as the inspired *dicta* of great leaders. Some modern religious systems, at least in theory, attempt to bypass the whole problem by divorcing the practical moral life from religious salvation. Holding that salvation is a purely religious problem solved by faith, predestination, or a unique personal religious experience, and consequently not dependent on human conduct, they regard particular patterns of ethical ideas and practices as relative, culture-bound products having no essential relation of origin to religious beliefs. On the other hand, some religious systems assign human reason a large role in the development of their ethical outlooks, both because it is held that the Creator's law can be discovered by reason in the nature of things, and because general moral principles can be logically applied to concrete situations only after all the elements in the situation have been analyzed. Thus, the ethical process is considered dynamic and existential in the sense that human reason, supplemented by principles drawn from religion, formulates patterns of ethical conduct in terms of the changing exigencies of the situation.

THE TRADITIONAL
ROMAN CATHOLIC APPROACH

As we have indicated, the discussion of the relation between religion and ethics implies some understanding of how members of the religious group regard the ethical process. It is assumed that the Catholic system involves a more or less distinctive view and consequently merits attention here. In practice, Catholic ethical positions tend to be formulated on the bases of principles derived from faith and reason, so that it would seem to follow that any adequate consideration of the Catholic approach must involve some understanding of both the philosophical and theological framework within which Catholic thinkers tend to operate.

Thus, *official* statements of the Catholic position on moral issues are generally presented with supporting arguments drawn from reason, tradition, and revelation. Moreover, it is evident that when Catholic moralists draw conclusions from the general principle that human conduct must conform to the order of right reason, their use of the term *reason* does not have the same connotations as the *ratio* of the Enlightenment. Rather, following a long scholastic tradition, they use the term to signify man's power to grasp reality, maintaining that he grasps reality not only in natural cognition but also by faith in the revelation of God. Their "order of reason," therefore, is the order that corresponds to the reality made evident to man through faith and knowledge.

On the other hand, Catholic thought has consistently vindicated man's natural ability to discover moral order and the norms for right moral conduct. According to their view, supernatural revelation is absolutely necessary for knowledge of some religious truths (mysteries), but unaided human reason is capable of discovering sufficient knowledge of general ethical principles to make judgments of value. However, because some of these principles can be discovered only with great effort, supernatural revelation is regarded as a practical necessity if they are to be known with ease, certitude, and without admixture of error by the generality of men. At the same time, by giving man definite information concerning the spiritual character of his soul, immortality, his purpose in life, God as Creator and Supreme Good, and Christ as Saviour, divine Son, and Teacher, supernatural revelation provides man with clear and certain knowledge of the essential elements of his origin, nature, and destiny. It thereby supplements the findings of reason, though men are capable of discovering the natural truths of religion and the essential norms of moral conduct without it.

Hence, Catholic thinkers argue that quite independently of any dogmas of faith or of truths known only through supernatural revelation, a definition of human nature and the qualities requisite for its perfection can be formulated in which all thinking men can concur. Furthermore, they maintain that on the basis of such natural insights, general views concerning the structures and purposes of essential human institutions can be developed, with the result that irrespective of divergent beliefs, consensus concerning the general form and functioning of the social order can be achieved. Consequently, even within a pluralistic society, a requisite unity of goals and action can be developed within the broad framework of those accepted premises concerning which all can agree.

The salient features of this approach may be stated as follows. Starting with the facts of experience, they maintain that we can apprehend something of the natures of things and the laws according to which these natures function by observing the energies and forces working in them as manifested in their actions and reactions to the external world.

For example, a grain of wheat develops into an adult plant, not by chance, but with remarkable regularity. Thus we observe that there are natures in nature, that natures are tendencies, and that human nature is no exception. Hence, the careful observation of man's behavior can teach us something about the tendencies of human nature and consequently about what is good for man.

Moreover, an investigation of the energies, drives, and impulses that we observe at work in man reveals that he is conscious of these tendencies and has some knowledge of the relations between them and their inherent ends. He is also aware that he has some control over when and how they shall operate and that he is not wholly free to act as he chooses in this regard. Rather, he is conscious of a kind of inner need or necessity, an ought, to follow a particular line of action. As we have indicated, this experience of moral consciousness in man is universal. How is it to be explained?

Catholic thinkers tend to develop their explanations along the following lines. First, the observed tendencies in man and their inherent ends are regarded as good in themselves because they are related to the development and perfection of his nature. Second, in man these natural tendencies do not proceed to the fulfillment of their goals instinctively but must be directed by man's highest faculty, the mind. Hence, the phenomenon of morality emerges in man because the tendencies of human nature are directed toward the achievement of their inherent ends through the ordering activity of the mind, not through the compulsion of instincts. Third, the human agent grasps intuitively that good is to be sought and evil avoided. This principle is not deduced but is understood immediately in experience. It constitutes the first principle in the practical order, and all subsequent judgments are arrived at by applying it to specific human actions in concrete situations. Fourth, since human nature is a unity, there is a natural harmony and hierarchy among its tendencies resulting in an order of ends, the existential achievement of which results in man's development and fulfillment. Thus, although the particular ends inherent in various human tendencies are good in themselves, they are partial goods and consequently their actualization is subordinated to the total good of the human agent, in regard to whom they appear as means.

In other words, when evaluating the ethical significance of specific human acts, Catholic thinkers proceed by observing the natural human tendencies and their inherent ends that are being actualized in these acts. They then study the relation between the realization of these partial ends and the integration of the human agent expressed in terms of his integral fulfillment as a rational creature. Inasmuch as right order requires that specific human actions serve the total development of the human agent, their ethical quality will depend upon this relation in a concrete situation.

It should be obvious that since the area of human relations is extremely complex, and we achieve our knowledge of human nature and its essential tendencies through limited observation, there is ample room for development in ethical perspective. The basic premise that good is to be done and evil avoided is readily grasped in experience, but the application of this principle to specific human acts, depending as it must upon our somewhat limited knowledge of human tendencies and complex social situations, is subject to imperfection, error, and cumulative development as we proceed to evaluate the more complex areas of human activity. Ethical judgments are practical judgments based upon insights into human situations. Like all the practical sciences, ethics derives its matter from experience and consequently must stay close to reality.

This approach to the solution of ethical problems is based on a long tradition in Western culture. Inasmuch as it assumes that Christian revelation completes but does not contradict the moral law that can be discovered by reason in nature and offers an authoritative interpretation of it, it provides a common platform for the discussion of current ethical issues. Catholic thinkers would insist, of course, on the community's need for supernatural assistance in living up to the requirements of the moral law, together with the practical necessity of an authoritative interpreter to guard it from all admixture of error, yet their approach provides a common starting point for all who believe human reason is capable of discovering order in nature.

SOME IMPLICATIONS OF PLURALISM

The implications of pluralism may be considered either in terms of the ongoing social system or the religious minority groups involved, and from both a positive and negative viewpoint. Let us begin with the implications for the social system. To place the problem in an adequate conceptual framework, we may assume that there are things that must get done in any society if it is to continue as a going concern. These functional prerequisites constitute the generalized conditions necessary for the maintenance of a given social system, and while the specific social structures established to actualize them may differ from society to society, they must be realized in one way or another if the society is to endure. Among the more obvious functional requisites are adequate adjustment to the environment, systematic and stable division of labor, a set of shared goals, and of means prescribed to attain them, a system for controlling disruptive behavior effectively, and provision for replacement, that is, for the adequate training of youth to fulfill essential adult roles.

Further, it may be assumed that there exists a requisite functional relation between various elements of a culture, in the sense that one cultural element requires the other either as a necessary condition or as an inevitable consequence. This means that a quality manifested in one department of a culture requires certain particular qualities in other departments. In practice, this means that the behavioral patterns of the group must facilitate or at least make possible the practical realization of its shared institutional objectives; and these specific objectives, in turn, must be so formulated as to render possible the fulfillment of its ultimate goals. Because change may be introduced at each of these three interrelated levels, and the institutions of advanced societies like our own tend to move toward increasing functional differentiation, the maintenance of some degree of integration presents a perennial challenge in large complex societies.

Thus, all religious groups must share concern for meeting the functional requisites of society, and this concern should constitute a unifying starting point and the basis for discussion. However, since even Christian groups may develop somewhat different moral attitudes and follow somewhat different approaches to the ethical process, some intergroup tensions and misunderstandings are perhaps inevitable as each group moves to translate its distinctive values into appropriate institutional objectives and adequately implementing behavioral patterns. Unfortunately, what is often overlooked in such circumstances is that socially pertinent values and their assumed functional requisites are related as ends and means. Hence, the functional requisites are not specifically predetermined by these ultimate values or goals except where there is only one means available for achieving a given end. When this necessary relation between ends and means does not exist, man, as a rational creature, can devise many different means for achieving a proposed goal. In a given cultural situation, the available means for attaining specific ultimate goals will depend on the character of related institutions, the past experience and customs of the group, and their resources in nature and in technological skills. We need only call attention to the varied types of political, economic, or family systems that have existed in different Christian communities to demonstrate the point we are making here.

It follows that Christian thinkers cannot *a priori* deduce from their conceptions of human nature and its ultimate purposes the details of the structure of human institutions and relations. Social institutions, together with the manifold implementing behavioral patterns associated with them, stand as means in terms of these ultimate goals. In constructing and maintaining a social system under change, we are consequently faced with the unending, arduous task of developing means that will adequately assure the realization of the values we cherish in accord with the moral means that we can approve. At best our efforts will represent little more than "cultural approximations" of the ideal. They will be approximations because their very relatedness to a given social milieu limits them to being but one expression of the ideal. They are subject to modification, both because our appreciation of moral values and knowledge of human nature is subject to growth, and because changes in the total social system may render ineffective some established patterns and call for the substitution of others.

Because moral values and norms become embodied in concrete social structures, religious groups face the perennial danger of identifying a given cultural attempt to embody or implement an abstract value with the value itself. In other words, a peculiar cultural implementation, that is, the historical institutions and associated patterned relations embodying a value, is thought to be as sacred as the value itself, and defended against change accordingly. Thus, feudalism, monarchy, traditional national, racial and social class distinctions, and so on, have been mistakenly identified with absolute values, though they represented only more or less adequate attempts to embody abstract values in concrete

institutional structures. The real evil of this seemingly en-
demic error is that it focuses attention and concern primarily on the defense of the *status quo* rather than the creative
confrontation, interpretation, and integration of inevitable
growth and social change. We have only to consider the convenient paralysis of the Christian conscience during the industrial revolution or in dealing with race relations to understand the danger involved.

Although pluralism may result in intergroup tensions, it
may also cause religion to be held in high esteem in society.
Because there is no established church, religious participation is voluntary; the maintenance of a given organized religious group necessarily encourages the active concern of
individual members; and religion itself is not identified with
the state, a specific social class, or a quasi-political organization including a good proportion of pseudo-members affili-
ated to promote secular purposes. Moreover, religious pluralism, both as fact and possibility, has served to generate
creative competition and rivalry, to strengthen ingroup solidarity, and to provide suitable vehicles of religious expression
for those dissatisfied members who, if there were only an
established church, might have become either anti-clerical
or anti-religious.

On the negative side, under conditions of pluralism, religion may tend to exert a minimum of influence on social
institutions and cultural goals, inasmuch as no single faith
or denomination is in a dominating position. As a result,
the churches emphasize the personal rather than social implications of their doctrine, and may continue to be highly
esteemed precisely because they do not "interfere" with the
secular pursuits of their adherents. As it has developed in
this country, moreover, religious pluralism has tended to
postpone the inevitable confrontation of religion with
science or modern social problems, at least, among the majority of the faithful. Since the public schools may not teach

religion, many students do not become aware of the need to integrate the implications of their religious beliefs and modern science, while no religious group feels called upon to spell out in any detail the relevance of religion when solutions to modern critical social issues are proposed. This separation or compartmentalization of religion and reality enables many to maintain quite inconsistent beliefs and attitudes, though it may also alienate some who seek to develop an integrated philosophy of life.

As a footnote, I might add that owing to their quasi-alienation as a merely tolerated minority in the past, American Catholics tended to focus their major efforts on assuring the preservation of their distinctive religious beliefs. Since they were allowed to assume little influence in running society, they could either ignore what was being done in this regard or enjoy the luxury of criticizing those who were responsible. This negative approach is no longer possible. As long as they were not responsible for the conduct of national affairs, they could assume, and often did, that they possessed adequate "answers" or solutions for the nation's problems. Implicit in this assumption was the belief that there was a "Catholic" social order, a "Catholic" form of social institution, and a "Catholic" structure of human relations.

By way of conclusion and as possible *points de départ* for further discussion I offer the following practical suggestions. In a rapidly changing pluralist society the various confessions should focus major concern on the clarification of their positive ethical positions rather than on their differences with others. To avoid rendering their religious beliefs culturally irrelevant through sterile withdrawal from the democratic process, they should also emphasize the grounds for agreement and cooperation inherent in the immediate exigencies of the general welfare. With sincere conviction that truth is hard to come by and all serious attempts to reach it merit respectful consideration, they should strive to enlarge their capacity to listen seriously to others. And finally, as they gradually acquire experience in living with pluralism, they must learn to practice considerate restraint in using political power to enforce their distinctive ethical views in the practical order.

THE APOSTLE PAUL AND THE INTROSPECTIVE CONSCIENCE OF THE WEST*

KRISTER STENDAHL

IN THE HISTORY of Western Christianity—and hence, to a large extent, in the history of Western culture—the Apostle Paul has been hailed as a hero of the introspective conscience. Here was the man who grappled with the problem "I do not do the good I want, but the evil I do not want to do is what I do . . ." (Rom. 7:19). His insights as to a solution of this dilemma have recently been more or less identified, for example, with what Jung referred to as the Individuation Process;[1] but this is only a contemporary twist to the traditional Western way of reading the Pauline letters as documents of human consciousness.

Twenty-five years ago Henry J. Cadbury wrote a stimu-

* The paper read at the Colloquium was an abridged edition of this article, which has in the meantime appeared in *The Harvard Theological Review*, 56:199–215 (1963).

[1] D. Cox, *Jung and St. Paul: A Study of the Doctrine of Justification by Faith and Its Relation to the Concept of Individuation* (New York, 1959). Attention should also be drawn to the discussion in *The American Psychologist* (1960), 301–304, 713–716, initiated by O. H. Mowrer's article "Sin, the Lesser of Two Evils"; cf. also the Symposium of W. H. Clark, O. H. Mowrer, A. Ellis, Ch. Curran, and E. J. Shoben, Jr., on "The Role of the Concept of Sin in Psychotherapy," *Journal of Counseling Psychology* 7:185–201 (1960). For an unusually perceptive and careful attempt to deal with historical material from a psychoanalytical point of view, see Erik H. Erikson, *Young Man Luther* (New York, 1958). Not only the abundance but also the "Western" nature of the Luther material makes such an attempt more reasonable than when it is applied to Paul, who, as Erikson remarks, remains "in the twilight of biblical psychology" (p. 94).

lating study, "The Peril of Modernizing Jesus" (1937). That book and that very title is a good summary of one of the most important insights of biblical studies in the twentieth century. It has ramifications far beyond the field of theology and biblical exegesis. It questions the often tacit presupposition that man remains basically the same through the ages. There is little point in affirming or denying such a presupposition in general terms—much would depend on what the foggy word "basically" could mean. But both the historian and the theologian, both the psychologist and the average reader of the Bible, are well advised to assess how this hypothesis of contemporaneity affects their thinking, and their interpretation of ancient writings.

This problem becomes acute when one tries to picture the function and the manifestation of introspection in the life and writings of the Apostle Paul. It is the more acute since it is exactly at this point that Western interpreters have found the common denominator between Paul and the experiences of man, since Paul's statements about "justification by faith" have been hailed as the answer to the problem which faces the ruthlessly honest man in his practice of introspection. Especially in Protestant Christianity—which, however, at this point has its roots in Augustine and in the piety of the Middle Ages—the Pauline awareness of sin has been interpreted in the light of Luther's struggle with his conscience. But it is exactly at that point that we can discern the most drastic difference between Luther and Paul, between the sixteenth and the first century, and, perhaps, between Eastern and Western Christianity.

A fresh look at the Pauline writings themselves shows that Paul was equipped with what in our eyes must be called a rather "robust" conscience.[2] In Phil. 3 Paul speaks

---

[2] The actual meaning of the Greek word *syneidesis*, usually translated "conscience," is a complex linguistic problem, see C. A. Pierce, *Conscience in the New Testament* (Naperville, Ill., 1955). The more

most fully about his life before his Christian calling, and there is no indication that he had had any difficulty in fulfilling the Law. On the contrary, he can say that he had been "flawless" as to the righteousness required by the Law (v.6). His encounter with Jesus Christ—at Damascus, according to Acts 9:1–9—has not changed this fact. It was not to him a restoration of a plagued conscience; when he says that he now forgets what is behind him (Phil. 3:13), he does not think about the shortcomings in his obedience to the Law, but about his glorious achievements as a righteous Jew, achievements which he nevertheless now has learned to consider as "refuse" in the light of his faith in Jesus as the Messiah.

The impossibility of keeping the whole Law is a decisive point in Paul's argumentation in Rom. 2:17–3:20 (cf. 2:1ff.); and also in Gal. 3:10–12 this impossibility is the background for Paul's arguments in favor of a salvation which is open to both Jews and Gentiles in Christ. These and similar Pauline statements have led many interpreters to accuse Paul of misunderstanding or deliberately distorting the Jewish view of Law and Salvation.[3] It is pointed out that for the Jew the Law did not require a static or pedantic perfectionism but supposed a covenant relationship in which there was room for forgiveness and repentance and where

---

general problem dealt with in this lecture is closer to the problem to which P. Althaus draws attention in his *Paulus und Luther über den Menschen*, 2 ed. (Gütersloh, 1951); cf. the critique by F. Büchsel, *Theologische Blätter* 17:306–311 (1938). B. Reicke, *The Disobedient Spirits and Christian Baptism* (Copenhagen, 1946), pp. 174–182, gives the meaning "loyalty" in 1 Peter 3:21; cf. Reicke, "Syneidesis in Rom. 2:15," *Theologische Zeitschrift* 12:157–61 (1956). See also C. Spicq, *Revue Biblique* 47:50–80 (1938), and J. Dupont, *Studia Hellenistica* 5:119–53 (1948).

[3] See esp. G. F. Moore, *Judaism*, III (Cambridge, Mass., 1930), 151. H. J. Schoeps, *Paul* (Philadelphia, 1961), pp. 213–218, voices the same criticism from the anachronistic point of modern Old Testament interpretation as carried out by M. Buber and others. Cf. however, M. Buber, *Two Types of Faith* (New York, 1951), pp. 46–50.

God applied the Measure of Grace. Hence, Paul should
have been wrong in ruling out the Law on the basis that
Israel could not achieve the perfect obedience which the
Law required. What is forgotten in such a critique of Paul
—which is conditioned by the later Western problem of a
conscience troubled by the demands of the Law—is that
these statements about the impossibility of fulfilling the Law
stand side by side with the one just mentioned: "I was
blameless as to righteousness—of the Law, that is" (Phil.
3:6). So Paul speaks about his subjective conscience—in
full accordance with his Jewish training. But Rom. 2–3
deals with something very different. The actual transgres-
sions in Israel—as a people, not in each and every individual—show that the Jews are not better than the Gentiles,
in spite of circumcision and the proud possession of the Law.
The "advantage" of the Jews is that they have been entrusted with the Words of God and this advantage cannot
be revoked by their disobedience (Rom. 3:1ff.), but for
the rest they have no edge on salvation. The Law has not
helped. They stand before God as guilty as the Gentiles,
and even more so (2:9). All this is said in the light of the
new avenue of salvation, which has been opened in Christ,
an avenue which is equally open to Jews and Gentiles, since
it is not based on the Law, in which the very distinction between the two rests. In such a situation, says Paul, the old
covenant, even with its provision for forgiveness and grace,
is not a valid alternative any more. The only *metanoia*
(repentance/conversion) and the only grace which counts
is the one now available in Messiah Jesus. Once this has
been seen, it appears that Paul's references to the impossibility of fulfilling the Law are part of a theological and
theoretical scriptural argument about the relation between
Jews and Gentiles. Judging from Paul's own writings,
there is no indication that he had "experienced it in his
own conscience" during his time as a Pharisee. It is also

striking to note that Paul never urges Jews to find in Christ the answer to the anguish of a plagued conscience.

If that is the case regarding *Paul the Pharisee,* it is, as we shall see, even more important to note that we look in vain for any evidence that *Paul the Christian* has suffered under the burden of conscience concerning personal shortcomings which he would label "sins." The famous formula "simul justus et peccator"—at the same time righteous and sinner—as a description of the status of the Christian may have some foundation in the Pauline writings, but this formula cannot be substantiated as the center of Paul's conscious attitude toward his personal sins. Apparently, Paul did not have the type of introspective conscience which such a formula seems to presuppose.[4] This is probably one of the reasons why "forgiveness" is the term for salvation which is used least of all in the Pauline writings.[5]

It is most helpful to compare these observations concerning Paul with the great hero of what has been called "Pauline Christianity," that is, with Martin Luther. In him we find the problem of late medieval piety and theology. Luther's inner struggles presuppose the developed system of penance and indulgence, and it is significant that his

---

[4] For a penetrating analysis of the original meaning of this formula in Luther's theology, and its relation to the Pauline writings, see W. Joest, "Paulus und das lutherische Simul Justus et Peccator," *Kerygma und Dogma* 1:270–321 (1956). See also R. Bring, "Die Paulinische Begründung der lutherischen Theologie," *Luthertum* 17:18–43; and Bring, *Commentary on Galatians* (Philadelphia, 1961); H. Pohlmann, "Hat Luther Paulus entdeckt?" *Studien der Luther-Akademie* n.f. 7 (1949). For a perceptive view of the role of Luther's conscience, see A. Siirala, *Gottes Gebot bei Martin Luther* (Helsinki, 1956), pp. 282ff.

[5] There is actually no use of the term in the undisputed Pauline epistles; it is found as an apposition in Eph. 1:7 and Col. 1:14; cf. the Old Testament quotation in Rom. 4:7, where Paul's own preference for "justification" is clear from the context, and the similar term "remission" in Rom. 3:25. Cf. my articles "Sünde und Schuld" and "Sündenvergebung," *Die Religion in Geschichte und Gegenwart* 6:484–489, 511–513 (1962), with a discussion of the absence of a common word for "guilt."

famous 95 theses take their point of departure from the problem of forgiveness of sins as seen within the framework of penance: "When our Lord and Master Jesus Christ said: 'Repent (*penitentiam agite*) . . . ,' he wanted the whole life of the faithful to be a repentance (or: penance)."

When the period of the European mission had come to an end, the theological and practical center of penance shifted from baptism, administered once and for all, to the ever repeated Mass, and already this subtle change in the architecture of the Christian life contributed to a more acute introspection.[6] The manuals for self-examination among the Irish monks and missionaries became a treasured legacy in wide circles of Western Christianity. The Black Death may have been significant in the development of the climate of faith and life. Penetrating self-examination reached a hitherto unknown intensity. For those who took this practice seriously—and they were more numerous than many Protestants are accustomed to think—the pressure was great. It is as one of those—and for them—that Luther carries out his mission as a great pioneer. It is in response to *their* question, "How can I find a gracious God?" that Paul's words about a justification in Christ by faith, and without the works of the Law, appears as the liberating and saving answer. Luther's unrelenting honesty, even to the gates of hell (cf. especially his *De servo arbitrio,* "On the Bondage of the Will"), his refusal to accept the wise and sound consolation from his spiritual directors, these make him into a Christopher Columbus in the world of faith, who finds new and good land on the other side of what was thought to be the abyss.

In these matters Luther was a truly Augustinian monk, since Augustine may well have been one of the first to ex-

---

[6] For this change and its effect on Christology, see G. H. Williams, "The Sacramental Presuppositions of Anselm's Cur deus homo," *Church History* 26:245–274 (1957).

press the dilemma of the introspective conscience. It has always been a puzzling fact that Paul meant so relatively little for the thinking of the Church during the first 350 years of its history. To be sure, he is honored and quoted but—in the theological perspective of the West—it seems that Paul's great insight into justification by faith was forgotten.[7] It is, however, with Augustine that we find an interpretation of Paul which makes use of what to us is the deeper layer in the thought of the great Apostle. A decisive reason for this state of affairs may well have been that up to the time of Augustine the Church was by and large under the impression that Paul dealt with those issues with which he actually deals: (1) What happens to the Law (the Torah, the actual Law of Moses, not the principle of legalism) when the Messiah has come?[8]—(2) What are the ramifications of the Messiah's arrival for the relation between Jews and Gentiles? For Paul had not arrived at his view of the Law by testing and pondering its effect upon his conscience; it was his grappling with the question about the place of the Gentiles in the Church and in the plan of God, with the problem Jew/Gentiles or Jewish Christians/ Gentile Christians,[9] which had driven him to that interpre-

---

[7] For early Pauline interpretation see K. Staab, *Pauluskommentare aus der griechischen Kirche* (Münster i. W., 1933); V. E. Hasler, *Gesetz und Evangelium in der alten Kirche bis Origenes* (Zurich, 1953); E. Aleith, *Paulusverständnis in der alten Kirche* (Berlin, 1937); P. G. Verweijs, *Evangelium und Gesetz in der ältesten Christenheit bis auf Marcion* (Utrecht, 1960); now also U. Wickert, "Die Persönlichkeit des Paulus in den Pauluskommentaren Theodors von Mopsuestia," *Zeitschrift für die neutestamentliche Wissenschaft* 53:51–66 (1962). For Paul and conscience in relation to Gnosticism, see F. L. Sagnard, *Clément d'Alexandrie: Extraits de Théodote* (Paris, 1948), pp. 247–249, and R. M. Grant's observations in *The Journal of Theological Studies* 7:310–311 (1956).

[8] For the Jewish background to the problem as the one relevant to Paul, see W. D. Davies, *Torah in the Messianic Age and/or the Age to Come* (Philadelphia, 1952); also H. J. Schoeps, *Paul*, p. 174, with reference to the talmudic tractate Sanhedrin 98a.

[9] It is significant that the contrast in Paul is between Jews and Gentiles, or Jewish Christians and Gentile Christians, but never be-

tation of the Law which was to become his in a unique way.[10] These observations agree well with the manner in which both Paul himself and the Acts of the Apostles describe his "conversion" as a call to become the Apostle to and of the Gentiles. This was the task for which he—in the manner of the prophets of old—had been earmarked by God from his mother's womb (Gal. 1:15, cf. Acts 9:15).[11] There is not—as we usually think—first a conversion, and then a call to apostleship; there is only the call to the work among the Gentiles. Hence, it is quite natural that at least one of the centers of gravity in Paul's thought should be how to define the place for Gentiles in the Church, according to the plan of God. Rom. 9–11 is not an appendix to chs. 1–8, but the climax of the letter.

This problem was, however, not a live one after the end of the first century, when Christianity for all practical purposes had a non-Jewish constituency. Yet it was not until Augustine that the Pauline thought about the Law and Justification was applied in a consistent and grand style to a more general and timeless human problem. In that connection we remember that Augustine has often been called "the first modern man." While this is an obvious generalization, it may contain a fair amount of truth. His *Confessiones*

tween Jews and Gentile Christians; see G. Bornkamm, "Gesetz und Natur: Röm. 2:14–16," in *Studien zu Antike und Urchristentum* (1959), pp. 93–118; cf. J. N. Sevenster, *Paul and Seneca* (Leiden, 1961), p. 96.

[10] Schweitzer was certainly right when he recognized that Paul's teaching about justification by faith had such a limited function in Paul's theology and could not be considered the center of his total view. "The doctrine of righteousness by faith is therefore a subsidiary crater . . ." *The Mysticism of Paul the Apostle* (New York, 1931), p. 225.

[11] J. Munck, *Paul and the Salvation of Mankind* (Richmond, 1959), ch. 1; see also H. G. Wood, "The Conversion of St. Paul. Its Nature, Antecedents and Consequences," *New Testament Studies* 1:276–282 (1954/55); and U. Wilckens, "Die Bekehrung des Paulus als religionsgeschichtliches Problem," *Zeitschrift für Theologie und Kirche* 56:273–293 (1959).

are the first great document in the history of the introspective conscience. The Augustinian line leads into the Middle
Ages and reaches its climax in the penitential struggle of an
Augustinian monk, Martin Luther, and in his interpretation of Paul.[12]

Judging at least from a superficial survey of the preaching of the Churches of the East from olden times to the
present, it is striking how their homiletical tradition is either
one of doxology or meditative mysticism or exhortation—
but it does not deal with the plagued conscience in the way
in which one came to do so in the Western churches.

The problem we are trying to isolate could be expressed in
hermeneutical terms somewhat like this: The Reformers'
interpretation of Paul rests on an analogism when Pauline
statements about faith and works, Law and Gospel, Jews
and Gentiles are read in the framework of late medieval
piety. The Law, the Torah, with its specific requirements
of circumcision and food restrictions becomes a general
principle of "legalism" in religious matters. Where Paul
was concerned about the possibility for Gentiles to be included in the messianic community, his statements are now
read as answers to the quest for assurance about man's salvation out of a common human predicament.

This shift in the frame of reference affects the interpretation at many points. A good illustration can be seen in

---

12 For the Augustinian interpretation see A. F. W. Lekkerkerker,
Römer 7 und Römer 9 bei Augustin (Amsterdam, 1942); cf. Ph.
Platz, "Der Römerbrief in der Gnadenlehre Augustins," *Cassiciacum* 5
(1938); also J. Stelzenberger, *Conscientia bei Augustin* (Paderborn,
1959); and Stelzenberger, "Conscientia in der ost-westlichen Spannung
der patristischen Theologie," *Tübinger Theologische Quartalschrift*
141:174–205 (1961). For the Greek background, see O. Seel, "Zur
Vorgeschichte des Gewissensbegriffes im altgriechischen Denken," in
Festschrift F. Dornseiff (1953), pp. 291–319. For a broad and instructive survey, which substantiates our view in many respects — but
reads the biblical material differently — see H. Jaeger, "L'examen de
conscience dans les religions non-chrétiennes et avant le christianisme,"
Numen 6:175–233 (1959).

what Luther calls the Second Use of the Law, i.e., its function as a tutor or schoolmaster unto Christ. The crucial passage for this understanding of the Law is Gal. 3:24, a
passage which the King James Version—in unconscious
accord with Western tradition—renders: "Wherefore the
law was our schoolmaster (R.V. and A.S.V.: tutor) to bring
us unto Christ," but which the Revised Standard Version
translates more adequately: "So that the law was our custodian until Christ came."[13] In his extensive argument for
the possibility of Gentiles becoming Christians without circumcision etc., Paul states that the Law had not come in
until 430 years after the promise to Abraham, and that it
was meant to have validity only up to the time of the
Messiah (Gal. 3:15–22). Hence, its function was to serve
as a custodian for the Jews until that time. Once the Messiah had come, and once the faith in him—not "faith" as a
general religious attitude—was available as the decisive
ground for salvation, the Law had done its duty as a custodian for the Jews, or as a waiting room with strong locks
(vv. 22f). Hence, it is clear that Paul's problem is how
to explain why there is no reason to impose the Law on
the Gentiles, who now, in God's good messianic time, have
become partakers in the fulfillment of the promises to
Abraham (v. 29).

   In the common interpretation of Western Christianity,
the matter looks very different. One could even say that
Paul's argument has been reversed into saying the opposite
to his original intention. Now the Law is the tutor *unto*
Christ. Nobody can attain a true faith in Christ unless his
self-righteousness has been crushed by the Law. The function of the Second Use of the Law is to make man see his
desperate need for a saviour. In such an interpretation, we
note how Paul's distinction between Jews and Gentiles is

[13] Cf. my article on Gal. 3:24 in *Svensk Exegetisk Aarsbok*
18/19:161–173 (1953/54).

gone. *"Our* Tutor/Custodian" is now a statement applied to man in general, not "our" in the sense of "I, Paul, and my fellow Jews." Furthermore, the Law is not any more the Law of Moses which requires circumcision etc., and which has become obsolete when faith in the Messiah is a live option—it is the moral imperative as such, in the form of the will of God. And finally, Paul's argument that the Gentiles must not, and should not come to Christ *via* the Law, that is, *via* circumcision etc., has turned into a statement according to which all men must come to Christ with consciences properly convicted by the Law and its insatiable requirements for righteousness. So drastic is the reinterpretation once the original framework of "Jews and Gentiles" is lost, and the Western problems of conscience become its unchallenged and self-evident substitute.

Thus, the radical difference between a Paul and a Luther at this one point has considerable ramification for the reading of the actual texts. And the line of Luther appears to be the obvious one. This is true not only among those who find themselves more or less dogmatically bound by the confessions of the Reformation. It is equally true about the average student of "all the great books" in a college course, or the agnostic Westerner in general. It is also true in serious New Testament exegesis. Thus, R. Bultmann—in spite of his great familiarity with the history of religions in early Christian times—finds the nucleus of Pauline thought in the problem of "boasting,"[14] that is, in man's need to be utterly convicted in his conscience.[15] Paul's self-understanding in these matters is the existential, and hence, ever valid center of Pauline theology. Such an interpretation is an

---

[14] R. Bultmann, *Theology of the New Testament*, I (New York, 1951), 242f.

[15] C. H. Dodd feels the difficulty in such an interpretation, but ends up with placing Paul's overcoming of his boasting somewhat later in his career, "The Mind of Paul," in *New Testament Studies* (Manchester, 1953), 67–128.

even more drastic translation and an even more far-reaching generalization of the original Pauline material than that found in the Reformers. But it is worth noting that it is achieved in the prolongation of the same line. This is more obvious since Bultmann makes, candidly and openly, the statement that his existential hermeneutic rests on the presupposition that man is essentially the same through the ages, and that this continuity in the human self-consciousness is the common denominator between the New Testament and any age of human history. This presupposition is stated with the force of an a priori truth.[16]

What in Bultmann rests on a clearly stated hermeneutic principle plays, however, its subtle and distorting role in historians who do not give account of their presuppositions but work within an unquestioned Western framework. P. Volz, in his comprehensive study of Jewish eschatology, uses man's knowledge of his individual salvation in its relation to a troubled conscience as one of the "trenches" in his reconstruction of the Jewish background to the New Testament.[17] But when it comes to the crucial question and he wants to find a passage which would substantiate that this was a conscious problem in those generations of Judaism, he can find only one example in the whole Rabbinic literature which perhaps could illustrate an attitude of a troubled conscience (bBer. 28b).[18]

---

[16] Bultmann, *Theology of The New Testament,* II (1955), 251; cf. also Bultmann, "The Problem of Hermeneutics," *Essays Philosophical and Theological* (New York, 1955), 234–261.

[17] P. Volz, *Die Eschatologie der jüdischen Gemeinde im neutestamentlichen Zeitalter* (Tübingen, 1934), pp. 111ff.

[18] Cf. also how F. Büchsel, who repeats this view in highly biased language, admits the lack of evidence for such an attitude: the Pharisee "vacillated between an overbearing confidence in his good works, which made him blind to his sinfulness, and a desperate anxiety before the wrath of God, *which, however, manifests itself only seldom*" (italics mine), *Theologisches Wörterbuch zum Neuen Testaments,* ed. G. Kittel, III (Stuttgart, 1938), 935. The examples, often quoted, from 4 Ezra 3–4 and 7–8 deal primarily with the historical theodicy and not with the individual conscience.

To be sure, no one could ever deny that *hamartia*, "sin," is a crucial word in Paul's terminology, especially in his epistle to the Romans. Rom. 1–3 sets out to show that all—both Jews and Gentiles—have sinned and fallen short of the Glory of God (3:19, cf. v. 23). Rom. 3:21–8:39 demonstrates how and in what sense this tragic fact is changed by the arrival of the Messiah.

It is much harder to gage how Paul subjectively experienced the power of sin in his life and, more specifically, how and in what sense he was conscious of actual sins. One point is clear. The Sin with capital S in Paul's past was that he had persecuted the Church of God. This climax of his dedicated obedience to his Jewish faith (Gal. 1:13, Phil. 3:6) was the shameful deed which made him the least worthy of apostleship (1 Cor. 15:9). This motif, which is elaborated dramatically by the author of the Acts of the Apostles (chs. 9, 22 and 26), is well grounded in Paul's own epistles. Similarly, when 1 Timothy states on Paul's account that "Christ Jesus came into the world to save sinners, of whom I am number one" (1:15), this is not an expression of contrition in the present tense, but refers to how Paul in his ignorance had been a blaspheming and violent persecutor, before God in his mercy and grace had revealed to him his true Messiah and made Paul an Apostle and a prototype of sinners' salvation (1:12–16).[19]

Nevertheless, Paul knew that he had made up for this terrible Sin of persecuting the Church, as he says in so many words in 1 Cor. 15:10: ". . . his grace toward me was not in vain; on the contrary, I worked harder than any of them —though it was not I, but the grace of God which is with me."

This his call to apostleship has the same pattern as the

---

[19] This theme is elaborated further in the Epistle of Barnabas 5:9, where *all* the Apostles are called "iniquitous above all sin," with a reference to Mk. 2:17.

more thematic statement that Christ died for us godless ones, while we were yet sinners (Rom. 5:6–11). We note how that statement is only the subsidiary conditional clause in an argument *e majore ad minus:* If now God was so good and powerful that he could justify weak and sinful and rebellious men, how much easier must it not be for him to give in due time the ultimate salvation to those whom he already has justified. Hence, the words about the sinful, the weak and the rebellious have not present-tense meaning, but refer to the past, which is gloriously and gracefully blotted out, as was Paul's enmity to Jesus Christ and his Church.

What then about Paul's consciousness of sins after his conversion? His letters indicate with great clarity that he did not hold to the view that man was free from sin after baptism. His pastoral admonitions show that he had much patience with the sins and weaknesses of Christians. But does he ever intimate that he is aware of any sins of his own which would trouble his conscience? It is actually easier to find statements to the contrary. The tone in Acts 23:1, "Brethren, I have lived before God in all good conscience up to this day" (cf. 24:16), prevails also throughout his letters. Even if we take due note of the fact that the major part of Paul's correspondence contains an apology for his apostolic ministry—hence it is the antipode to Augustine's Confessions from the point of view of form—the conspicuous absence of references to an actual consciousness of being a sinner is surprising. To be sure, Paul is aware of a struggle with his "body" (1 Cor. 9:27), but we note that the tone is one of confidence, not of a plagued conscience.

In Rom. 9:1 and 2 Cor. 1:12 he witnesses to his good conscience. This tone reaches its highest pitch in 2 Cor. 5:10f.: "For we must all appear before the judgment seat of Christ so that each one may receive the retribution for what he has done while in his body, either good or evil. Aware, therefore, of the fear of the Lord, we try to persuade men, but to God it is clear [what we are]; and I hope that it is clear also to your conscience." Here, with the day of reckoning before his eyes, Paul says that the Lord has approved of him, and he hopes that the Corinthians shall have an equally positive impression of him, and of his success in pleasing the Lord (5:9). This robust conscience is not shaken but strengthened by his awareness of a final judgment which has not come yet. And when he writes about the tensions between himself and Apollos and other teachers, he states that "I have nothing on my conscience" (1 Cor. 4:4; N.E.B.—literally "I know nothing with me"; the verb is of the same stem as the word for conscience); to be sure, he adds that this does not settle the case, since "the Lord is my judge," but it is clear from the context that Paul is in little doubt about the final verdict. His warning against a premature verdict is not a plea out of humility or fear, but a plea to the Corinthians not to be too rash in a negative evaluation of Paul.

Thus, we look in vain for a statement in which Paul would speak about himself as an actual sinner. When he speaks about his conscience, he witnesses to his good conscience before men and God. On the other hand, Paul often speaks about his *weakness,* not only ironically as in 2 Cor. 11:21f. In 2 Cor. 12 we find the proudly humble words, "But He said to me: 'My grace is sufficient to you, for the power is fulfilled in weakness.' I will the more gladly boast of my weakness, that the power of Christ may rest upon me. For the sake of Christ, then, I am content with weaknesses, insults, hardships, persecutions, and calamities; for when I am weak, then I am strong" (vv. 9–10). The weakness which Paul here refers to is clearly without any relation to his sin or his conscience. The "thorn in the flesh" (v. 7) was presumably some physical handicap—some have guessed at epilepsy—which interfered with his effectiveness and, what was more important, with his apostolic authority, as we can

see from Gal. 4:13, cf. 1 Cor. 11:30. Sickness was seen as
a sign of insufficient spiritual endowment. But there is no
indication that Paul ever thought of this and other "weaknesses" as sins for which he was responsible. They were
caused by the enemy or the enemies. His weakness became
for him an important facet in his identification with the
work of Christ, who had been "crucified in weakness"
(2 Cor. 13:4; cf. also 4:10 and Col. 1:24).—In the passage from Rom. 5, mentioned above, we find the only use
of the word "weak" as a synonym to "sinner," but there these
words helped to describe primarily the power of justification
as a past act (and the New English Bible consequently
renders it by "powerless"). This is the more clear since the
third synonym is "enemy" (v. 10), and points to Paul's
past when he had been the enemy of Christ.

Yet there is one Pauline text which the reader must have
wondered why we have left unconsidered, especially since
it is the passage we mentioned in the beginning as the proof
text for Paul's deep insights into the human predicament:
"I do not do the good I want, but the evil I do not want to
do is what I do" (Rom. 7:19). What could witness more
directly to a deep and sensitive introspective conscience?
While much attention has been given to the question
whether Paul here speaks about a pre-Christian or Christian experience of his, or about man in general, little attention has been drawn to the fact that Paul here is involved
in an argument about the Law; he is not primarily concerned about man's or his own cloven ego or predicament.[20]
The diatribe style of the chapter helps us to see what Paul
is doing. In vv. 7–12 he works out an answer to the semi-

---

[20] The confusion caused by psychological interpretations, and the
centrality of the Law in Rom. 7, was seen in the epoch-making study
by W. G. Kümmel, *Römer 7 und die Bekehrung des Paulus* (Leipzig,
1929); cf. C. L. Mitton, *Expository Times* 65:78–81, 99–103, 132–
135 (1953/54); and E. Ellwein, *Kerygma und Dogma* 1:247–268
(1955).

rhetorical question: "Is the Law sin?" The answer reads: "Thus the Law is holy, just, and good." This leads to the equally rhetorical question: "Is it then this good (Law) which brought death to me?" and the answer is summarized in v.25b: "So then, I myself serve the Law of God with my mind, but with my flesh I serve the Law of Sin" (that is, the Law "weakened by sin" [8:3] leads to death, just as a medicine which is good in itself can cause death to a patient whose organism [flesh] cannot take it).

Such an analysis of the formal structure of Rom. 7 shows that Paul is here involved in an interpretation of the Law, a defense for the holiness and goodness of the Law. In vv. 13–25 he carries out this defense by making a distinction between the Law as such and the Sin (and the Flesh) which has to assume the whole responsibility for the fatal outcome. It is most striking that the "I," the *ego*, is not simply identified with Sin and Flesh. The observation that "I do not do the good I want, but the evil I do not want to do is what I do" does not lead directly over to the exclamation: "Wretched man that I am . . .!", but, on the contrary, to the statement, "Now if I do what I do not want, *then it is not I who do it*, but the sin which dwells in me." The argument is one of acquittal of the ego, not one of utter contrition. Such a line of thought would be impossible if Paul's intention were to describe man's predicament. In Rom. 1–3 the human impasse has been argued, and here every possible excuse has been carefully ruled out. In Rom. 7 the issue is rather to show how in some sense "I gladly agree with the Law of God as far as my inner man is concerned" (v. 22); or, as in v. 25, "I serve the Law of God."

All this makes sense only if the anthropological references in Rom. 7 are seen as means for a very special argument about the holiness and goodness of the Law. The possibility of a distinction between the good Law and the bad Sin is based on the rather trivial observation that every man knows that there is a difference between what he ought to do and what he does. This distinction makes it possible for Paul to blame sin and flesh, and to rescue the Law as a good gift of God. "If I now do what I do not want, I agree with the Law [and recognize] that it is good" (v. 16). That is all, but that is what should be proven.

Unfortunately—or fortunately—Paul happened to express this supporting argument so well that what to him and his contemporaries was a common sense observation appeared to later interpreters to be a most penetrating insight into the nature of man and into the nature of sin. This could happen easily once the problem about the nature and intention of God's Law was not any more as relevant a problem in the sense in which Paul grappled with it. The question about the Law became the incidental framework around the golden truth of Pauline anthropology. This is what happens when one approaches Paul with the Western question of an introspective conscience. This Western interpretation reaches its climax when it appears that even, or especially, the will of man is the center of depravation. And yet, in Rom. 7 Paul had said about that will: "The will (to do the good) is there . . ." (v. 18).

What we have called the Western interpretation has left its mark even in the field of textual reconstruction in this chapter in Romans. In Moffatt's translation of the New Testament the climax of the whole argument about the Law (v. 25b, see above) is placed before the words "wretched man that I am . . ." Such a rearrangement—without any basis in the manuscripts[21]—wants to make this exclamation the dramatic climax of the whole chapter, so that it is quite

[21] In a similar fashion even the standard Greek text of the New Testament (the Nestle edition) indicates that ch. 7 should end with the exclamation in v. 25a, and ch. 8 begin already with v. 25b. But the New English Bible retains v. 25b as the concluding sentence in ch. 7.

clear to the reader that Paul here gives the answer to the great problem of human existence. But by such arrangements the structure of Paul's argumentation is destroyed. What was a digression is elevated to the main factor. It should not be denied that Paul is deeply aware of the precarious situation of man in this world, where even the holy Law of God does not help—it actually leads to death. Hence his outburst. But there is no indication that this awareness is related to a subjective conscience struggle. If that were the case, he would have spoken of the "body of sin," but he says "body of death" (v. 25; cf. 1 Cor. 15:56). What dominates this chapter is a theological concern and the awareness that there is a positive solution available here and now by the Holy Spirit about which he speaks in ch. 8. We should not read a trembling and introspective conscience into a text which is so anxious to put the blame on sin, and that in such a way that not only the Law but the will and mind of man are declared good and are found to be on the side of God.

We may have wasted too much time in trying to demonstrate a fact well known in human history—and especially in the history of religions: that sayings which originally meant one thing later on were interpreted to mean something else, something which was felt to be more relevant to human conditions of later times.

And yet, if our analysis is on the whole correct, it points to a major question in the history of mankind. We should venture to suggest that the West for centuries has wrongly surmised that the biblical writers were grappling with problems which no doubt are ours, but which never entered their consciousness.

For the historian this is of great significance. It could, of course, always be argued that these ancients unconsciously were up against the same problems as we are—man being the same through the ages. But the historian is rightly anxious to stress the value of having an adequate picture of what these people actually thought that they were saying. He will always be suspicious of any "modernizing," whether it be for apologetic, doctrinal, or psychological purposes.

The theologian would be quite willing to accept and appreciate the obvious deepening of religious and human insight which has taken place in Western thought, and which reached a theological climax with Luther—and a secular climax with Freud. He could perhaps argue that this Western interpretation and transformation of Pauline thought is a valid and glorious process of theological development. He could even claim that such a development was fostered by elements implicit in the New Testament, and especially in Paul.

The framework of "Sacred History" which we have found to be that of Pauline theology (cf. our comments on Gal. 3:24 above) opens up a new perspective for systematic theology and practical theology. The Pauline *ephapax* ("once for all," Rom. 6:10) cannot be translated fully and only into something repeated in the life of every individual believer. For Gentiles the Law is *not* the schoolmaster who leads to Christ; or it is that only by analogy and a secondary one at that. We find ourselves in the new situation where the faith in the Messiah Jesus gives us the right to be called Children of God (1 Jn. 3:1). By way of analogy, one could of course say that in some sense every man has a "legalistic Jew" in his heart. But that *is* an analogy, and should not be smuggled into the texts as their primary or explicit meaning in Paul. If that is done, something happens to the joy and humility of Gentile Christianity.

Thus, the theologian would note that the Pauline original should not be identified with such interpretations. He would try to find ways by which the Church—also in the West—could do more justice to other elements of the

Pauline original than those catering to the problems raised by introspection. He would be suspicious of a teaching and a preaching which pretended that the only door into the Church was that of evermore introspective awareness of sin and guilt. For it appears that the Apostle Paul was a rather good Christian, and yet he seems to have had little such awareness. We note how the biblical original functions as a critique of inherited presuppositions and an incentive to new thought.[22] Few things are more liberating and creative in modern theology than a clear distinction between the "original" and the "translation" in any age, our own included.

[22] For a fuller treatment of these issues, see my article "Biblical Theology" in *The Interpreter's Dictionary of the Bible,* I (Nashville, 1962), 418–432.

SOME REFLECTIONS ON THE INTROSPECTIVE CONSCIENCE FROM NEW TESTAMENT DATA

DAVID STANLEY, S.J.

D R. S T E N D A H L ' s view that Paul's was essentially a "robust" conscience and that Romans 7:7–25 is incorrectly understood when interpreted as evidence of exaggerated introspection or scrupulosity is, I believe, an accurate one. There is, moreover, in the New Testament generally a notable absence of that tendency to overemphasize introspection which has at times been evinced by the spirituality of the Christian West. I wish to illustrate this briefly by some observations on certain key passages in the New Testament.

In the first place, the lack of this tendency to probe into the introspective conscience may be explained by the privileged position of the first-generation Christians. To judge by the attitude of several New Testament writers, the Christian of the apostolic age did not seriously envisage the possibility of a relapse into sin after conversion. *Metanoia,* the total reorientation of one's religious life to Christ, which was the object of the primitive kerygma, was considered the decisive act of one's Christian existence. By faith, the believer severed himself definitively from his old sinful ways. Through this act of complete self-commitment to Jesus Christ a man was justified or made righteous; and his life henceforth was one wholly consecrated to the risen Lord. The belief in the impeccability of the Apostles, a prominent datum in Catholic tradition, may be considered a vestigial remnant of this New Testament viewpoint.

Certain New Testament authors of the second generation do indeed envisage the possibility of a relapse into the state of sinfulness, but recoil in horror at the very idea. "It is impossible to restore again to repentance those who have been enlightened . . . if they then commit apostasy, since they crucify the Son of God on their own account and hold him up to contempt" (Heb. 6:4-6). And again, "if we sin deliberately after receiving the knowledge of the truth, there no longer remains a sacrifice for sins . . ." (Heb. 10:26). The author of 1 John urges his readers to pray for sinners, but explicitly excludes "deadly sins" (1 Jn. 5:13-17). James also reckons with the fact of sin within the Christian community, and he urges confession of sin and an attempt to reform the sinner (Jas. 5:15, 19-20). Moreover, Matthew records a Logion of Jesus concerning the admonition and correction of a sinning member of the community (Mt. 18:15-17); and Paul warns his Corinthians against falling back into their old pagan habits of vice (1 Cor. 6:8-11).

The Christian of the apostolic age was certainly aware of his sinful tendencies, but as a general rule the term "sinner" is reserved in the New Testament for those who stand outside the Gospel and have not yet accepted the Good News of Christian salvation. It is in this sense that Luke represents Peter, at the moment of his call from Jesus, as applying the term to himself (Lk. 5:8; cf. also the publican in Lk. 18:13). The Lucan parable of the Prodigal Son, in which the younger brother probably symbolizes the Gentiles, betrays the same point of view, as does Paul's statement in Romans 5:8 (cf. also Gal. 2:15-16).

It is to be observed, however, that in the *Pater noster,* the Christian prayer *par excellence,* the petition for forgiveness of sins is an acknowledgment by the members of the Church of actual sinfulness. Further, it should be remembered, if we are to assess correctly this inadvertence to the introspective conscience (particularly in the Gospels), that the psychological element has been eliminated habitually in almost all the Gospel narratives—as the form critics rightly point out. I am thinking of the classic example of a vocation story in the Synoptics (Mk. 1:16–20). In this regard the story of the rich young man (Mk. 10:17–22) is a rare exception. This lack of attention to the psychological dimension may be taken as an indication of the absence of the introspective conscience, in the sense in which Dr. Stendahl has defined it, amongst Christians of the apostolic period; and the New Testament's use of the term "conscience" confirms this impression. The word is used of a "weak" conscience (1 Cor. 8:10, 12), or of a "good" conscience (2 Cor. 1:12), of a "clear" conscience (1 Pt. 3:16, 21), or of the testimony of conscience (Rom. 2:15). And it is interesting to observe that, in the pericope about the woman taken in adultery, the phrase "accused by their conscience" (Jn. 8:9) is almost certainly a later interpolation. The Catholic tradition already alluded to, regarding the confirmation in grace of the Apostles, may well stem from the memory in the consciousness of the Church of this lack of psychological data in the New Testament.

I should like now to recall a text in Paul which, like the passage examined by Dr. Stendahl, has not infrequently been misinterpreted as evidence for a scrupulous or introspective conscience on the part of the Apostle, that is, 1 Cor. 4:4: "I am not conscious of anything in myself; but I am not on that account justified." This has been taken to mean concern about some "secret" or forgotten sins, thanks to which a man may not be in the state of grace although he thinks he is. The context of the passage, however, makes it certain that Paul is merely asserting that no human judgment—even that of an individual concerning himself—can render a man just, but only the creative judgment of God and of the risen Lord (cf. 1 Cor. 4:3–5).

In concluding, I should like to point out another interpretation of Romans 7:7–25, which may serve as a confirmatory argument for Dr. Stendahl's view of the robust nature of Paul's conscience. The interpretation to which I refer is basically that proposed by Père Stanislas Lyonnet, S.J., in his notes on Romans in the *Bible de Jérusalem.*

The passage is to be considered as a dramatic re-presentation of the assertions made in Romans 5:12–21 concerning the function of sin in Israel's salvation-history. The "Ego," presented as the protagonist in the drama, is Adam, inasmuch as he is first parent of the human race and, therefore, embodies the collective experience of humanity. The pericope is concerned chiefly with a psychological description of Adam's fall, but it also depicts his state of mind both before and after his act of disobedience to the divine command. On this view, the prohibition, "Thou shalt not covet" refers, not to the Decalogue, but to God's injunction in Gn. 2:16–17. The reaction of the Woman (Gn. 3:6) as she contemplates the fruit is depicted precisely as a contravention of this divine taboo. "The Woman saw . . . that the tree *was desirable* for its gift of wisdom." From Romans 7:11, it is clear that Sin (a personification, which is another actor in the drama) is to be identified with the serpent of Genesis. Paul's remark, "Sin deceived me," is an exact reproduction of the Septuagint version of the Woman's admission (Gn. 3:13): "The serpent deceived me." The references to the death of "Ego" (Rom. 7:9, 11) are a reminiscence of God's threat (Gn. 2:17): "The day you eat of it you shall surely die." The statement by "Ego," "I was once alive without law," is best understood as a description of Adam's paradisiac existence before the imposition of the divine prohibition regarding the tree. Finally, the vivid picture of "Ego" as a victim of diabolical possession

(Sin = the serpent = the devil) in verse 17 ("It is not I who do these things, but Sin indwelling in me") recalls subsequent remarks by the author of Genesis on the evil effects of Adam's rebellion (cf. Gn. 6:5; 8:21).

THE PROBLEM OF CONSCIENCE AND THE TWENTIETH-CENTURY CHRISTIAN

CHARLES E. CURRAN

EVEN a superficial reflection shows the existence of moral conscience. Man experiences the joy of having done something good or the remorse of having done something evil. He recognizes an imperative to do this or avoid that. A more profound analysis distinguishes moral conscience from social pressure or even a religious imperative.[1]

Moral conscience has many meanings. St. Paul describes conscience as a witness or judge of past activity, a director of future action, the habitual quality of a man's Christianity, and even as the Christian ego or personality.[2] This paper will discuss the problem of antecedent conscience, that is, conscience as pointing out to the Christian what he should do in the particular circumstances of his life.

HISTORICAL SUMMARY

Scripture reveals Christianity as a dialogue or covenant relationship between God and his people. Christian tradition frequently refers to conscience as the voice of God telling man how to respond to the divine gift of salvation. Both the reality and the concept of moral conscience have

[1] Jacques Leclercq, *Les grandes lignes de la philosophie morale* (Louvain, 1953), pp. 7–13.
[2] C. Spicq, "La conscience dans le Nouveau Testament," *Revue Biblique* 47:55–76 (1938). Cf. C. A. Pierce, *Conscience in the New Testament* (London, 1955).

evolved in the course of salvation history. Two reasons explain the evolution. First, God speaks to primitive man in one way and to more mature man in another way. Second, only when man has acquired a certain degree of maturity can he reflect on his own subjective states.[3]

In the beginning of salvation history, conscience (the reality, not the word) appears as extrinsic, objective, and collective.[4] Theophany, however, gives way to angelophany, and finally to human prophets who speak in the name of God.[5] The prophets, the conscience of Israel, stress interior dispositions and begin to mention individual responsibility (Jer. 31:29–30; Ez. 14:1–8). They look forward to the day when God will plant his law in the innermost part of man (Jer. 31:33–34; Ez. 36:26–27; Psalm 50:12). Since the prophets insist on God as the first cause, conscience is not the voice of man but the voice of God who speaks to man.

St. Paul, with his emphasis on the internal and subjective dispositions of man, brings into Christian thought the term conscience (*syneidesis*), which originally appeared in Democritus and was developed by stoic philosophy.[6] Paul, while adopting the uses of the term in pagan philosophy,

[3] For the general lines of the evolution by which God brought his people in the Old Testament to both self-knowledge and a knowledge of the true God, see Marc Oraison, *Love or Constraint?* (New York, 1959), pp. 152–163.

[4] The characteristics of a primitive conscience in general are aptly described by Richard Mohr, *Die Christliche Ethik im Lichte der Ethnologie* (Munich, 1954).

[5] Theophany abounds in the first chapters of Genesis. There is some dispute among Scripture scholars on the exact nature of the "Angel of Yahweh" which appears in Gen. 16:7; 22:11; Exodus 3:2; Judges 2:1. Even if the expression here refers merely to God in a visible form, such an expression indicates a "sophisticated" reluctance to speak of a pure theophany. In the Old Testament, angels exercise the same twofold function as conscience; namely, they make known the will of God and serve as guides both for individuals and the whole people of God.

[6] Spicq, pp. 51–55; Pierce, pp. 13–53. Also Th. Deman, *La Prudence* (Paris, 1949), pp. 479–487.

introduces the notion of conscience as the director of human activity—antecedent conscience.[7] Commenting on the different Pauline uses of the term conscience, the Fathers of the Church explicitly make the last step in the interiorization of conscience. Conscience now becomes the voice of the human person himself and only mediately and indirectly the voice of God.[8]

Scholastic theology of the thirteenth century first considered scientifically, as opposed to the pastoral approach of the Fathers, the nature of moral conscience. Is it a faculty? A habit? An act? The Thomistic school distinguished conscience, the judgment of the practical reason about a particular act, from *synteresis,* the quasi-innate habit of the first principles of the moral order. St. Bonaventure placed more emphasis on the will especially with regard to *synteresis.* The subjective voice of reason was open to God through the mediation of law.[9]

Unfortunately, the scholastic synthesis succumbed to the dangers of sterile intellectualism, the nominalistic tendency to extrinsicism, and the increasing influence of positive juridic sciences. The decree of the Council of Trent again legislating the necessity of annual confession of sins ac-

---

[7] Eric D'Arcy, *Conscience and its Right to Freedom* (New York, 1961), pp. 8–12; Pietro Palazzine, *La Coscienza* (Rome, 1961), pp. 63–71; Deman, pp. 488–489. Spicq maintains that the concept of an antecedent conscience was known by Paul's contemporaries, but it is certain that Paul contributed most to its development (pp. 63–67). Among the texts cited as instances of Paul's referring to antecedent conscience are: 1 Cor. 8; 10:25–33; Rom. 13:5.

[8] The affirmation is made by Antonio Hortelano in unpublished notes. Hortelano refers to the following citations from *Cursus Completus Patrologiae,* ed. J. P. Migne (Paris). Augustinus, "Tractatus in Joannem," *PL* 35, col. 1382; Origenes, "Commentarium in Epistolam ad Romanos," *PG* 14, col. 895; Basilius, "Homilia XIII," *PG* 31, col. 432.

[9] Odon Lottin, *Morale Fondamentale* (Tournai, 1954), pp. 163–165, 221–228. The author summarizes here the conclusions derived from his multivolumed historical study, *Psychologie et Morale aux XIIe et XIIIe siècles* (Gembloux).

cording to their number and species orientated moral theology (and the question of conscience) toward the judgment seat of the confessional rather than toward the living of the Christian life.[10]

In this light one can better understand the famous controversy of the seventeenth and eighteenth centuries about the question of a probable conscience. When I am not certain about the existence of a law, am I obliged to follow the doubtful law? Today the vast majority of moral theologians accept some form of a mitigated probabilism, which maintains that only a law which is certain can oblige a subject.[11] As a result of the controversy, *De Conscientia* became a separate and well-developed treatise in the manuals of moral theology. Among the benefits accruing to moral theology from such a development are the balance and equilibrium finally attained, the precise terminology acquired, and the realization that conscience must consider the many problems of daily living.

However, the defects of the manualistic treatises on conscience are great. Briefly, legalism, extrinsicism, impersonalism, and an ethic of obligation characterize such considerations of conscience. Positive law and objective considerations are greatly exaggerated. Conscience becomes

[10] There is no complete and authentic history of moral theology. Nor can there be until more particular studies are made. For the best available study of the development of moral theology of this time, see Bernard Häring and Louis Vereecke, "La Théologie Morale de S. Thomas d'Aquin à S. Alphonse de Liguori," *Nouvelle Revue Théologique* 77:673–692 (1955). Also Louis Vereecke, "Le Concile de Trente et l'enseignement de la Théologie Morale," *Divinitas* 5:361–374 (1961).

[11] Most of the manuals of moral theology accept such a probabilism. In practice, the antiprobabilists do not differ much from those who espouse simple probabilism. Outside the manuals, there is a reaction against the legalistic mentality of probabilism which has taken different forms. Cf. Th. Deman, "Probabilisme," *Dictionnaire de Théologie Catholique*, vol. XIII (Paris, 1936), col. 417–619; also Deman, *La Prudence*; Georges Leclercq, *La Conscience du Chrétien* (Paris, 1947), pp. 127–197; P. Rousselot, *Quaestiones de Conscientia* (Paris, 1947), pp. 51–80.

negative, oppressive and sin-orientated.[12] The dire consequences are not restricted merely to the intellectual and
theoretical plane. History and empirical studies show that
the linking of introspection and a legalistic approach to
morality provides fertile ground for the formation of the
scrupulous conscience.[13] Unfortunately, in everyday Catholic life, the average Catholic equates Christian morality with
Mass on Sunday, no meat on Friday, and the need to obey
what the Church teaches about sex.

In the last few decades theologians have begun to react
against the manualistic treatment of conscience. Under the
influence of the Thomistic renewal, authors now stress the
virtue of prudence and the subjective element which cannot be found in any of the books on cases of conscience.[14]
In keeping with the return to the primitive sources of Scripture and the Fathers, which is characterizing all theological
investigation today, theologians consider conscience in the
light of charity, or the responsibility of the Christian before
the call of God, or as an anticipation of the eschatological
judgment.[15]

---

[12] The increasing awareness of the need for a renewal of moral
theology in the last few years stems from these negative characteristics
present today in most manuals. For a brief review of the recent
literature on the subject of renewing moral theology, see John C. Ford
and Gerald Kelly, *Contemporary Moral Theology* (Westminster, Md.,
1958), pp. 42–103. It is my personal belief that the authors have not
paid sufficient attention to the part played by the Tübingen school of
theology nor do they seem fully to appreciate the need for a life-
centered and not confessional-orientated moral theology.

[13] Juan García-Vicente, "Dirección pastoral de la escrupulosidad,"
Revista de Espiritualidad 19:514–529 (1960). Also, *Cahiers Laennec*
20 (June 1960) which is totally concerned with the question of
scrupulosity.

[14] Deman, *La Prudence,* especially pp. 496–514. Perhaps Deman
overemphasizes prudence at the expense of conscience. For a very
satisfying discussion of the relation between prudence and conscience,
see Domenico Capone, *Intorno alla verità morale* (Naples, 1951). A
fuller bibliography on the relation between prudence and conscience is
given by Josephus Fuchs, *Theologia Moralis Generalis* (Rome, 1960),
p. 169.

[15] Bernard Häring, *The Law of Christ,* I (Westminster, Md., 1961),

Outside the pale of theology, two divergent tendencies —exaggerated interiorization and over objectivization— have destroyed the true notion of conscience. Ever since Descartes, philosophers like Montaigne, Rousseau, and Kant have overemphasized the subjective element. Existentialism, the last step in the tendency, makes subjective conscience the center of the whole world, completely cut off from God or any other subject. On the other extreme, conscience is merely a function of physiological factors (Chauchard), psychological factors (Freud), or sociological factors (Durkheim).[16]

THE NATURE OF CONSCIENCE

Guided by the lessons of history, one can better understand the nature of conscience, its function, and its formation. Catholic theologians generally distinguish *synteresis*, moral science, and conscience. Adopting a synthetic approach, we can define *synteresis* as the power of conscience situated in the inmost part of the soul (*scintilla animae*). In its rational aspect, *synteresis* tends to the truth, so that man almost intuitively knows the fundamental principle of the moral order—good is to be done and evil is to be avoided. In its volitional aspect, *synteresis* tends toward the good and the expression of such a tendency in action.

Moral science is the knowledge of the less general principles of the moral law which man deduces from the primary principles. The category of moral knowledge also includes whatever man knows from revelation or authority.

91–213; René Carpentier, "Conscience," *Dictionnaire de Spiritualité*, vol. II (Paris, 1953), cols. 1548–1575; Gérard Gilleman, "Eros ou agapè, comment centrer la conscience chrétienne," *Nouvelle Revue Théologique* 72:3–26, 113–135 (1950).

[16] For a critique of such opinions based on theological principles, see Palazzine, pp. 217–275. Also, Jacques Leclercq, *Christ and the Modern Conscience* (New York, 1962), pp. 7–104.

It pertains to the objective, the conceptual, the essential order.

Conscience is the concrete judgment of the practical reason, made under the twofold influence of *synteresis,* about the moral goodness of a particular act. Conscience forms its judgment discursively from the objective principles of the moral order; but at the same time, there is also a direct connatural knowing process. The dictate of conscience is concrete, subjective, individual, and existential.

Conscience tells man what he should do. Man's "ought" follows from his "is." Man's actions must affirm his being. St. Paul makes Christian existence the foundation of Christian morality. The Christian is baptized into the death and resurrection of Christ. Consequently, he must die to self and walk in the newness of life (Rom. 6). Man's existence is a loving dependence on his God and a communion with his fellow men. Human endeavor must express this twofold personal relationship.

Conscience and human freedom are not completely autonomous. In practice man rejects the complete autonomy of conscience. In the eyes of the world Adolf Eichmann and the Nazis were guilty of crimes against humanity despite the plea of a clear conscience. Conscience must act in accord with the nature of man. The greatest possible freedom for man, the greatest possible happiness consists in the fulfillment of his own being.

The judgment of conscience expresses with regard to a particular act the fundamental tendency of man to truth and good. The basis of Christian morality, however, is not man's relation to an abstract principle, but to a person, *the* person, God. Since he first loved us, God has freely given us his love, his friendship, our salvation. Scripture uses the words faith and love (*pistis, agape*) to express man's acceptance and response to God's gift. Like Christ himself, man's external actions must manifest this love. At the same time man's actions dispose him to enter more intimately into the mystery of divine love. The ultimate norm of Christian conduct is this: What does the love of God demand of me in these concrete circumstances? Love, as a complete giving of self and not a mere emotion, seeks always the will of the beloved.

THE FORMATION OF CONSCIENCE

God speaks to us through the very existence he has given us: creation, salvation, our talents, abilities—and even weaknesses—and the existential circumstances of our situation. In other words, the will of the beloved is made known to us through his "laws"—the law of the Spirit, the natural law, positive law, and the law of the situation.[17]

The primary law of the new covenant is the internal law of the Spirit, the law of Christ, the law of love. Even Christ, however, found it necessary to express his law in external rules; but the demands are comparatively general, for example, the beatitudes.[18]

God also speaks to man through the human nature he has given him. The natural law, as theologians call it, is primarily a dynamic, internal law. Since it is the very law of man's existence and being, it has an absolute character.[19] Christ, at least implicitly, affirmed the value of the natural

[17] The word *law* is not a univocal term. Unfortunately, the coercive characteristic which essentially belongs to external positive law has been illegitimately transferred to the law of the Spirit and the natural law.

[18] Some of Christ's laws are materially determined and particular; for example, with regard to divorce, adultery, or even the thought of adultery. For an explanation of the general and more formal demands of Christ as the expression of a mentality or tendency rather than a determined material command, see C. H. Dodd, *Gospel and Law* (Cambridge, Eng., 1951), pp. 73–83.

[19] A good description of the natural law with regard to its internal and historical character as well as its relation to the law of Christ is given by J. Fuchs, *Le Droit Naturel: Essai Théologique* (Tournai, 1960).

law within the framework of the new covenant.[20] The law of nature is assumed into the law of Christ, for all nature was created according to the image of Christ and all nature exists for Christ.[21] From the first principle of the natural law, more objective, detailed rules of conduct are formulated.

Unfortunately, many Catholic theologians have exaggerated the natural law. It is not the primary law for the Christian. Some have succumbed to the temptation of using the natural law as a club. Others have overextended it in attempting to prove the moral certitude of mere hypotheses. Many still tend to codify completely the natural law and thus rob the natural law of its dynamic character.

Living in human society, the Christian is also the subject of human law, both civil and ecclesiastical. Such law is purely external and consequently seen as an infringement on human liberty. Since positive legislation is not absolute, it does not oblige when in conflict with the interest of the higher laws.

God has called each person by his own name. In one sense, every individual is unique; every concrete situation is unique. The Christian's answer to the divine call must respond to his individual circumstances.

Conscience is a supernaturally elevated subjective power of man. The law of Christ and the natural law are primarily internal laws. Why, then, is it necessary to have detailed, particular, external expressions of these laws? Why a code? Man's love of God is not yet perfect. Fallen human nature still experiences the tendency to self and not to God. Spiritual schizophrenia is a necessary characteristic of earthly

[20] Mt. 5:27–48; Mt. 19:3–12; Mt. 19:17–20; Mk. 7:20–23; Lk. 12:57.

[21] For Christ as the exemplar of all creation and nature, see Col. 1:15–20; 1 Cor. 8:6; Eph. 1:3–10. Theologians speak of Christ as the final cause of all creation because of the same texts as well as John 1:1–14 and 1 Cor. 3:22–23.

Christianity. Even the impulsive reaction of the human will of Christ was to avoid the sacrifice willed by his Father.[22] Love of God is by its nature a self-sacrificing love. Man in his present state cannot know perfectly what are the demands of love of God. Particular, external expressions of the law of love and natural law have a value only insofar as they point out the minimum and basic demands of the law of love. Code morality is not opposed to an ethic of love.[23]

External laws, if considered without any relation to the internal law, can be even an occasion of sin (Gal. 3:19; Rom. 5:20–21; 7:5–23). The external law is static and very incomplete. It does not and cannot express the totality of man's relationship to God. The vast majority of the decisions of conscience pertain to matters where there are no determined external expressions of law. Thus far we have not been speaking of the positive human laws which are primarily external. Here, too, self-sacrificing love of God and respect for the common good move man to obey positive law despite its inherent imperfections, unless such positive law runs counter to a higher law.

The formation and training of conscience include much more than the mere knowledge of external formulas of law. Insistence on external law is the haven of the insecure (neuroticism, scrupulosity) or the shallow (legalism, Phariseeism). Christian morality is ultimately love, an "I-thou" relationship between God and man. By meditating on true values, the Christian grows in wisdom and age and grace.

---

[22] Mt. 26:39. Theologians, interpreting the different acts of the will of Christ in this passage, distinguish between the *voluntas ut natura* and the *voluntas ut ratio*. Christ's human will impulsively shrank from suffering. He could accept suffering only insofar as he saw it as the will of his Father.

[23] For the Catholic, the *magisterium* or teaching function of the Church gives an authentic interpretation of Christian morality. Doctrinal and moral pronouncements constitute just one aspect of the teaching office of the Church. The whole Church in the lives of all members must bear living witness to the truth.

Likewise, the formation of conscience must take into consideration the findings of many of the positive sciences. For example, what purports to be religious obedience might in reality be the manifestation of an inferiority complex. Such a formation, joined with the virtue of prudence acquired in daily Christian experiences, prepares conscience to hear the call of God's love.

Time permits the mention of only two important characteristics of Christian conscience: communitarian and creative. A communitarian conscience recognizes man's relation with his fellow men in the kingdom of God. A communitarian conscience avoids excessive individualism and the opposite extreme of mass hypnosis. A creative conscience, attuned to the Spirit, throws off the shackles of stultifying legalism. A true Christian conscience leads man to make Christianity and Christian love "the light of the world and the salt of the earth"—a positive commitment to the kingdom of God in its reality both as the city of God and the city of man.

Reality is complex. The problems of conscience are complex. Frequently, there are no easy solutions. After prayerful consideration of all values involved, the Christian chooses what he believes to be the demands of love in the present situation. The Christian can never expect to have perfect, mathematical certitude about his actions. The virtue of humility preserves him from falling into the opposed extremes of introspective anxiety and mere formalism. Neurotic anxiety has no place in Christianity. Christianity is fundamentally a religion of joy—of man's participation in the joy and triumph of the resurrection. The paradox of Christianity is that joy comes through self-sacrificing love.

For the Christian who has made a commensurate effort to form his conscience correctly, the dictate of conscience is an infallible norm of conduct. Even though the action itself is not in objective conformity with the divine will, the Christian's conduct is pleasing to God, for it stems from a pure heart.[24]

The opposition that conscience experiences between Christian law and Christian freedom, between love and code morality, stems from man's imperfect love of God and wounded human nature. In reality, there is no dichotomy. The Christian law is the law of love—"the law of the Spirit, [giving] life in Christ Jesus, has delivered me from the law of sin and death" (Rom. 8:2). Conscience leads man to participate ever more deeply in Christian love and freedom until the Christian reaches his final destiny where love, joy, freedom, and conformity with God's will are one.

[24] During the probabilism controversy, antiprobabilists frequently cited the opinion of St. Bernard that a person following an erroneous conscience in good faith commits sin. Bernard's opinion stems from his mystical insistence on conscience as the voice of God. Consequently, any error or deviation can be attributed only to the bad will of man. Philippe Delhaye, *Le problème de la conscience morale chez S. Bernard* (Namur, 1957), especially pp. 44–45.

INTEGRITY OF HEART:
A COMMENT UPON
THE PRECEDING PAPER

PAUL L. LEHMANN

FATHER CURRAN has introduced his discussion of "The Problem of Conscience and the Twentieth-Century Christian" by remarking that "even a superficial reflection shows the existence of moral conscience." Let me, accordingly, begin by remarking that even a superficial reflection shows the *nonexistence* of moral conscience.

This reversal exhibits, on the face of it, a contradiction. But the contradiction would be misunderstood if it should be supposed that the inversion of Father Curran's remark were intended as a denial of it. Of course, a superficial reflection shows the existence of a moral conscience! But the same superficial reflection shows its nonexistence! The contradiction exposes a fundamental ambiguity inherent in the phenomenon of conscience. The ambiguity is that the conscience is neither as obvious nor as expendable as analysts of the conscience are inclined superficially—and even *axiomatically*—to suppose. Quite coincidentally, I learned this all over again this morning as I was leaving the hotel for the concluding section meeting of the Colloquium. While waiting for the elevator, my attention was arrested by voices which indicated a serious and vigorous conversation in progress. The speakers were invisible to me but appeared to belong to the hotel's maintenance staff. The point at issue was apparently a personal decision of some kind about which one of the speakers was voicing his uncertainty. Ad-

dressing himself to this perplexity, the other speaker de-
claimed: "I don't know whether you should drink or not.
All I know is that you should do what God and nature tell
you."

The tutelage from which this moral counsel has pro-
ceeded would scarcely be difficult to identify—especially
in these parts. However, lest it be supposed that this "grass
roots moral theology" is the fruit only of Roman Catholic
moral reflection and guidance, I hasten to add that if one
were to amend that corridor conversation by substituting
the word "Bible" for the word "nature," one could pass from
the ethical wisdom and unwisdom of Rome and Trent to the
ethical wisdom and unwisdom of Wittenberg, Geneva, and
Massachusetts Bay without detecting the slightest pruden-
tial or behavioral difference. The consciences of Catholics
and of Protestants alike have bogged down in the deadening
gap between the strident certainties claimed for moral insight and counsel and the daily occasions and responsibili-
ties of decision-making. "God and nature," or "God and the
Bible" have become bearers of moral clarity and guidance
as a "consummation devoutly to be wished," but in practice
"honored more in the breach than in the observance." As
Mr. G. K. Chesterton once put it in a different context but to
the same point—referring to his father and his grandfather,
he remarked: "As liberals they believed in progress; but as
honest men they often testified to deterioration."

In our time, then, the phenomenon of the conscience exhibits an ambiguity between precept and practice in the
actual process of decision-making which seriously calls into
question the enterprise of Moral Theology. If the discussions of this Colloquium had not conspicuously shown that
Christian candor and Christian fraternity are compatible, I
should have found myself drawing back from putting the
matter so forthrightly. Even so, I seem to myself both un-
gracious and ungrateful toward the discovery that at many

points of ethical analysis and on many specific ethical issues
Father Curran and I have been of like mind and on the same
side of the matter under debate. When a moral theologian
goes as far as Father Curran has, in the paper he has just
presented to us, toward a recognition of the perplexities of
conscience and of the need for a Moral Theology without
manuals (I hope I have not overextended his argument),
is it not intransigeant and merely arbitrary to turn aside
from such a demonstration of self-criticism and of reconstruction and to insist upon a shift of the discussion to quite
another context and to quite other grounds?

It will be understandable if, in the brief time allotted to
me, I forego fuller comment upon those matters which I
particularly appreciate in Father Curran's paper, or upon
the points of agreement between us. The purpose and spirit
of this Colloquium will be more appropriately served by
indicating as clearly and concisely as I can, what a shift of
the discussion of conscience to quite another context and to
quite other grounds involves. In a word, it involves the question whether Moral Theology can either adequately or properly deal with the ethical reality and function of conscience.
In my judgment, the answer to this question must be negative. The presuppositions, method, and conceptual distinctions which constitute the science of Moral Theology cannot exhibit the ethical reality of conscience or guide the
conscience in its function of giving ethical significance to
the making of decisions.

Moral Theology presupposes a view of grace and sin, of
nature and human nature, of being and virtue, and of the
role of reason in the determination of the good, of the good
will and of right actions which is fundamentally tangential
to the ambiguity of conscience to which we have alluded at
the outset. The tension between moral certainty and uncertainty is only one form of the persistent perplexity afflicting
the conscience in action. Mention may also be made of the

tension between freedom and obedience, between love and law, between a conscience tranquil in the assurance of forgiveness and a conscience tormented by conviction of sin. Father Curran has rightly noted these tensions and the corrections which they require of the tight and formal schematisms of the manuals of Moral Theology. But he has not sufficiently considered the fact that these tensions do not so much *pose* the problems of conscience which it is the task of "moral science" (to use his phrase) to clarify and correlate as *expose* the strain upon a faculty of judgment which can never forge a functional ethical bond between the *directional requirements* and the *complexities* of decision-making. The gap between the ethical claim and the ethical act, or between ethical integrity and ethical disobedience is the persistent perplexity afflicting the conscience. So long as the conscience is understood as a faculty of judgment, however sanctified and enlightened a faculty of judgment, this perplexity cannot be escaped. A remark of Sigmund Freud about Immanuel Kant goes to the root of this perplexity and may be extended to include the enterprise of Moral Theology as a whole. "The philosopher Kant," Freud declared, "once remarked that two things continually reassured him of the existence of God: the starry heavens above and the moral conscience within us. The stars are unquestionably superb. But where conscience is concerned, God seems to have been guilty of an uneven and a careless piece of work." (I have quoted from memory.) One can only welcome the lengths to which Father Curran goes in the direction of a nonmanualistic, more adequately personalistic analysis of the nature and function of conscience by moral theologians. Yet the ambivalence of his own language, moving as it does between Scripture and Reason, between covenant-relation and "first cause" and "the mediation of law," between "charity" and "*synteresis*," suggests the enormous tenacity of the conceptual apparatus which produced

the manuals of moral theology and the virtual impossibility
within that context of giving ethical reality to conscience.

Suppose, however, that we took the Scriptures as seriously as Father Curran evidently wishes to do. What pros-
pects for giving ethical reality to conscience would be open
to us? The covenant tradition, the prophets, and Jesus and
Paul seem to exhibit another way of getting at the ethical
reality of conscience. This is evident from a not unimportant semantic consideration, namely, that the Scriptures as
a whole make conspicuously little use of the word "conscience" and speak instead of the "heart." This semantic
variation is not a distinction without a difference. It is a
sign of a quite different way of looking at decision-making
and of understanding what is ethically real. The stress now
falls upon the activity of God in creating, sustaining, and
redeeming a human community of God's choosing and of
God's perfecting. The stress falls upon a total personal response, "from the heart," not primarily through a faculty of
judgment, but to what God is doing in the world to make
and to keep human life human. What is ethically real is
what gives and sustains and fulfills the human shape of
human life. This is what God is doing, what man is called
to do. God's doing, by word and act, provides for man's
doing, by word and act, a context within which the directional requirements and the complexities of decision-making
can be meaningfully conjoined. In this context, the conscience is fundamentally not a faculty of judgment but a
living personal bond between God and man and neighbor.
This bond is at once the focal point of sensitivity to what is
human and the spring of all right action.

Thus, the ethical reality of conscience is, in a striking
phrase of Calvin's, "nothing other than inward integrity of
heart." When the heart, or with Calvin we may now also say
"conscience," is free from all "the righteousness of the law"
—whether natural or moral, rational or juridical—then, the

heart is open to and ready for the doing, on earth as it is in heaven, of the will of God. Then, all things, whether goods and services, circumstances and needs, science, culture, and politics, become instrumental to the knowledge of God and the service of God, whose service is "perfect freedom."

This means, I suppose, that ultimately ethics is more akin to art than to metaphysics. For the price which metaphysics pays for its admirable clarification and ordering of the conceptual description of the nature of reality, of virtue and of obligation, is loss of sensitivity to what is concretely and fundamentally human. Art, on the other hand, is the province of sensitivity both to nature and to man where what is concretely and fundamentally human is continually taking shape and being reshaped. Since ethics is concerned with the human shape of reality, it continues to depend upon art for the nourishment of sensitivity to light and shade, to form and configuration; and, in turn, to nourish art with the human substance of its creativity. The biblical context within which conscience acquires its ethical integrity is confirmed in artistic creativity as an alternative to the noble inadequacy of the enterprise of moral theology.

THE ECUMENICAL MOVEMENT: A LAYMAN'S VIEW

NATHAN M. PUSEY

I T M A K E S me very happy that Harvard could provide a setting for this Roman Catholic-Protestant Colloquium. A university such as this must necessarily, at this point in cultural development, be a secular institution, but the word "secular" does not need to be used in a pejorative sense. As I use it, I mean only that Harvard cannot belong to any one group, denomination, or church—certainly not that Harvard is hostile to, or would exclude religion. Although the Harvard Divinity School exists within a secular university, it is itself a Protestant theological school. Similarly, in the Harvard Memorial Church the services of Protestant worship continue an unbroken tradition of more than 300 years going back to our founding.

We are a secular institution because we now have within our community not only a great variety of Protestants, but many Roman Catholics, many Jews of differing beliefs, some Orthodox Christians, at least a few Muslims, Hindus, and Buddhists, a great multitude of agnostics and, I suspect, at least a few avowed atheists. Under such circumstances, I am sure you will agree that the modern university's discarding or outgrowing secularism must wait upon an advance in ecumenicity enormously beyond anything yet achieved or even dreamed to be feasible. But at the same time it makes the modern university an unusually favorable site for discussions like these.

I am not only happy that Harvard could provide a setting for the Colloquium. I am also profoundly grateful to all of you who came here from other places and from another tradition, charitably and thoughtfully, to make this encounter possible. We have learned through your kindness; we are grateful for your many contributions; and we have come to like you. We are grateful to Cardinal Cushing for his ready acknowledgment of the value of such a meeting, and for all he has done with characteristic kindliness and industry, not only to make the gathering possible, but to contribute to its success.

We are especially grateful to Cardinal Bea, that great and endearing statesman of his Church, whose quick mind and whose zestful and loving spirit have been an inspiration to us all. As thoughtless of self as an early Apostle, he has come a far journey to bring us a hopeful message of new life which we have long needed to hear. There can be no question that he will remain in our memories. It is our prayer that his message will also remain and contribute to be a guide to us.

Dean Miller asked me as a member of the Central Committee of the World Council of Churches to say something tonight about the ecumenical movement as a Protestant layman sees it. I interpret this assignment less as an invitation than as a command—and here I am. I hope the Lord will forgive me, for I am surely a layman among the learned!

I begin with a show of learning from my past. For the classical Greeks the word "oikumene" meant the inhabited as opposed to the physical world. The term described the world where people lived—or, to be strictly honest, the narrower world where *Greek* people lived. The non-Greeks, the barbarians, apparently were not quite people. Later the Romans used a similar term to signify "the Roman world," though this, as they developed it, came to be a very big world indeed. Only slowly, and in the minds of but a few, did the idea take on wider applicability.

Today as we use the word, it has a religious connotation. But it still needs stretching because, for example, you Roman Catholics have your ecumenical movement, and we Protestants have ours. However, the Colloquium offers a clear indication that already at least a few from both camps (Is it wrong to use the word "camp" when we are talking about a cold war which has endured for 400 years?) are beginning to wonder if these movements can not only grow strong each in itself but also, at the same time, come together in some wider, more creative association. Archbishop Temple, thinking in these broader terms, said of the ecumenical movement that it was "the great new fact of our time."

The formative old facts of our time have now become painfully apparent to everyone. The worldwide spread of the industrial revolution based on the advance of science and technology has engendered everywhere a deep yearning for social change and economic development. We have seen everywhere a need for stable governments and at the same time too frequent inability of peoples to secure or maintain such governments. With the end of western colonialism there has been a resurgence of nationalism followed by the flounderings of newly independent peoples (nearly a billion of them) living in woeful political immaturity. Add to these the population explosion, the fear of a new economic colonialism, the spread of subversion and distrust and the consequent destruction of open societies, the polarization of power between East and West, the development of monstrous new weapons of war, and the intensification of the danger of conflict. And along with these unhappy trends there has been a continuing displacement of refugees and migrations of peoples, oppression of the weak by the strong, callous treatment of those who are not of our kind, and continuation of the age-old blights of poverty, hunger, ignorance, and disease, not least of mental disease. Yet at the same time there has been a vast hungering for learning—or for the fruits of learning.

The new fact in all this, Archbishop Temple tells us, is the ecumenical movement, which is perhaps nothing other than a fresh, vivid renewal of awareness that the Church is involved in all of life—that the Church is relevant, and that it has an inescapable responsibility, opportunity, and possibility within itself. My task this evening is to say something about what this movement means to me.

In the Protestant world the ecumenical movement goes back to a meeting in Edinburgh in 1910, but my own experience in the movement is rather recent in origin. I first heard about it in the years right after World War II, when I came on the booklet "Man's Disorder and God's Design," which had been prepared as a working paper for the First Assembly of the World Council of Churches held in Amsterdam in 1948.

By a combination of circumstances I found myself a delegate of my church at the Second Assembly held in Evanston, in 1954. One episode from that meeting stands out in my memory. This was the righteous indignation, indeed the anger, shown by an African bishop who rose in the assembly to denounce the condition of the Church which permitted three pitifully small competing denominational churches to stand at a crossroads in a single destitute African village, each professing to offer to the hungry and bewildered Africans an inclusive way to salvation, professing in a cacophony of voices, and with little awareness of the villagers' true need, to be speaking in the Lord's name.

At that Assembly I was elected a member of the World Council's Central Committee and, having been re-elected in Delhi, have been a member ever since. What I know of the ecumenical movement I have learned from this experience, owing much for my instruction to the friends I have made there from many lands and churches.

The ecumenical movement appears to me to be first of all a stirring, a quickening, a renewal of life within the churches. It incorporates a fresh and heightened sense that in some fashion the Christian Church must not only be relevant, but to be this, must also be one in Christ, that back of all our divisions there is *the* Christian Church, a universal Church which has work to do, and that we can be fully Christians only as we become part of that Church. There is no group of us in which there does not exist a troubled awareness of the deep need to understand how this might be so, and a feeling that we must do what we can to make it so. There is also a fresh realization that we are all of us, the whole people of God, priests and laity alike, responsible ministers in every aspect of the Church's work. At another level we have also been coming to see, our vision here stimulated by the great cultural developments of our time, that the Church's place is neither here nor there, on this continent or on that, or with this class and not that, but with all peoples everywhere.

The vision that has broken upon us afresh in this century is nothing less than one of the whole inhabited globe, and of every association of people within it, of the whole human family, as both actually and potentially the Household of God. With this has come a sense of shame that our actions have been so seriously out of joint with this deepest purpose of our existence, and a dawning realization that, in our complacencies and self-righteous assurances, not only have we done little to advance the Kingdom of God but that, professing to act in Jesus' name, we have actually done much to thwart it.

Cardinal Bea has done well to remind us that if this vision which now quickens us to new life is to be productive of any lasting good, we shall need to be clear in our minds, as well as on fire in our hearts. In time, probably over a long span of time, we shall need to work down beneath the fellowship to a more precise understanding of the nature of that fellowship which in any acceptable sense can be called the Church.

It seems to me that virtually everyone who has spoken in this Colloquium has been aware of, and has emphasized the difficulty of this task. It cannot be a question of simply retracing steps, of running away from our separations, of pretending they do not exist, never occurred, or are not important. Such childish avoidance of trouble and difficulty cannot offer an acceptable solution, even if it were possible. Rather we must struggle forward from where we are—out of the horribly uncomfortable thickets where we find ourselves to paths and trails which will lead to major related avenues, and, hopefully, finally to the one broad highway defined by our Lord, where we can be one and live together in unity and love. In time it seems to me this must be seen to be a highway not only for Catholics and Protestants, and the Orthodox; somehow there will have to be found there a place also for Muslims and Jews, and for Hindus, Buddhists and all the rest, not by denial of the faith or by watering it down, or by eroding it, but, in the Lord's time, by understanding it more deeply and accepting it more widely.

In the summer of 1954 Lesslie Newbigin, then Bishop in Madura, South India, gave a speech at the University of Chicago in which he spoke of "The Household of God." I should like here to paraphrase and quote freely from that important and moving speech. Bishop Newbigin began by saying that within India the notion that all religions are in essence one has become almost an axiom of thought. He expressed sympathy with this development, saying that, when one remembers both the evils that have been inflicted upon India by the strife of religious communities and the terrible sterility of the purely secular education which has been imparted in government schools, one can be moved by this noble effort to teach the rising generation a universal, nonsectarian religion.

We do not need to go to India to encounter this attitude of mind, the desire to find a faith above all little, partial faiths. It is very well known in the West.

But though Bishop Newbigin could understand why people in India hoped to find a suprafaith, he did not commend the effort. Rather he was using the fact to make clear an essential truth about Christianity. He was saying that the attempt to lose oneself in mystical union with the Ultimate, in a separated and segregated region above the turmoil and struggle of this world, is not an acceptable path for a Christian. He was trying, with all the force he could command, to make clear what he takes to be the essential inescapable this-worldly character of Christianity. "So God loved *the world* that he gave his only begotten Son to the end that all that believe in him should not perish but have everlasting life." Bishop Newbigin said there is an irreconcilable difference between Christianity and Hinduism (and by implication then between Christianity and any religion that would try to escape the conflicts of culture by turning away from those conflicts). His point was that this difference turns on "whether we regard the multiplicity and change which characterize human life as a mere veil which has to be torn away (or avoided) in order that we may have access to ultimate reality, or whether we regard them as the place where we are to meet with and know and serve the divine purpose." In the Christian view it is in this Household of God, the world of men—a world of all men—that we are "*to meet with* and *know* and *serve* the divine purpose."

If we accept this view of the world, we shall not despair of our pluralisms, but rather welcome the challenge that lies precisely in the midst of them (in family, society, city, state and church) and know that, if we are obedient, it is in the midst of these that we must endeavor to find, or be willing to be found *of*, God. What Christianity demands is not a leap into togetherness, but the creation of community. For this there are no short cuts. As Cardinal Bea has said, it will require a long and difficult, and perhaps we should add recurring, effort of mind and will.

In sum, stated succinctly, what the ecumenical movement seems to me to be trying to do is to call all of us to more Christ-centered lives. He who has brought us together here, He who, we believe, will draw us more closely together with the passage of time, is the Lord Jesus Christ. It is our conviction, in the words of another, that "His vicarious death on a lonely hill contains the power to create a community of men from every tribe and tongue and nation and people."

The Third Assembly of the World Council of Churches was held in the autumn of 1961 in New Delhi. Its theme was "Jesus Christ, the Light of the World." I gather this theme was chosen at least in part because of the extraordinary significance that has always been attached to the word "light" in virtually all religions, including those of the East. Adherents of many religions would agree with the statement of the John of the Epistles (1 John 1:5) when he said, "This is the message we have heard from him and proclaim to you, that God is light and in him is no darkness at all." It was the purpose of Delhi to suggest to any who cared to listen that Jesus Christ is that light, and that it is open to all men.

A preliminary paper circulated before Delhi sought to say something helpful about Jesus Christ as Light, and about our need for him, by setting him over against the familiar darkness of our world. (I did not note, and I do not know, the author of the following passage, but I should like to introduce it here.) "When the Church chooses to witness more wholeheartedly to Jesus Christ as the Light, it will discover more fully the shape of the darkness. The boundary between the two realities does not coincide with the line between Christians and non-Christians. It does not follow the frontier between one religion and all others. It does not support the cultural chasm between a Christian West and a non-Christian East. It does not recognize the various curtains which anxious societies stretch around their borders. Then where is the line between light and darkness?

"The answer is given by the very presence of *The Light.* He came to his own and his own received him not. His light meets this darkness most sharply in that terribly public spot named Golgotha. Darkness is here defined. It is what blinds men to his presence. It is the self-righteous hate or the in-turned love which cannot accept his out-turned love. It is the passion for power and wealth which sees in his cross the most terrible weakness and poverty. It is the exclusiveness of men who think that the world should belong to them because they represent the right ancestry, the elite class, the strongest nation, the holiest religion. It is the fear which sees in death the end of hope. It is the utopian dream of security for the few and the cynical assurance of doom for all. Such darkness cannot tolerate the invasion of such a Light. When the Light defines darkness in this way it cuts through the false securities of the world . . . From the cross the Light shines with a pitiless glare upon our divisions and antipathies."

It appears that an understanding of that Light must be won anew in each generation—in some sense, anew, again and again, in each human heart. The ecumenical movement represents a growing and a widening recognition of this truth of our existence.

It has been a great joy to be able to begin to talk about this matter here this year with our Roman Catholic brethren. A learned Presbyterian friend of mine once said, "Our time is one of God's springtimes." Let us hope that it may be so. But for our part, it seems to this one Protestant layman (as I am now more confident than ever before it does also to many Roman Catholic friends), that it is our role, while we wait upon His mercy, to endeavor to be guided by Cardinal Bea's wise injunction, "to practice the truth in love; and so grow in all things, in Him who is the Head, Christ."

THE SEMINAR DISCUSSION SUMMARIES

SEMINAR I. BIBLICAL STUDIES:
RECORD AND INTERPRETATION*

Promptly at 9 a.m. on the morning of March 28, 1963, approximately forty-five Roman Catholic and Protestant scholars sat down together behind tables arranged in a large square within the Braun Room of Harvard Divinity School. It was immediately apparent that a majority of the group were acquainted with one another. We had met on previous occasions in meetings of learned societies; some had participated in joint projects; the two American members, one Catholic and one Protestant, of the international group preparing the Dead Sea Scrolls for publication were present. All were acquainted with one another's books and articles on biblical subjects. The chairman, Professor Stendahl, took special note of this fact, for it marked a difference between our seminar and the others. In the area of biblical study ecumenical discussion at a scholarly level is already far advanced. The barriers have been down for some time, and we met as friends who did not need to be overly self-conscious of our differences.

Catholic biblical scholars have often pointed to *Divino Afflante Spiritu, Encyclical Letter of Pope Pius XII on the Promotion of Biblical Studies* (1943), as having provided the encouragement and the charter of freedom to engage actively in all forms of textual, exegetical, and historical re-

---

* The writer was greatly aided in the preparation of this chapter by his colleague, Krister Stendahl, who was Chairman of the Seminar, by David M. Stanley, S.J., of the State University of Iowa, and by two Harvard graduate students, S. Dean McBride, Jr., and Roy B. Ward, Jr. They took careful notes of the proceedings in the seminar and prepared digests from each day's discussions. These have been of very substantial assistance in giving precision to memory.

search. An examination of the successive issues of the *Cath-olic Biblical Quarterly* since that time provides eloquent testimony to the extraordinary development in the range, quality, and amount of scholarly work being done. The rapid growth in the number of well-trained teachers of Scripture in Catholic educational institutions is equally well marked. While to Protestants *Humani Generis, En-cyclical Letter of Pope Pius XII Concerning Some False Opinions Which Threaten to Undermine the Foundations of Catholic Doctrine* (1950), appears to condemn the very biblical work which *Divino Afflante Spiritu* had encouraged, it has by no means been so interpreted in Catholic biblical circles. To be sure, there are those who do not wholly ap-prove of the modern biblical movement, but the same situa-tion exists in Protestantism. Gregory Baum, O.S.A., in his address at the Colloquium mentioned a pamphlet, entitled "Rationalism and Catholic Exegesis," which was circulated among all the bishops of the Ecumenical Council in Rome in October 1962. It tried to show that the work of biblical scholars was, in effect, "denying the historicity of the divine events of salvation."[1] Yet the profound effect which the biblical movement has had on the Roman Catholic Church was made clear in the Ecumenical Council during the frank and critical debate on the schema concerned with Scripture and Tradition.[2] Cardinal Bea is reported to have com-mented on the original draft of the schema that it contained many references "to the scripture scholars; yet there was only one favorable mention—all the rest were held suspect." It was his judgment, however, that the schema was the work of a particular group and "not what the better theologians today think."[3]

Protestants, for their part, are somewhat too comfortably

[1] See pages 71–90 for the address of Father Baum.
[2] *Ibid.*, page 78.
[3] See Xavier Rynne, *Letters from Vatican City* (New York, 1963), p. 149.

aware that the development of modern historical criticism is something for which they and their ancestors have been responsible. As one of the seminar participants put it, biblical historical criticism is the product ultimately of the Protestant Reformation and of the period of the Enlightenment.[4] Rejecting many things in the Roman Catholic Church which were felt to be accretions not to be found in the Bible, Protestants affirmed the principle of *sola scriptura*: that is, what is essential to the Church is to be derived from Scripture alone.[5] Yet what actually happened in the multiplication of Protestant divisions is that *sola scriptura* came to mean Scripture as interpreted in a given Church tradition. In the course of time, the variety of faith and order in the churches finally raised the question as to what the Bible actually taught. If Scripture stands over the Church, then it also stands over these traditions in interpretation. The vast literary and historical effort, together with the archaeological recovery of the biblical world, has meant a greatly increased accuracy in the interpretation of biblical literature within its own time, its own historical context, and its own geography. This is now providing a ground for unity and a checkrein on divisive tendencies. No one Christian group can now claim that its teaching and polity are *the* system taught in Scripture. The historical study of the Bible is taking us behind Protestant provincialism, behind the Reformation itself, and behind the medieval and patristic developments. For this reason it plays a reconciling role, not only between Protestants and Catholics, but also between Christians and Jews. The fact that this new avenue has its roots in secular historical sciences does not make it less significant for the ecumenical movement. It, nevertheless, faces Christians with the fact that it is not only Christ as he is known in the churches but secular research outside the

---

[4] See the paper of W. D. Davies, pages 110–151.
[5] See the address of James M. Robinson, pages 91–109.

churches which has supplied us with one strong incentive to new *rapprochement.*

With regard to the actual state of Roman Catholic biblical study, a member of the seminar said that in archaeology and the ancillary sciences, and in textual criticism, Catholic scholarship was making important contributions. As for exegetical work, the French series, *Etudes Bibliques,* and the recently completed *La Sainte Bible* (well known as the *Bible de Jérusalem*) are very significant. In English, however, much is to be done because one can point to scarcely a single Catholic exegetical work of exceptional merit. For some time, the speaker continued, he personally had been urging that a start be made on something important, even if it were only concerned with the briefest of biblical books, such as Jude or James! Catholic Scripture teachers were abreast of Protestant exegetical work. He did not think, however, that the reverse was true. Here and there one could indeed point to important Catholic contributions to individual problems, totally bypassed or overlooked in, for example, many of the articles in the recent *Interpreter's Dictionary of the Bible* (1962).

This remark triggered a discussion which involved the central issue before the group during its three morning discussions. An author of one of the articles mentioned in the *Interpreter's Dictionary* who was present readily admitted his failure and stated that in the future Protestants generally would have to pay far closer attention to Catholic work. Yet he wondered whether some slight excuse might be offered by the feeling of unreality he has repeatedly experienced about some Catholic exegetical work. An article will begin at a given point, survey in great detail the various views and issues being held and discussed, and then return to the same point at which it began. To an outsider this seems to be "going through the motions" of scholarship, rather than arriving at results based on the investigation itself. This raised

the question as to the freedom of the Catholic scholar in relation to the authority of the Church.

The following summary of the discussions during the
three-day period is arranged roughly according to the order
of their discussion, the first two items being treated on the
first day. The repetition of topics, as the conversation returned to them from different perspectives, will be noted.

I. THE FREEDOM OF
THE BIBLICAL SCHOLAR

The question of the freedom of the biblical scholar was
undoubtedly uppermost in the minds of the Protestants
present. This, of course, was occasioned by their impression
of the authoritarian nature of the Catholic Church. Can
freedom of scholarly inquiry exist if limits are set in advance
as to what may or may not be discovered as historical
"truth"? During the lengthy discussion of this question the
following impressions emerged:

(1) Catholic scholars by no means felt impeded in their
exegetic and historical work by the Church's dogma.

(2) Indeed, it is possible that Protestants do not really
understand the actual working of the Catholic Church and
its conception of authority.

(3) It is certainly clear that Protestant scholars have
often been inclined to forget their own involvement in, and
limitation by, theological, philosophical, and cultural currents, and by less formalized but equally restricting pressures of their churches.

(4) The historical method itself has had a history and
an intimate involvement with philosophical and theological
presuppositions.

(5) Protestants today have generally become far more
aware of, and articulate about, Church tradition. The
Church's scholarship, while insisting on its freedom to use
the historical method in investigating Scripture, neverthe-

less labors within a context of commitment to the Church and to a given Church tradition.

In one presentation in the seminar a Catholic scholar, after an analysis of the current state of biblical study in his Church, said that Catholic exegesis tends toward "middle-of-the-road" positions on most issues and could not be said generally to be adventuresome. In New Testament study, for example, it was more inclined to the views of C. H. Dodd and Vincent Taylor in England and of Oscar Cullmann and Joachim Jeremias in Germany than to the type of position espoused by Rudolf Bultmann and his followers. In Old Testament study it was more inclined on the whole to the positions espoused by W. F. Albright and his students than to those at the center of discussion in Germany today. The reasons for this were threefold:

(1) Catholics hold to a strong belief in the inerrancy and inspiration of Scripture. This does not mean that there is no human element in the Bible or that there are no mistakes in the transmission of tradition, but it does affirm that Scripture is of divine origin. Precisely how God is to be understood as the author of the Bible, or how inspiration is to be defined, is difficult to articulate. Yet to state that there is some truth in the term "inerrancy" is to affirm a special relation of God and Scripture, even when that relation is difficult to formulate.

(2) Roman Catholic biblical scholarship feels a responsibility to theology. Dogma in the Roman Catholic Church serves a negative function by preventing certain types of "adventurism." Implicit in this assertion is faith in God as the God of history. Consequently, the dogmatic position as developed in history can serve as a guide and as a corrective. It does not, however, close off exegesis from fresh understandings, nor does it impel scholars to read the fully developed doctrines of the later Church back into the New Testament.

(3) There is a special concern for the "salvific" value, the saving truth to be found in Scripture for our day. In Catholic thought it is the Church which "demythologizes" Scripture, that is, which translates the Gospel into terms and forms which are meaningful for today. The Church as a whole, in its life and worship, in its sacraments and liturgy, makes the transfer between an ancient literature and modern life. Liturgy thus forms a guiding factor in exegesis. In the context of this definite commitment to the Church, its life and its teaching, however, one could not say that respect for tradition actually constitutes a controlling factor in exegesis. An examination of the best Catholic work would reveal a real objectivity in historical exegesis.

Discussion of the question of freedom in commitment promptly elicited from many of the Protestant participants the observation that they continually face a similar problem of relating historical scholarship to dogmatics. No man can divorce himself from the past or from his commitments. History has within it both continuity and discontinuity, and the historian himself is involved in both. While it is common to consider theology and history as entirely separate disciplines, reflection will indicate that they are always involved in each other, and can be considered as separable only within the "faculties of the soul." On the one hand, there is the commitment to a specific historical method. Yet this commitment will always be in dialogue with our philosophical and theological commitments, so that method and meaning must be seen to be related and continually facing and interacting with each other.

At one point in the discussion it was noted that both Protestant and Roman Catholic exegesis not infrequently failed to recognize the critical distance between the Scripture and ourselves, that is, the critical function of the Scripture to which we are subject. A proposal was then made for a critical study of the Bible which consciously rejects the aim of making the material relevant. The objection to this supposedly "liberated" approach to exegesis was quite general in the group. It was simply that historical work without presuppositions is not possible.[6] Nevertheless, there is a sense in which the interpreter must attempt to disentangle the descriptive task of expounding what an ancient writer believed and said from the authority which his words had subsequently and should have today. Descriptive study is possible because of common tools with which to work. These have enabled common discourse, not only between Roman Catholic and Protestant scholars, but also between both and agnostics.

II. THE PROBLEM OF
EVENT AND INTERPRETATION

The discussion, having begun with a Protestant's query as to how a member of an authoritarian Church could be free to do critical biblical research, thus ended with a general consensus that freedom within the context of commitment was a common problem to all. At that point the conversation turned to one facet of the question concerning the authority of Scripture.

The initial presentation of a Roman Catholic biblical scholar had referred to the special problem now existing as to the manner in which the Bible's authority is to be acknowledged and stated. No small part of the history of the Church has had to do with the interpretation and proclamation of the Gospel, together with an exposition of what it means and implies in the idiom of a given age. During the past century and a half, the development of the discipline of history in the Western world has had a radical effect on the human mind, and upon how we look at life. Classical

---

[6] One member of the group at this point recalled a work with the following title: "An Unbiased History of the Civil War from a Southern Point of View"!

Christian theology was developed in a world whose reality was considered to be an unchanging rational structure. Abstract concepts evolved through logical procedures could expound and interpret such a reality, and particulars could be given order within the framework of the whole. Christianity could thus be presented as a system of doctrine which was capable of rational defense. Today we are inclined to say that we know little about human life or institutions unless we know their past, the story of how they came to be what they now are. This story is full of variety, of change, and movement. It is not easily systematized or treated in an abstract manner.

In this atmosphere the modern movement in biblical theology has been emphasizing the event-character of the biblical revelation. In the Scriptures God's manner of revealing himself has not been through a system of "truths," but in and through historical happenings which are understood and confessed to have a special religious character. Indeed, biblical worship centered in a "kerygma," in the proclamation of God's mighty acts which were seen as the creative center of the history of Israel and the nascent Church. Current biblical study, in its emphasis upon history, has thus been much concerned with the biblical interpretation of earthly events as revealing the divine activity, on the one hand, and on biblical literature as deriving from a community whose worship celebrated this activity, on the other.

The initial speaker, in describing Catholic exegesis as possessing a "middle of the road" character, referred to this situation when he spoke of the current emphasis on the acts of God as creating a theological problem, unless it is emphasized that there was always a community, a congregation who saw, heard, and interpreted. The Exodus of Israel from Egypt was God's event of salvation, but there is also the community which confesses it as such. The resurrection of Christ as God's event implies a voice of interpretation in the worshipping community. "The God who speaks interprets the God who acts."[7] On the other hand, most Catholic exegetes disagree with the position of the great German New Testament scholar, Rudolf Bultmann, in his skepticism as to whether we can actually get behind the kerygma of the early Church to the person of Jesus of Nazareth. The time span covered by the oral tradition between the death of Jesus and the writings of the Apostle Paul and the four Gospels is too short to make possible an assumption that all that we have about Jesus was the creation of the worshipping community. Furthermore, a Catholic would affirm divine guidance of the early disciples so that the development of the early Church can be affirmed as under the guidance of the Holy Spirit. Thus, the interpretation of Jesus' parables as given in the Gospels can be received as normative by the Church.

With these affirmations, a majority of those present, Protestants as well as Catholics, were generally agreed. A Protestant scholar, however, suggested that difficulties begin when modern scholarship discovers that there is quite often more than one level of interpretation present in the Scriptures. Close study of a given parable, for example, may reveal that various interpretations have been given it, and that the final context for it in the written Gospel was surely not the original interpretation of the parable as intended by Jesus. Which level of meaning is normative for the Church?

The discussion of this problem revealed that a simple answer was impossible, and that suggestions toward a perspective did not divide along confessional lines. The following are among the remarks advanced to the problem:

(1) Historical research in uncovering background ma-

---

[7] An intentional word play on the title of a series of lectures by G. Ernest Wright, *God Who Acts, Biblical Theology as Recital*, Studies in Biblical Theology, no. 8 (London and Chicago, 1952).

terial has rediscovered many lost meanings so that we have found what was then obvious to the people who heard the parables. By historical means we have advanced farther in the attempt to distinguish the original from the subsequent interpretation(s).

(2) In modern scholarship there has been a primitivistic tendency, so that the nearer one gets to the original, the more authoritative it should be assumed to be.

(3) This can be defended theologically on the basis of the dogma of the Incarnation. The more authoritative interpretation is that of Jesus himself when that can be determined.

(4) Yet one cannot dismiss the interpretation(s) of the canonical Gospels as irrelevant or unimportant. Different periods tend to stress different aspects of the biblical variety of materials because of the changing needs and circumstances of the Church. So it was in the time when the Gospels took form, and so it has been ever since.

(5) On the basis of the dogma of the inspiration of Scripture, one could claim that later canonical interpretations are of equal value with the original since they are divinely guided. The attempt to use only the original tends to lose sight of the wide relevancy of the material.

(6) Perhaps the parables of Jesus are not the best example in Scripture of the point at issue. One can certainly point to various levels of interpretation of the great events in the Old Testament. In different situations different facets of meaning within an event may be found important. The great events have, as it were, a "field of meaning" adhering to them, so that they are a rich resource whose meaning is never exhausted. Consequently, no one "interpretation" can be said "to be on the same level" as the event which gives rise to it. The event as so conceived is original and serves as the guide to, and critic of, its interpretations. The apostolic community was concerned first of all in proclaim-

ing the whole event of Jesus Christ, and not simply his words.

(7) The New Testament's interpretation of the Old Testament is accepted as valid, but one does not thereby downgrade the meaning of the Old Testament in its own right. The New Testament does not swallow up the meaning of the Old, but the latter as "the cradle of Christ" belongs to the interpretation of the Christ-event.[8]

This discussion may be considered an illustration of the difficulty of pinpointing precise historical layers or levels for precise definitions of infallible authority. The vitality and movement of the biblical sense of reality resists overly rigid restriction in formulae. In general, it seemed to be agreed within the group that there have been primitivistic tendencies which deny the historical dialogue between and among the levels of interpretation and which falsely may set up an antithesis between Jesus and the Church.

III. THE EFFECT OF SCRIPTURAL STUDY ON THE AUTHORITATIVE STRUCTURE OF THE CHURCH

The question of the authoritarian structure of the Roman Catholic Church continued to trouble the Protestants. If the structure is fixed and authoritative, how can the work of the biblical scholar have any real effect upon it? At one point in this discussion, one of the Roman Catholic participants, the first ordained Catholic scholar to be appointed to the religion department of a state university in this country, told of the situation in his school where his Protestant colleague was by no means as free as he wished to be. As a Roman Catholic the speaker said that he could and did teach in much the same manner as his Presbyterian colleague. He experienced no difficulty, and his sense of free-

[8] See further, for example, Bernhard Anderson, ed., *The Old Testament and the Christian Church* (New York, 1963).

dom was complete. His colleague, on the other hand, was continually encountering criticism from conservative students with regard to his views, perhaps because they felt more threatened by one in their own tradition. In this case, therefore, the Protestant was definitely limited by an authoritative structure.

The opening paper on the second day by a Protestant scholar[9] pointed to several areas of discovery which have brought Protestant scholars to somewhat different standpoints from those traditionally held by certain Protestant denominations:

(1) Critical study has brought to Protestants an awareness of the discipline and order which characterized the structure of the Early Church. The image of the New Testament Church as an unstructured, gathered congregation, ruled solely by the Spirit without conscious structure, has had to be revised.[10]

(2) The rediscovery of the role of "law" in the Old Testament and in primitive Christianity has necessarily modified the emphasis on nonlegalistic aspects of Pauline theology. Indeed, the speaker, having been asked to take one topic

---

[9] See the paper of W. D. Davies on pages 110–151.

[10] A classic depiction of the Early Church as a completely charismatic community without the normal structures of law and organization is given by Rudolf Sohm in his *Kirchenrecht* (Leipzig, 1892). He attempted to show how the Catholic Church emerged with precisely the opposite form wherein the charismatic was completely replaced by a formal, legalized structure, and the spiritual "kingship" of Christ was externalized into the authoritarian monarchical organization of the Roman Church. It is now recognized, of course, that the role of law and authority is far greater and more complex in the Bible than such a view assumes, though it has been commonly held by the "low church" branches, or "gathered congregations," of Protestantism. The writer has attempted to show that the role of the Spirit in the New Testament, as in the Old, is more of a "political" than a "spiritual" concept. It marks the fulfillment of eschatological expectations which had their rootage in the pre-monarchic conception of Divine *government* in Israel, wherein God ruled directly, the Spirit being his agent for accomplishing his will *within* human beings: see G. Ernest Wright, *The Rule of God* (Garden City, N.Y., 1960), ch. vi.

and to explore it with exegetical depth, held that "law and tradition" in the Pauline epistles can be shown to derive from both the person and the teaching of Jesus. These were Paul's authority and they became for him what the law was for Judaism. Thus, while "justification by faith" was indeed a dominant motif in Pauline teaching, it should not be taken to exclude an understanding of the Christian as under the "law of Christ."

(3) The Protestant's opposition of Scripture and Church cannot be justified in the overly simplified manner in which it has often been attempted. The canon itself was formed by the Church as an expression of the faith of the Christian community.

Protestants, therefore, have gone too far in citing the Apostle Paul in order to deny the Catholic emphasis on the authority of the Church. In many ways Paul exercised the authority of a bishop over a number of Christian communities.

Yet, a Protestant enquired, how far can one go in asserting that the hierarchal structure of the Roman Catholic Church is a simple extension of the authority of the first Apostles? The question of authority is very complex; a simple analogy does not operate between law and tradition in Pauline thought and law and tradition in contemporary Catholicism. Is not the history of the Church, in the Catholic view, to be understood as involving revelation of ultimate truth, expressed in the dogmatic statements of the Church? The authority of the Church is grounded in the fact that the Catholic cannot conceive of the possibility that the entire course of the Church has erred. It is the Church as a whole which is infallible. Accordingly, no real tension should exist between hierarchy, theologian, and exegete. All stand within the framework of the Church's authority and participate in it as organs of the Church.

The question then arose as to the nature of authority in

Protestantism. This, the Protestants agreed, is very difficult to define because it is conceived somewhat differently by the various traditions. The ultimate authority is the living God who is actively at work in the Church and in the world. Traditionally, it is the Reformation principle of *sola scriptura* as expressed through the "preaching of the word," the *viva vox evangelii*, that constitutes authority for Protestantism.

At this point, a Catholic enquired as to how the Protestant biblical scholar relates himself to this authority? If Scripture itself is the authority, then there is no external basis by which the exegete can judge the validity of his work. He is faced with the perpetual task of striving after divine truth revealed in the Scripture without ever being able to grasp it unambiguously. A Protestant response was to the effect that ultimate authority rests with the providence of God, and, if there is always a contingent and ambiguous element in the Christian's knowledge of him, as in the work of the exegete, then that is something which belongs to the very nature of finite existence because of the manner in which God has chosen to reveal himself. Authority is only imperfectly revealed in the continual dialogue between Scripture and Church. In other words, while the interpretation of Scripture is *under* the authority of the Church for the Catholic, that interpretation is *an instance of* the authority of the Church for Protestantism.[11]

Is the Protestant scholar, then, able to exercise more freedom in his work than the Catholic precisely because he often stands in a less formalized dogmatic framework? The return of the discussion to the question of freedom brought with it similar remarks as were made on the first day about the fact that the methodology used can never be divorced completely from the cultural context in which the Protestant

[11] See further below, and also the paper of James M. Robinson on pages 91–109.

lives nor from the theological axioms which he holds. The fact that he is not always aware of his stance is a serious limitation on his claims to objectivity. The Catholic scholar, on the other hand, has to be aware of the framework in which he works. Yet, as one spokesman put it, he is in a sense set free by the security which the framework offers. He is limited only in those areas affecting "faith and morals," and these, theoretically, do not pertain to the specific historical problems dealt with by the exegete.[12]

Nevertheless, Protestants continued to be troubled by aspects of the Catholic dogmatic structure which in theory would seem to qualify the results of historical investigation. In the past the Catholic Church has used exegesis in an attempt to justify dogmatic statements which have no firm scriptural basis. Furthermore, the "objectified metaphysics," the philosophical mode of thinking in Catholicism, seems to run counter to an empirically oriented conception of historical criticism.

The main point to which the conversation led was this: Insofar as the Roman Catholic Church has a fixed dogmatic structure, is it not impossible for the work of the biblical exegete to affect it in any real way?

Protestant exegesis, even though deeply affected by theological and philosophical developments, has had a more direct impact on Protestant dogmatics. Along with the acceptance of the historical criticism of the Bible went the casting off of much of the dogmatic framework which characterized the major Protestant groups involved in the Reformation. It is doubtful that the churches could return to such a framework. Even as late as a generation ago, one could assume that a basically similar outline would have been used in the average course in theology within a majority of

12 See further Heiko Oberman, "Quo Vadis, Petre? The History of Tradition from Irenaeus to 'Humani Generis,'" *Harvard Divinity Bulletin* 26:1–25 (July 1962).

the Protestant theological seminaries for the training of clergy. Today one can no longer do so. Both historical criticism and the clearer realization of the dynamic or event-character of revelation have destroyed the older structure of dogmatics, and it is not yet clear what will take its place. The systems of the great Protestant theologians of the past and present generation are carefully studied, but none of these systems appears to have set the theological house in the order desired by a majority of the younger theologians. Is it possible to say, Protestants enquired, that no analogous development in Catholicism is possible? Surely, the framework of the Church cannot be overthrown by exegesis? Is there not a major structural difference between Roman Catholicism and Protestantism at this point?

Catholic spokesmen were unwilling to go quite as far as these queries seemed to imply. Of course, the dogmatic framework of the Church is unchangeable. Yet, at the same time, it would be inaccurate to say that Catholic exegesis is irrelevant to dogma, for it certainly serves to enrich the Church's understanding of dogma. As Pope John XXIII expressed it to the Second Vatican Council, while the dogma itself does not change, the words used and the manner of exposition do change and should be contemporary. Furthermore, a particular dogma as given historical expression at a specific time was then directed to a special situation where error needed correcting and where positive truth needed restatement. Yet, it must not be assumed that the particular aspect of the dogma stressed at a given moment exhausts its truth, or that all its aspects are mentioned. It is too early to assess the full effects of the new Catholic exegesis on the dogmatic structure of Catholicism; the revolution could well have many similarities to that of the last one hundred years in Protestantism. The first months of the Second Vatican Council could be understood as suggesting that such a revolution is indeed underway.

IV. THE NATURE OF THE CHURCH AND ITS EFFECT UPON BIBLICAL EXEGESIS

On the final morning, attention was turned to the address of James M. Robinson which had been given on the preceding afternoon. This paper had provoked a considerable amount of conversation. A number of persons, especially among the Roman Catholics, had expressed approval of the general thesis and seemed to feel that Professor Robinson's distinctions had indeed articulated an important area of difference between the Protestant and Roman Catholic Churches, as well as the role of scriptural studies in both.

Robinson's search was for "the appropriate hermeneutical principle" which would interpret and distinguish the confessions. By this he meant the manner in which, or the means by which, the Church at any given moment relates itself to its situation in the world. *Sola scriptura* as the formal principle of the Reformation suggests that Protestantism is being itself only when the Bible is being interpreted as presenting a reality that is contemporary and relevant. On the other hand, the Second Vatican Council shows us the Roman Catholic Church actively engaged in being the Church. "It is indeed the interpretation of Scripture, rather than the Third Assembly of the World Council of Churches, that is the hermeneutical principle of Protestantism most appropriate to serve" as the comparison and contrast to the Second Vatican Council. For the Protestant, the Church is the Church only when the Word is being validly proclaimed. For the Roman Catholic, on the other hand, it is the whole Church that mediates the reality of salvation to the contemporary situation. Revelation is objectified and actualized in the event of the sacraments. For Protestantism, "reality happens as Word"; for Roman Catholicism, "reality is metaphysically institutionalized."

For the former, valid interpretation is the essence of the Church; for the latter, it appears as "an appendix to an already achieved contemporaneity of salvation in the Church as institution."

The initial Catholic response to the paper in the seminar was directed to the implication that scriptural study was only "an appendix" and, therefore, not central to the work of the Roman Catholic Church. It was asserted that biblical scholarship was indeed a genuine and crucially important task. Within the Church there is a dialogue between the human, institutional side and the divine side (Scripture, tradition, liturgy, outstanding men and women). The scholar is a participant in this dialogue and his work forms a part of it. On the other hand, Protestants should understand the complexity and the many currents flowing within the Roman Church. It is not a solid, inflexible, or rigid structure which can easily be captured in a capsule definition. Were this not true, the Catholic scholar would indeed be very circumscribed in his work. Yet, in this country, he is able to speak and write with complete freedom. At the same time, it should be stated that Catholics practice "an economy of truth" with reference to the faithful. This means that statements must fit the situation, and that in certain contexts truth should not be presented in its fullness or entirety, lest it be misunderstood.

Another Catholic participant said frankly that in his opinion Robinson's paper came close to presenting the true situation. Roman Catholic biblical scholarship is subject to a *magisterium* which can mean freedom or, at certain times, restriction. Thus scriptural scholarship is an expendable item precisely because of the nature and role of the Church.

Response from the Protestant side was too varied to summarize adequately. The following, however, are a few of the points suggested by speakers who wished to modify

Robinson's attempt to state "the hermeneutical" principle of Protestantism:

(1) In both Old and New Testament times there was a community, a "people of God," before there was Scripture. The "Word" of God came to this people who understood that their very existence as a community was the saving work of God. The canon of Scripture is their testimony to this remarkable divine activity. Consequently, the *sola scriptura* of the Reformation cannot serve as a complete expression of the essence of Protestantism. The Church as the redeemed of God, as the People of God, as the servant of God—only this is the Church which hears and proclaims the "Word." An exclusive emphasis on *sola scriptura* suggests a definition of the Church and its task which lacks structure, and it expresses itself in certain types of biblical theology today which stress the proclamation (the kerygma) within the context of the worshipping community apart from the structural elements of "peoplehood," the establishment of which forms the true setting and origination of the kerygma.

(2) *Sola scriptura* is a tendential aspect of the Reformation, even when its importance is affirmed. It has always been a particularly useful weapon in controversy, but by itself it is not an adequate basis for a statement of Protestantism's "hermeneutical principle." The dominant Protestant groups have always had a strong ecclesiology and an emphasis on the importance of the sacraments, even though the latter are reduced in number to two.

(3) The "hermeneutical principle" proposed pushes toward a doctrine of the invisible Church and toward an understanding of history that is marked by discontinuity.

(4) If the basic characterizing principle of Protestantism is the valid interpretation of the "Word," an ambiguity exists since both "Word" and "Church" are constituents of "the body of Christ."

Professor Robinson's reply, supported by others, included the following:

(1) He did not intend to make a dichotomy between "Word" and "Church," but rather to point to the hermeneutical principle in each case which sheds light on what the Church is.

(2) The "Word" is not to be defined too narrowly. It means event and interpretation, so that event has something to say, and, indeed, speech itself is event. Furthermore, he would not wish to discount the communal aspect of the "Word."

(3) To discount the hermeneutical principle of the "Word" on the basis that it is used especially in times of crisis would destroy the authority of the Reformation, since it was a movement arising out of crisis. The "Word," the *sola scriptura,* as the formal principle of the Reformation is evidenced, for example, in much Protestant church architecture where the pulpit has traditionally been central.

(4) There is continuity in history if one accepts G. Ebeling's definition of Church history as the history of the interpretation of Scripture, the term "interpretation" being used in the wide sense defined in the first part of Robinson's paper.

This conversation between Protestants is of a type that always arises whenever the question of the nature of the Church is discussed. It suggests, however, that not all Protestants would regard the ecumenical possibilities between themselves and Roman Catholics exclusively set forth within the principles of Professor Robinson's paper!

The discussion on the third morning was so fast-moving that the above issues were scattered throughout much of the session. Meanwhile, other subjects came up briefly and were set aside as the group moved along with its central theme for the morning.

One brief colloquy occurred when a Protestant raised the

issue of "intellectual honesty" at the Catholic's statement
that dogma never changes—it is only rephrased or restated
—or when the image of the even-flowing course of doctrine
is publicly presented. The typical encyclical, for example,
will begin by tracing the history of its subject in previous
encyclicals, and tries to quote the words of previous pontiffs
as sustaining texts for what is actually something quite new.
Is it not obvious that *Divino afflante Spiritu* was a radically
new departure and that *Humani generis* derived from a conservative group which did not like it? Yet both encyclicals
were issued by the same pope.

Catholics replied that encyclicals indeed had a special
form and manner of expression that must be understood,
that caution is in order when using translations of encyclicals and that one must avoid oversimplified interpretations
of them, that some Catholics are complaining of too many
pronouncements coming from the hierarchy, and that it
must be remembered that the dogmas of the Catholic Church
are considered as only partial depictions of truth, though
one does not mean by this that they are fallible. Protestants
on their part admitted their own desire to preserve the continuity of tradition, even when particular points in the
tradition were being criticized. Thus, for example, it is not
infrequent that a Protestant scholar will use traditional
language and say by it something most untraditional, or will
praise nineteenth-century liberals and then extract a special
joy in showing how wrong they were.

It perhaps could be said that for most of the group, Professor Robinson's paper pointed to the basic issue of division
between Catholics and Protestants. That is in the conception of the Church. Yet it is difficult for Protestants to enter
into dialogue with Roman Catholics on the subject, because
they, themselves, in their various traditions, hold variant
conceptions of the nature of the Church.

Finally, in a concluding summary, it was noted that

hermeneutics had been at the center of the concerns of the seminar. The task of both biblical scholars and theologians alike is that of interpretation. In future dialogue one important area of continued conversation lies in the area of semantics. Common problems and concerns are often discussed in different contexts and with differing terminologies because of our variant histories. Most encouraging to the whole group, however, was the discovery that no issues were found to divide it which did not bend and interpenetrate and which were not subject to understanding analysis and discussion. The discussants were frank and open, and we parted with new appreciation and respect for one another and for our respective traditions.

G. Ernest Wright
Harvard University

SEMINAR II.
SYMBOL AND SACRAMENT*

IT WAS apparent from the beginning of our discussions
that there had been substantial development in the liturgical thought of both Catholics and Protestants since the
sixteenth century. All of us had read of some of these
changes, but we were now to talk about them at length.
We hoped thus to discover how Catholic and Protestant
regarded their own recent clarifications of liturgical theology
and practice, as well as their attitudes toward recent developments in the other branch of Christendom. We were led to
explore the regions of agreement at the beginning, for only
on the basis of our common faith and common traditions
could the differences be seen in their proper perspective. Some Catholics were surprised to find that in the non-
liturgical churches there had been a steady movement toward incorporating in the service of Holy Communion some
of the traditional moments that had long been in the Catholic and Episcopal liturgies: from the *Sursum Corda* and the
Gloria to the prayers of the Canon. As Fr. Gerald Ellard
observed in our first session, Catholic worship is becoming
more Protestant and Protestant worship more Catholic.
When the seminar was over many members said that they
had been surprised and were delighted over (1) the free-

* The author of this summary wishes to acknowledge the substantial
help that he has received from Roman Catholic members of the seminar
—in particular Frs. Von Euw and Sheehan of St. John's Seminary, Fr.
Callahan of Weston College, and especially the Very Reverend Damasus
Winzen, O.S.B., of the Mount Saviour Monastery in Elmira, New York.
The assistance of two graduate students of Harvard Divinity School,
Mr. William Arnold and the Reverend David Clark, who acted as
scribes of the proceedings, is also gratefully acknowledged.

dom and the depth of the discussion and (2) the extent of the areas of agreement.

Fr. Gerald Ellard of St. Mary's Seminary, Kansas, read the paper on the first morning, basing his remarks largely on Chapter I of the schema already adopted in the first session of the Second Vatican Council. He quoted at length from the Vagaggini commentary on that chapter, which had been published in the February 1963 issue of *Worship*. This document calls for "liturgical reform" under norms not yet completely stated. "The liturgical outlook is now a force sweeping through the Church . . . The liturgical question stands out as intimately tied to whatever is vital in the Church today."[1]

Fr. Shawn Sheehan, of St. John's Seminary, Brighton, Massachusetts, summarized the basic attitudes of this chapter in the following manner:

(1) The primacy of the Father's Will.

(2) Christ making the Father's Will effective and giving the Father the worship due from man.

(3) In the Church Christ continues the sanctification of men and involves men in his own worship of the Father.

(4) The liturgy is the summit of the Christian Church and the source of its power. (One Protestant wanted to qualify the word "source" by "proximate".)

(5) Moral and apostolic actions are the fulfillment of the obligations contracted by participation in the liturgy.

This summary along with Fr. Ellard's paper became the initial basis of the discussion. Concerning this summary,

[1] On December 7, 1962, the Vatican Council, by an overwhelming vote (2,162 to 46) adopted the first chapter of the schema *De sacra liturgia*. The full text of Chapter I will not be made public until it is officially promulgated, but on December 8, 1962, there appeared in the semiofficial daily *L'Osservatore Romano* a full comment on Chapter I prepared and signed by the Reverend Cyprian Vagaggini, O.S.B. An English translation of this commentary appeared in the February 1963 issue of *Worship* 37:153–164. It should be clear that all quotations are from this article.

and the published commentary in *Worship,* three comments should be made:

(1) They provide a corrective to the Protestant interpretation of the Catholic theory of the Atonement (Anselm) that it was the human Jesus who offered perfect obedience and by his suffering and death satisfied the divine justice. These points make clear the unity of the Trinity in the work of redemption. "God was in Christ reconciling the world to himself" (2 Cor. 5:19).

(2) The Christ involves believers in the act of worship. This insight strikes many Protestants as novel, although it is implicit in much Protestant writing on the theology of the liturgy, as well as in many of the classic Protestant prayers. But it is seldom explicit in the thought of Protestant clergy or laity, who regard public worship as an important part of the life of the Church, yet as a collective human response to the divine Word. If we take seriously the metaphor of the Church as "the body of Christ"; and especially if we take seriously the Pauline word, "The Spirit helps us in our weakness; for we do not know how to pray as we ought, but the Spirit himself intercedes for us with sighs too deep for words" (Romans 8:26); or if we consider our Lord's promise: "where two or three are gathered in my name, there am I in the midst of them" (Matthew 18:20) —then a new dimension will enrich Protestant worship. As in all areas of faith, Protestant and Catholic need to beware of premature claims to perfection in worship. One Protestant observed that all worship is idolatrous: we tend to worship our idea of God. Only when we recognize our danger of idolatry and acknowledge the divine rebuke even when we draw near to him can we in a measure be freed from the dangers of idolatry.

One Protestant called attention to Cranmer's oblation, now used in several Protestant orders of Holy Communion: "Here we offer and present unto Thee, O Lord, ourselves, our souls and bodies, to be a reasonable, holy and lively [living] sacrifice unto Thee."[2] He asked, "Would this be acceptable to Catholics?" Yes, was the reply, provided it was incorporated into and made a part of the offering of Christ to the Father.

(3) New also to some Protestants in the seminar was the thought that the very act of participation in the Eucharist creates new obligations. One Protestant remarked that this insight already appeared in Luther's (1519) "Treatise on the Blessed Sacrament":

> God gives us this sacrament, as much as to say, "Look, many kinds of sin are assailing you; take this sign by which I give you my pledge that this sin is assailing not only you but also my Son, Christ, and all his saints in heaven and on earth. Therefore take heart and be bold. You are not fighting alone. Great help and support are all around you."
>
> As love and support are given you, you in turn must render love and support to Christ in his needy ones. You must feel with sorrow all the dishonor done to Christ in his holy Word, all the misery of Christendom, all the unjust suffering of the innocent, with which the world is everywhere filled to overflowing. You must fight, work, pray, and—if you cannot do more— have heartfelt sympathy.
>
> There are those, indeed, who would gladly share in the profits but not in the costs. . . . They will not help the poor, put up with sinners, care for the sorrowing, suffer with the suffering, intercede for others, defend the truth, and at the risk of [their own] life, property and honor seek the betterment of the Church and of all Christians.[3]

Here is a conception of the Church that is breath-taking in its scope.

The first substantial agreement in our seminar was manifest at this point: worship is the act of the entire community. Fr. Willebrands of Rome reported that part of the discus-

---

[2] From the first English *Book of Common Prayer* (1549).
[3] *Luther's Works*, XXXV (Philadelphia, 1960), 53, 54, 57.

sion at the Vatican Council was centered on the Old Testament people of God as a worshipping community. He added that although the first chapter of the schema does not mention the priesthood of all believers, this thought is basic to that chapter. Fr. Ellard added that the "royal priesthood" of all believers must never be taken as a figure of speech.

Yet, it now seems plain that we were not understanding each other at this point. There is no blinking the difference in views about the ministry. One Lutheran observed that in the Roman Church the priesthood is interpreted in terms of office, whereas in the Lutheran Church it is in terms of function. Professor Cyril Richardson remarked that the difference occurs among Protestant churches, too. In some, the minister is doing what in principle any layman could do, while in churches with a high view of ordination the clergyman is doing what no layman could do. Fr. Sloyan remarked that the way was now open for conversations about ordination between Catholics and Protestants who hold a high view of the work of the ministry.

Fr. Damasus Winzen said after the Colloquium was over that both Catholics and Protestants agree that there is a difference between the Church as it is today and the Kingdom of God. It is the difference between promise and fulfillment, analogous to the difference between the Old Testament conception of the people of God and the New Testament doctrine of the Church. It had always seemed that the Catholic Church had anticipated the Kingdom, whereas the Protestants had emphasized the poverty, the "not yet" of the Church. Now it seems that just the reverse is true. In Catholic thought, the sacramental priesthood belongs to the Church on earth: it is a mark of her imperfection, her humility. The priesthood is instrumental, not an end in itself, an instrument in the hands of the Lord of the Church until he comes. In the heavenly Church the fullness of his presence replaces all other instruments. It was in this context that Fr. Winzen said he did not expect to wear a Roman collar in heaven!

Protestants, on the other hand, seem to have a much more pronounced and audacious anticipation of the Kingdom than the Catholics. It is because of the presence of the New Age in the Church that a special sacramental priesthood has no room in the Church. It is for the same reason that the presence of the Christ at the Eucharist is the presence of the Risen Saviour, and that this is the reason why the Eucharist is not a sacrifice but a banquet, a participation not in the Cross but in the glory. To many Catholics it seems that the prerogatives of the Kingdom of Heaven were being anticipated, not by the legitimate delegation of a few, but by the common usurpation of all. Fr. Winzen further pointed out that St. Paul clearly stated an authority that put him above others, one which was not delegated to him by the members of the community, but by Christ.

On one point there was no misunderstanding between the seminar participants: the "priesthood of all believers" means that the laity should participate in the liturgy with understanding and thus belong to the Church as a worshipping community. Chapter I of the Vatican Council Schema is specific. In the celebration of the Mass, the "presence and participation of the people will be preferred to a quasi-individual and private form (no. 27)." It calls for the "active participation of the faithful . . . in responses, the acclamations and the hymns (no. 31)." The rites should be "clear and simple, in general easily understood by the people (no. 34)." It recognizes "the necessity of a homily and of a liturgical catechesis (no. 35)."

Protestants do not present a united front on the place of the laity in worship. But there was general agreement that there is a pressing need for a clearer understanding by the laity of the history and of the theological significance of the various elements in the service of Holy Communion.

In each of the three sessions of the seminar the thorny question of the "Real Presence" was openly discussed. One Protestant said that his church needed a sharper doctrine of the presence of the Christ in the Eucharist. Professor Richardson observed that in the ancient liturgies the Logos descended on the baptismal font and on the bread and wine. Why was it that the water was not changed, whereas the elements of Holy Communion were? Fr. Von Euw in response said that all the recognized ancient liturgies—especially those of the East—did stress the descent of the Holy Spirit upon other sacramental elements, for example, the oils for consecration and the baptismal water. The ancient traditions of preserving these elements in reverent places (ambries, etc.) are still found even in Roman Catholic liturgical laws. But the mode of the presence of the Spirit in these elements was usually recognized as quite different from the mode of Christ's presence in the Eucharist.

Fr. Winzen added that while the water of baptism is set apart as "sacred," that is, withdrawn from profane and reserved for sacramental usage, the presence of the Spirit in the water is not an enduring one, but restricted to the very act of the sacrament. But cleansing is not the same as eating; the mode of presence in the Eucharist is established by the words of Christ: "Take, eat, this is my Body, which is given for you."

Which body is present in the sacrament, asked a Protestant theologian, the earthly, broken body on the Cross or the glorified body? If the former, then the act of the Eucharist is a sacrifice. If the latter, then the Eucharist becomes a remembrance. He observed that in Calvin the Christ is present in his resurrected, not his crucified body. This gives Calvin's doctrine an eschatological character; the crucifixion is remembered but the resurrection and the future judgment are now present in the sacrament.

Fr. Callahan of Weston College replied that the Christ

who is present in the sacrament is the Christ who is now in heaven, a glorified Christ who bears in his body the marks of his crucifixion. The mode of his sacramental presence differs from the mode of his heavenly presence, but it is the same glorified Christ who is present both in heaven and in the Eucharist. Catholics believe the Eucharist to be both a remembrance and a sacrifice. It is the sacramental re-presentation (but by no means a repetition) of the once-for-all sacrifice of Calvary whose salvific power it communicates to the present worshipping congregation.

Another Catholic speaker, referring to the *substantia et species* of the sixteenth century (and of St. Thomas), said that the former referred to the "inner reality of Christ" while the latter refers to the space and time limitations of the bread and the wine. One Protestant theologian was quick to exclaim, "This is just what John Calvin was saying!" It seemed for a moment that Thomas Aquinas and John Calvin were shaking hands before our eyes! But some Protestants objected that this obscured the radical difference between Creator and creature. There was a closer meeting of minds when the Real Presence was interpreted in terms of the dramatic action of the liturgy. Patristic and Eastern precedents were cited for such an association.

Dean Miller remarked that time is abrogated in the mystery of Holy Communion as it is in myth and symbol. There was no dissent when Prof. Richardson summarized the discussion under this formula: In the Eucharist there is made present at this moment of time the eternal reality of the historical act so that we participate in it and share in its efficacy.

There was lively discussion over the words in the title of the seminar. It was pointed out that the modern distinction between "sign" and "symbol" does not touch medieval usage, where "sign" participates in the nature of that to which it points. The word "sacrament" was called into question.

Chapter I of the schema on worship at the Second Vatican Council had spoken of the Christ in such a way that he could be called the foundation sacrament. Did this mean that the Christ himself is the supreme sacrament? A Lutheran objected: Surely, this is metaphor. Christ is much more than sacrament. The first chapter had also spoken of "that sacrament which is the whole Church herself," deriving her sacramental nature and work from the Christ. Asked a Presbyterian: Will you accept the sacraments as visible words? Fr. Ellard: Yes, if "words" be set in single or double quotation marks, indicating that their power is derived from the Word.

At this a Baptist theologian called for clarification. Which meaning of "sacrament" is basic, which derived? One Catholic remarked that the technical theological meaning of the word "sacrament" has its sole paradigm in the Incarnation and is correctly used only of those rites of his Mystical Body, the Church, through which Christ confronts the faithful in the present exercise of his incarnational activity. Another Catholic reported at length on the work of Dom Odo Casel (of Maria Laach) who pointed out that the Latin *sacramentum* served as a translation of the Greek *mysterion*. This approach opened a better understanding of the organic unity of the entire Christian *mysterion,* as St. Paul understands the word: "A revelation made by God to man through acts of god-manhood, full of life and power; it is mankind's way to God made possible by this revelation."[4]

The eschatology of the Eucharist was discussed at the last session. While the early Church did have a backward look in its liturgy, "Do this in remembrance of me," there was also a strong reference to the consummation, "until he comes" (1 Cor. 11: 24, 26). Even if, with Lietzmann, we regard the *agape* as an alternative celebration, having no

[4] Dom Odo Casel, *The Mystery of Christian Worship* (Maryland, 1962), p. 13.

reference to the death of the Christ, it also has a clear reference to both past and future: the remembrance of the meals with the Lord in the days of his flesh and the anticipation of the Messianic banquet. In our day the Eucharist tends to be confined to its backward gaze at the very time when the world despairs of the future and hope is weak. Is there a way of restoring the eschatological hope in the Eucharist, either by changing the biblical selections or by a prayer expressing Christian hope?

One Eastern rite Catholic observed that all the Eastern liturgies contain a strong eschatological emphasis. Fr. Von Euw pointed out that the many references to the Holy Spirit in Eastern liturgies have an eschatological emphasis. One Lutheran said that we should beware of making a "fad" out of the rediscovery of the eschatological; that we should not obscure the many eschatological references which have always been present in Western rites and which have had a proper theological order. Fr. Sheehan pointed to the *Gratias agamus,* the *Sanctus* and the *Benedictus qui venit* as making clear that the Kingdom is both realized and anticipated.

Fr. Damasus Winzen contrasted the Orthodox, Roman Catholic, and Protestant approaches to eschatology in the liturgy. He characterized the Orthodox approach as synthetic, purposely and constantly interweaving references to the historical, the liturgical, and the eternal. An example of such a synthetic interpretation in primitive Christianity is provided by catacomb paintings of banquet scenes, which cannot be clearly described as *agape* meals, or Eucharists, or Heavenly Banquets, precisely because they represent all three at the same time. He characterized the Roman Catholic approach as analytic, that is, carefully distinguishing between the historical, the sacramental, and the heavenly reality, without, however, neglecting their unity. The Protestant approach was described by Fr. Winzen as an emphasis on the "not-yet" with regard to the Kingdom. He associated this with the Zwinglian separation of Spirit and matter, which he saw as the exaggeration of dangerous tendencies within Roman Catholicism also. When attempts have been made in Western Christianity to make the epiclesis more distinct, this has been done at the expense of understanding the epiclesis as the continuing action of the whole Canon.

One follower of Calvin recalled the historical difficulties in Western Christianity's attempt to hold in proper balance Christ's presence in the Eucharist in relation (1) to the historical events of the Incarnation and the Crucifixion, and (2) to the "not-yet" of the Kingdom. Emphasis on the past, once-for-all event has led to preoccupation with death, whereas emphasis on the Risen Christ has tended to obscure the historical and make eschatology a matter of completely future hope. Fr. Callahan said that this was a false dilemma in the light of New Testament eschatology, for the latter involves a divine vitality which is partially conveyed to us now and will attain its full vigor at the Parousia. He illustrated the idea by noting that the Eucharist was instituted in, and draws its present efficacy from, the historical context of Christ's life, death, and resurrection; but when it is communicated to the present-day faithful the Eucharist brings us into the sacramental presence of Christ risen in glory and is the efficient pledge that we are called to share fully in that glory. Jesus Christ is the sacrament of God; through Jesus Christ's continuing sacramental activity the Trinity links the man of faith to the salvation history of the past, vivifies him with grace and love for that of the present, and fortifies him with hope for an even greater future. Dean Miller recalled that there is a difference between human and divine time. The meaning of "once-for-all" is properly understood in terms of "all-for-once." One Catholic interpreted the *hapax* of *Hebrews* as combining death and resurrection, the temporal and the eternal. He admitted that the

Council of Trent was preoccupied with Calvary, but pointed out that Trent's formulations are neither final nor exhaustive.

At this stage Professor Richardson summarized the Protestant position as follows: (1) Protestants believe that Catholics put too much emphasis on the "heaven-is now," not enough on the "not yet." The latter emphasis points to the tentative character of all human achievements and structures, even in the Church. (2) Catholics fail to appreciate fully the prophetic role which has played so large a part in Protestantism. The prophet speaks out in God's freedom to challenge man's sin even in his religious achievements, and to direct him both to God's grace and to that final goal of righteousness which is only partially incorporated in the actual dogmas, institutions, and actions of the Church.[5]

In the latter part of the last morning, some time was given to the possibility of a common lectionary in all the churches. One Protestant expressed the hope that when the Catholic Church undertakes a revision of its lections in a two- or three-year cycle some way might be found for informal consultation with the leaders of Protestant bodies, such as the World Council of Churches. Dean Douglas Horton expressed scepticism, recalling that theological perspectives are involved and that attempts to work out a common lectionary even between related Protestant bodies have come to grief in the past. The seminar, having no ecclesiastical status, however, could and did express the hope that the members of the Vatican Secretariat present would take the suggestion informally to Cardinal Bea. At least a start could be made. If a common lectionary could be made available, individual churches could use their own versions of the Bible. There was brief discussion of first attempts in various parts of the Christian world to work toward a com-

[5] But see Fr. Winzen's comment above, made after the Colloquium was over.

mon version of the Bible and of attempts at a common hymnal. It was recalled that in hymnals now in use we have already achieved a large measure of ecumenicity.

Throughout the discussions there was a freedom that was itself an expression of mutual confidence. Protestants did not hesitate to point to elements in the Catholic tradition that they found objectionable; Catholics used the same freedom. Yet the criticisms were based more on underlying theology rather than on practice. For example, no Catholic asked why Protestant churches did not observe the Eucharist every Sunday. Nor did any Protestant ask why the Catholic Church had not made more progress toward conducting the Mass in the vernacular. Nor was there much Protestant criticism of the seven sacraments of the Catholic Church. Fr. Ellard did say in his opening paper that every Catholic child learns about the seven sacraments in his catechism. Yet he also said that Luther and Calvin were right in putting the main emphasis on the two sacraments of baptism and holy communion; he even called them "traditionalists" in holding this view.

A sobering note recurred in reference to the conflict in ways of thought between the symbolic and the descriptive, the religious and the naturalistic. Dean Miller said that the matter-of-fact world in which we live has little place for symbol or sacrament. The Church seems to our contemporary culture to speak a strange language. Yet, not far beneath the superficial immediacy of modern man are deep anxieties to which the liturgy can and must speak.

Fr. Stransky of Rome added that in our current world culture, where we are bombarded daily by words urging us to buy this or that, modern man has built up such a resistance to words that he has forgotten how to listen, especially when person-to-person language is appropriate. He has lost receptivity to God. Even modern piety marks a strange renewal of Pelagianism, the tendency to act before listening.

This report, as every member of the seminar would want, must end with a tribute to Fr. Gerald Ellard, S.J., who devoted a full life to liturgical renewal in the Church that he deeply loved. Most of us had never met him before the seminar convened. He combined a comprehensive, rigorous, and precise knowledge of the field with an extraordinary gentleness of spirit. In those three days his leadership was invaluable: he opened many doors for all of us. After he attended a late Saturday afternoon Mass, we drove him, with others, to the banquet that ended the Colloquium. He seemed deeply contented. His last comment at the seminar was to the effect that those three days together had been like a Pentecost, with a fresh outpouring of the Holy Spirit. Monday afternoon he died in a Boston hospital.

Father Callahan of Weston College wrote this in a letter:

When I read of the death of Father Ellard it occurred to me that he must have lived his last days on earth in great contentment. He had spent more than thirty years of his life laboring that the liturgical and sacramental life of the baptized might be more meaningful among the people of God. In God's Providence Father Ellard spent the last days of his life at a gathering where the charity and the devotion to truth and freedom which that liturgical and sacramental life ought to promote were most obviously in evidence. When I learned of his death I recalled that his closing remarks at the seminar meeting on Saturday morning included a recognition of the Pentecostal Spirit that pervaded the *Colloquium*. I am sure it is not presumptuous to feel that the same Spirit which he has now encountered in heaven moved him to make that remark.

> J. Harry Cotton
> Harvard Divinity School

SEMINAR III. REFORMATIO*

THE TITLE *Reformatio* was chosen for the third seminar in the Roman Catholic-Protestant Colloquium not, as might be thought, in order to emphasize the narrow and scholarly nature of the approach but rather to broaden the subject of the seminar so as to include not only the sixteenth-century Protestant Reformation, with which the English term "reform" is often associated, but also the whole background and tradition of reform in the medieval Church. The two papers presented to the seminar by Prof. Ladner and Prof. Schmidt, which are printed elsewhere in this volume, were concerned with the idea and reality of reform from the eleventh to the fifteenth century and showed clearly that medieval *reformatio* was important in its own right and not simply as the background of the Protestant Reformation. The discussion among the members of the seminar ranged yet more broadly. It concentrated in the period of the Middle Ages and Reformation, down to the Council of Trent, but it also touched on the issue of reform in the early and in the contemporary Church.

It is impossible to condense into a few pages all the points that were raised during the discussion, which lasted many hours during the three mornings of the Colloquium and included over a hundred contributions by almost thirty participants in the seminar. Even a simple transcript would

---

* This paper has been read by the Rt. Rev. J. Joseph Ryan, a Professor at St. John's Seminary, Brighton, Massachusetts, who made certain suggestions which were incorporated into the text but who otherwise stated that in his judgment the report is faithful to the spirit and tenor of the discussions, "as well as to the wide-ranging substance of its hundred-odd interventions." The Harvard graduate students who took notes on the proceedings to assist the writer were E. David Willis and David B. Evans. A special word of gratitude is due them for their assistance.

give a false tone of finality to opinions uttered in a spirit of give and take or of inquiry. Many remarks were made on the spur of the moment, without the opportunity to consult works of reference, and might have been corrected or revised after further investigation and consideration. In the following account, therefore, I have not tried to reproduce the discussion as it took place but to examine the methods by which the problem was studied and to summarize the principal points that emerged during the discussion. I cannot speak of any conclusions, because the seminar attempted only to discuss the issues arising from the papers and the general problem of *reformatio* and not to arrive at any definite agreement. The views expressed here of any general agreement are based upon my subjective impressions of the sense of the meeting; but I shall try not to overgeneralize and to indicate both individual opinions and areas of disagreement.

Three types or levels of approach to the problem of *reformatio* were apparent in the discussion. They often overlapped and were not always clearly formulated by the participants, but they represent three distinct aspects of the question, on different levels of abstraction and concreteness. The first, and most abstract, level was methodological and was concerned with the meaning of the term *reformatio* and the nature of reform. The second level was also theoretical, but more historical: the causes of the need for reform and the methods of reform, as seen by contemporaries. The third level was specifically historical and dealt with the history of reform: how the church and society have been reformed and who were the reformers. The distinction between these aspects is in some respects artificial, but they are a useful basis for studying and summarizing the discussion.

It was clear from the beginning that the term "reform" is used in very different meanings by theologians, ecclesiologists, historians, and laymen. Most simply, the difference can be seen in the terms "reform" and "re-form," with a hyphen, which are distinguished in the dictionaries and carry very different implications. "Reform" may be said to look backward to a perfect form or state that has been changed or corrupted but may hopefully be restored. "Re-form," on the other hand, is a forward-looking term and implies a change from one form into a new and different one. "Reform" without the hyphen is thus associated with "restoration," "renewal," "rejuvenation," and "rebirth," whereas "re-form" is more like "re-shape" and "innovate," which has distinctly pejorative implications for many Roman Catholic, Orthodox, and Protestant Christians.

The distinction between backward-looking and forward-looking reform was never clearly drawn in the discussion, but it is very important in order to understand both the role of *reformatio* in the history of the Church and some of the differences between the members of the seminar. The backward-looking reform is associated with the incarnational view of the institutional Church as the body of Christ. It is an ideal form, and any change or falling away, in the Augustinian sense, is evil. Reform is thus the work of recovering and restoring the perfect form that has been lost. Forward-looking reform is entirely different. It is associated with an eschatological view of the Church, which stresses its final end rather than its original form and looks to the future rather than to the past. This type of reform accepts the necessity and desirability of change and even of innovation and resembles in many respects the modern concepts of development and adjustment. Both of these views of *reformatio* are strongly historical, but in different ways. One stresses a point in the past, where the Church should strive to remain or to return to; the other stresses changing circumstances in the present and the future, in accordance with which the Church must change.

The importance of this changing historical background was frequently emphasized during the discussion, but its importance was variously assessed by members of the seminar. For those who assumed that reform looks backward, the historical change involved the loss of the original perfection, and they searched both for the causes of corruption and the ways of restoration. This view of reform often makes use of the naturalistic and biological metaphors of decay and old-age. Reform is then seen as a sort of rejuvenation. The corruption may also be seen as the result of specific human weaknesses, above all of pride, concupiscence, and ignorance. In either case it involves a definite break with the past. For other members of the seminar it was clear that *reformatio* need not involve the decay or corruption of an originally perfect form. At most, they accepted the inevitable imperfection of all human institutions, which men must strive at all times to improve. Reform for them was a process of adjustment to changing conditions, looking toward the final end. They emphasized that the Word of God is active in the Church, not only in the past but also in the present, re-forming in the true sense of the term. Thus, eschatology, as one member put it, transmutes the idea of reform as restoration into the idea of reform as innovation.

Besides this distinction of looking backward or forward, there are methodological distinctions in the views of the nature and the object of reform. Philosophically and theologically, "form" is unchanging, the inner determining principle of a thing, as distinct from its externals and accidents; and in this sense to reform means to change fundamentally the nature of a thing. For backward-looking reformers, this form is the ideal state in which the Church and Christian society were created, the Platonic idea, which they must try to recover. For eschatological, forward-looking reformers, although the innermost form is unchanging, it is linked to potentiality, in Aristotelian terms, and there is constant development and change. Both types of reformer have to distinguish, although not always consciously, between the substance and the accidents, the internals and the externals, of the object of reform. They must determine the nature of the form, the unchanging inner substance which they seek to restore or to uncover; and in practical terms they must decide what can and what cannot be reformed.

The nature of any reform will therefore depend both on its direction and on its object. Dogmas, institutions, and individual persons can all be the object of reform, but in different ways, and historians must distinguish between dogmatic, institutional, and, in individuals, moral and intellectual reforms. There was some lively discussion in the seminar over the possibility of dogmatic reform; and the distinction between essentials and externals, especially wording, was sharply drawn. Reformulation was here used in a new sense, suggesting a change in the wording but not in the essence of a dogma. There was agreement among the Roman Catholic members of the seminar that the inner truth of a dogma cannot be changed, but some were of the opinion that its verbal expression, as Cardinal Bea suggested in his third lecture, might be reformulated. The dogma might thus be set, according to one theologian, in a broader doctrinal context, and its inner truth more clearly brought out.

There was more general agreement on the possibility of institutional reform, but not on its scope. Change in the Church, one participant maintained, must involve change in the world, and true reform must be of the kingdom of God. Here again the distinction between the inner form and the outer accidents of both ecclesiastical and secular institutions is essential. One member of the seminar suggested that reform in the Church is basically a manifestation of its deepest nature, as if it were (the simile is mine, not his) an onion, off of which the reformers peeled the outer layers as they became outmoded, eventually to reveal its inner heart. The form may thus appear to change, but it has always been there. Most institutional reform, however, is concerned not with internals but with externals, above all with the correction of abuses.

Unlike dogmatic and much institutional reform, personal reform, both moral and intellectual, must be concerned with essentials. The Christian in baptism becomes a new man in the deepest sense of the term and is re-formed in Christ, although his external appearance may remain unchanged.

It was clear from the discussion in the seminar that these methodological distinctions were necessary in order to understand the significance of *reformatio,* both in the past and in the present, because it means different things and works in different ways. It can be directed backward or forward, be concerned with essentials or externals, and have as its object dogmas, institutions, or persons. The confusion of these various directions and types of reform—so as to maintain that a dogma can be reformed in the same way as an individual—can lead only to misunderstanding.

The theory of reform, historically considered, has tended to concentrate on the problems of how the ideal form of the early Church has been changed and corrupted and on how it should be reformed. This question was studied by Dr. Schmidt in his paper "Who Reforms the Church?"; he was concerned with the answers given to this question by Occam, Wyclif, Hus, and other theorists, and by men of action in the late Middle Ages and Reformation period. The discussion, in particular, brought out the connection of medieval nominalism with ideas on the nature of the Church and reform and how the pressing problems of the Church at that time stimulated reforming theory.

Most members of the seminar clearly thought of reform as the recovery of an ideal form, and various ways were suggested in which this form had been lost. Some saw it, as mentioned above, as a natural process of aging and decay; others, as the result of human weaknesses, above all of pride, which is at the same time the principal cause of corruption and the principal obstacle to reform. To counteract this continual process of falling away, one member suggested, the Church has ordinary as well as extraordinary methods of reform. The sacramental system, for instance, is a constant reform which sustains individual Christians and repairs their corruption. The diocesan bishop is likewise responsible for the constant institutional reform of his diocese. More general and deep-seated troubles, however, must be the object of occasional and extraordinary *reformatio.*

The author of all reform, theologically speaking, is God himself, and it is often said that the Church, as a divine institution, reforms itself. The triune nature of God is here associated with some of the methodological distinctions mentioned above, since as three Persons God is active in the Church in different ways. The idea of the creation of the Church in the image of Christ naturally stresses the backward-looking type of reform, seeking to restore the lost ideal. As the Holy Spirit, however, God is active in the Church and the world today, and eschatological reformers rely heavily on the doctrine of the Holy Spirit and of his reforming activity in individuals and institutions.

God as a reformer acts through as well as in created institutions and individuals, and there was considerable discussion in the seminar over the *locus* of reforming activity in the Christian community. The relative importance of *charisma* and *auctoritas* came up on each day of the seminar, and there was a strong tendency to contrast reform and authority and to assume that reform always starts with charismatic individuals outside the hierarchy, although it may be approved and supported by the ecclesiastical authorities. One member of the seminar mentioned, however, that the reforming role of the small group, both within and outside the Church, should not be lost sight of in this polarization of charismatic individuals and the authoritative hierarchy.

Individual reformers might be either members of the lower clergy, laymen, or even schismatics and heretics who are outside the official Church. Their prime characteristic is that they are unofficial and unexpected, and the character of their reforms cannot be predicted. The roles of teachers, lawyers, and laymen were especially discussed. One member of the seminar stressed that reform must start with education and that in the late Middle Ages, especially in the conciliar period, the universities and professors took a prominent part in the movements for reform. Another discussed the canon lawyers, who were often pictured as obstacles to reform but who in fact played an important part in the development of institutions and the application of the working of Christ in the Church. Particular interest was shown in the distinction and respective roles of the clerical and lay elements in the Church. Up until the eleventh and twelfth centuries, for instance, monks were usually regarded as neither clerics nor laymen but as a distinctive third order of society, and the strict modern distinction of clerical and lay is a product of the Investiture Contest. A member of the seminar pointed out that in the early Church the laity participated in what would now be considered clerical decisions and that the spiritual authority of inspired laymen only gradually became institutionalized in the office of the bishop and, finally, in the pope. The reforming activity of nonclerical monks and laymen, and of schismatics and heretics, is thus itself part of the historical development of the Church.

The question of the motives of these individual, or unofficial, reformers was also raised, but it was not discussed at length. Schismatics and heretics are obviously moved by some deep spiritual discontent to seek a reformation of both institutions and individuals, and sometimes also of dogmas. One speaker mentioned the possibility of exterior pressures and subconscious motivations. A fundamentally orthodox reformer, whose motives are primarily moral, may be driven into an extreme position by official opposition and even seek refuge in more basic reforms, affecting the substance of existing institutions, than he originally had in mind. Power factors may also play a part, and it was pointed out that shifts in the *locus* of power (as from the lay rulers to the hierarchy, and from the bishops to the pope in the eleventh century) may affect the movements of reform. Other members of the seminar disagreed. They accepted that the element of power could not be disregarded in either secular or ecclesiastical institutions, and the desire for power might be in some cases legitimate, but they felt that movements of reform were motivated basically by moral rather than by power factors.

The role of the hierarchy in reform, though generally considered less important than that of charismatic individuals and groups, was not entirely neglected. Authority rarely initiates reform, but it must judge the validity of individual reformers and movements of reform. The Roman Catholic members of the seminar in particular agreed that the Church must decide the nature of legitimate reform and that, for instance, in order to be legitimate, any institutional reformer must accept the validity of visible ecclesiastical institutions.

This point raised the important question of the nature and *locus* of final authority within the Church, which was called by one participant the principal area of disagreement between Roman Catholic, Orthodox, and Protestant Christians. During the conciliar period, as Dr. Schmidt brought out in his paper, even some Roman Catholics opposed papal absolutism and sought a broader basis for final authority in the Church in the totality of believers expressed through a council. They emphasized the role of the pope as the servant of the servants of God, which, though nothing new, had been in abeyance during the twelfth and thirteenth centuries, and they returned to the ministrative rather than dominative aspects of the papal position. Besides the papal and conciliar theories, the spiritual authority of pious monks and laymen, particularly of secular rulers, was recognized in various Christian traditions, and the *locus* of authority to validate reform is not therefore as clear as it might be. Institutional reform is obviously the particular province of the hierarchy; dogmatic reform (or reformulation), of the theologians; moral reform, of the ministers and preachers; and intellectual reform, of the teachers. These differing roles and authorities have been recognized to some extent in certain Protestant churches, but they have never been clearly distinguished in theory or in practice and have contributed to the confusion of many reforming movements.

The discussion of the theory of reform thus overlapped and interlocked with the study of specific reformers and movements of reform from the eleventh to the sixteenth centuries. In the first paper presented to the seminar Dr. Gerhart Ladner examined the reforms associated with the names of Pope Gregory VII (Hildebrand) and Francis of Assisi. He emphasized that the Gregorian reform, of which the Investiture Controversy was a central aspect, was the first general institutional reform, "in head and members," as it was later called, in the history of the Western Church. He associated it with the monastic and evangelical movements of the eleventh and twelfth centuries, out of which the Franciscan reform grew during the pontificate of Innocent III. Both from his paper and from the discussion it was clear that Gregory and Francis are central and characteristic figures, although in different ways, in the *reformatio* of the Middle Ages.

Gregory emerged primarily as an institutional reformer, in the methodological terms outlined above, but it is not certain whether he was principally concerned with the reform of externals and the correction of abuses or with a real change in the structure of the Church, above all by the exclusion of lay elements. According to some members of the seminar, Gregory's reform marked the first emergence of a real ecclesiastical party and a split of the Church into two branches, one clerical, which now included the monks, and the other lay, the *congregatio fidelium*. This view was apparently too extreme for other participants, who argued that Gregory was not trying to exclude all lay participation in ecclesiastical affairs but only the quasi-clerical functions of secular rulers, especially their control over ecclesiastical appointments. They pointed out that Gregory regarded himself not as an innovator but as a restorer and renewer and that he had a deep respect for canon law. Whatever his view of himself, however, it was pointed out that in practical terms Gregory introduced some fundamental changes into the structure of the Church and laid the basis for later medieval hierarchism.

In one area at least it was agreed that Gregory was an innovator. That was his relations with and concern for the East, which was discussed by several participants. Gregory's letters to the eastern emperors were said to have prefigured the crusades. At the same time his reforms in the West initiated a new period of Greek-Latin relations. They were misunderstood by the Greeks, it was said, whose image of the Latin Church was dominated by the corruption of the ninth and tenth centuries and for whom the Gregorian reform led the Latin Church further from, rather than nearer to, reunion. The Greek sense of continuity contributed to their view of the reforms as innovations, or changes away from the ancient forms, and they distrusted the tendency toward papal absolutism. The Latin theologians at the same time were suspicious of the Greek theological traditions.

Francis of Assisi was a different type of reformer from Gregory VII. He summed up the strivings toward repentance and poverty of the spiritual movements of the twelfth century, which sometimes led into heresy, and emerged with the most powerful and attractive movement of personal moral reform of the entire Middle Ages. His predominantly moral rather than institutional concern may account, according to one participant, for the fact that Francis is one of the very few Western medieval saints who is honored in the East. For the student of medieval *reformatio,* Francis is the supreme example of the charismatic individual reformer whose reform springs from outside the hierarchy, and almost from outside the institutional Church. Yet the history of his reform is the best corrective for too sharp a separation of *auctoritas* and *charisma,* because Francis himself, unlike many contemporary reformers, always respected authority and the hierarchy, above all in the person of Innocent III, who approved and supported the Franciscan reform. The institutional Church of the thirteenth century, thus, came to include, though admittedly in a modified form, many of the spiritual ideals which in the twelfth century tended to develop outside the Church. Many of the most effective movements of reform, indeed, have depended on the cooperation of the authoritative and charismatic factors and cannot be described as coming exclusively either from inside or from outside the hierarchy.

One of the central topics on this level of historical discussion was Luther and the Protestant reformers and their relation to the medieval tradition of *reformatio.* There were, of course, considerable differences of opinion among the members of the seminar, but it was clear that Luther marked a new departure in several respects. In at least one, his rejection of hierarchism, he actually reacted against one of the principal objects of some earlier reformers. Above all, however, several participants emphasized that Luther was concerned less with institutional and moral reform, as were the medieval reformers, some of whom had also rejected hierarchism, than with doctrinal reform. In itself, it was said, Luther's desire for reform was medieval, but his type and methods of reform were far from traditional. The distinction between the Gospel and the law, and between faith and morals, underlay his entire reform, and although this in itself was not new, it acquired in his teachings a new dynamic force which emphasized the helplessness of the individual before the Divine. The result was a reformation that affected the very essence of the Church and its teachings.

The seminar did not continue its discussions into the problems of contemporary *reformatio*, but a few points were made which may be summarized here by way of conclusion. The problem of reform is at the heart of the ecumenical movement, and many of the remarks made in the seminar have a direct bearing on the contemporary Christian dilemma. Above all, Christians, today, must distinguish clearly between essentials and externals and decide what can and what cannot be changed in existing institutions and dogmas. To this extent, the problem of reformers in the Middle Ages is the problem of reformers today. We too must deside whether to look backward or forward for the essential nature of the Church, and we must learn from the study of the history of reform that reform may come from both outside and inside not only the hierarchy but also the official Church—from unexpected as well as from expected reformers. Thus for many contemporaries Pope John XXIII was seen as embodying the perfect combination of *charisma* and *auctoritas*, who brought to the highest position of ecclesiastical authority a personal zeal and individual vision. A true contemporary reformation cannot be concerned simply with the abolition of abuses. It must indeed distinguish and preserve the essential truths of the Christian revelation and tradition, but on this basis it must be ready to face with new answers the present problems of Christendom. It must take account, as one speaker emphasized, of both old and new elements and face firmly, for instance, the continued separation from the Jewish people, who were first elected by God and from whom he has never withdrawn his electing grace. *Reformatio* today is not simply an undoing of the past, a tearing down of the barriers that have grown up within God's community, essential as this is, but also a creative realization of God's will for his community in the future.

Giles Constable
Harvard University

SEMINAR IV. CONSCIENCE IN A PLURALISTIC SOCIETY: THEOLOGICAL AND SOCIOLOGICAL ISSUES*

THAT PLURALISM is a pervasive fact of modern society and that it poses perplexing questions for the religious conscience was made apparent in the seminar proceedings by the character of the discussions themselves. The varieties of approach, method, language, and point of view exhibited in the conversations demonstrated the conspicuous absence of any commonly accepted ethical frame of reference *within as well as between* the Protestant and Catholic groups. In other words, the seminar faced great difficulty in coming to terms with pluralism because of the very pluralism or diversity of contemporary American religious thought, as well as because of the complexities inherent in the problem itself.

At the same time, it was the "pluralistic" and "open-ended" character of the conversations which gave some promise of new levels and possibly new kinds of consensus between Protestants and Catholics. If the participants seemed often to be talking past or around one another, if the course of their exchanges seemed to meander uncertainly, there was very little allegiance to doctrinaire systems of thought. Positions could not be sorted out neatly and con-

---

* The writer must express his indebtedness to the Rev. Theodore M. Steeman, O.F.M., for his willingness to be consulted about this chapter. The Harvard graduate students who acted as scribes in this seminar were Dorothy Corbett, Herbert D. Long, and Max L. Stackhouse.

sistently lined up against one another. Very little attempt was made to move clearly and rigidly from theological assumptions to social and ethical analysis. On the contrary, there was a notable desire on the part of both groups to face one another afresh and to speak in terms that were free of the old clichés. This lack of doctrinaire thinking gave the discussions a vitality and spontaneity impossible when opinions are settled and minds made up. Pluralism is not only the problem but also, in part, the hope of seminars like this one.

Of course, much to the disappointment of the press and the public, "popular issues," such as birth control and federal aid to education were scrupulously avoided. Had they been discussed, opinions would no doubt have been rapidly polarized, and the open character of the discussions lost. It is quite clear that a Roman Catholic-Protestant "dialogue" cannot be ultimately satisfactory without facing up to these immediate questions. They are, perhaps, a kind of litmus test regarding the degree and nature of consensus among Catholics and Protestants. Still, the seminar determined at the outset that, in the words of the statement of purpose, "to lapse into discussion of such questions prematurely can only impair a common exploration of many of the underlying assumptions and presuppositions that shape and guide ethical thinking in modern industrial society."

The statement of purpose defined the concern of the seminar as follows: "A critical examination and evaluation of theological and sociological thinking regarding the question of conscience. An attempt will be made to consider the mutual impact of theology and sociology upon one another, as well as to investigate the problems and points of strain that emerge from their encounter. It is hoped that such investigation will help each confession understand the dimensions of ethical thought and action, and to perceive what

is at stake in arriving at a common approach to ethics."
While, as has already been implied, the discussions ranged
far and wide, and while they did not yield any conclusions,
at least three general problem areas were tacitly accepted
as constituting the fundamental issues "at stake in arriving
at a common approach to ethics." These were (1) the character of American religious pluralism, (2) the problem of
natural law, and (3) the problem of conscience. Because
these issues are likely to haunt every Protestant-Catholic
conversation concerned with ethics, it is perhaps worthwhile
to piece together some of the pertinent reflections of the
seminar and briefly to elaborate the implications of these
reflections.

AMERICAN PLURALISM

There were two aspects to the discussions of pluralism.
In the first place, the analytical question arose as to the
character of American pluralism. There was no question
that at *some* level it is valid to speak of a "religious consensus" in the United States. The seminar would, generally,
have agreed with Professor Talcott Parsons' analysis of the
American religious situation. There exists, says Parsons, "a
common matrix of value-commitment which is broadly
shared between denominations, and which . . . has, in the
American case, been extended to cover a very wide range. Its
core certainly lies in the institutionalized Protestant denominations, but with certain strains and only partial institutionalization, it extends to three other groups of the first importance: the Catholic Church, the various branches of Judaism,
and, not least important, those who prefer to remain aloof
from *any* formal denominational affiliation. To deny that
this underlying consensus exists would be to claim that
American society stood in a state of latent religious war.
Of the fact that there are considerable tensions every responsible student of the situation is aware. Institutionaliza-

tion is incomplete, but the consensus is very much of a reality."[1]

The seminar agonized, however, over the *content* and *nature* of the consensus in this country. Were there, the participants were asking, beliefs and doctrines common both to Catholics and Protestants which can and do support our democratic system? Does something in the logic of the Christian tradition—which both groups share—drive toward a religiously "open society"? Or, is the American pattern a pragmatic accommodation to the deep-seated and unalterable conflicts among the various religious bodies? Moreover, what is the direction of American pluralism? These questions received positive and negative responses from both groups. One Protestant perceived the emergence of a grand new pattern of uniformity, a "triumph over diversity," as he put it. He implied that the area of agreement among Protestants and Catholics was already very broad, and that a further *rapprochement* was inevitable and very far-reaching in its implications. Some Catholics as well as other Protestants took vigorous exception to his conclusions. It was felt, for example, that American society, far from moving in the direction of uniformity, was in fact developing a diversity in thought and belief that would make contemporary America look like the Middle Ages.

At bottom, the question emerged as to whether the basic consensus among Catholics and Protestants lay at the *theological* level, the *pragmatic-institutional* level, or somewhere in between. It was argued, for example, that theological divergence between Protestants and Catholics is the place for the dialogue to begin. All institutional and practical differences are really outgrowths of basic conflicts in belief. One Catholic social scientist, however, was reasonably convinced

---

[1] Talcott Parsons, "Christianity and Modern Industrial Society," in *Sociological Theory, Values, and Socio-Cultural Change,* E. A. Tiryakian, ed. (Glencoe, Ill., 1963), pp. 33–70.

of a religious value-consensus among most Americans, and he urged a consideration of institutional adjustments and compromises. Quite obviously, in future discussions it will be terribly important to demarcate as sharply as possible the various levels at which consensus may take place among religious bodies. Some sort of common analytical frame of reference will help to clarify the complexities and confusions that lurk in such considerations as these.

All of the essentially analytical observations as to how much and what kind of pluralism we have in America introduced the second aspect of the problem, namely, how desirable, after all, pluralism actually is. This matter touches the heart of the Protestant-Catholic encounter, and while the thread of discussion was particularly tangled, it may be well to dwell for a moment on a few of the points that were raised or implied. If it is true, as was indicated by some along the way, that pluralism is in a positive sense the fruit of Protestant belief and action, that it is for Protestants an "article of faith" and not just an "article of peace," then a high *religious* evaluation of pluralism may be expected from Protestants. What is more, the values of voluntarism (capacity to *choose* one's religious affiliation) and toleration (respect for the right of the other to choose and live by his affiliation), which attend a system of denominational pluralism, may likewise be expected to receive strong religious sanction. On the other hand, there is by no means any fixed "Protestant" view on the question of diversity and pluralism, as is demonstrated by the current ecumenical concern for unity among the churches.

From this the crucial question arises whether there can, in fact, be a stable system of denominational pluralism without a strongly positive and fundamental religious legitimation of that system. To quote Professor Parsons again, "the genuine institutionalization of the constitutional protection of religious freedom cannot be confined to the secular side; it must be accepted as *religiously* legitimate as well."[2] Matters like these obviously involve historical, theological, and sociological discussions of the profoundest kind, discussions which the seminar had neither the time nor the predisposition to pursue. Nonetheless, the problem of the relation between religious belief and social organization underlay much of the conversation, and before any helpful conclusions may be arrived at, that problem will have to be dealt with.

Certainly, the implicit and complex conflict between some Protestants and Catholics in the seminar over this point indicates the need for an exceedingly careful and probing evaluation of assertions like Fr. Richard J. Regan's in his recent book, *American Pluralism and the Catholic Conscience*: "The dogmatic intolerance of a Catholic belief . . . is compatible with the political tolerance of democratic government."[3] The need for such an evaluation is underscored by the arresting comments in this regard of Professor Parsons: "From a sociological point of view there can be little doubt that the rise of the Catholic Church to its present position has introduced what we sociologists call a 'structural strain' of considerable proportions into American society, that there is no easy solution for the problems involved, and that perhaps above all simple tolerant 'good will' and avoidance of prejudice is not enough . . . The structure of the Church itself, and the kind of relation to secular society which is best adapted to it, are in certain respects out of harmony with the main structure of American society . . . Furthermore, through the claim to control all matters of faith and morals the church as an organization has a certain tendency to encroach on the freedom of

2 *Ibid.*
3 (New York, 1963), p. 72.

the individual as that is conceived in relation to our basic doctrine of the separation of Church and State."[4] These are strong words, and they may, in the course of further discussion and encounter, be proved wrong both theologically and sociologically. Yet, it is precisely such assertions as these which must be faced up to in future conversation. As has been hinted, the possible conflicts here articulated by Professor Parsons were latent throughout the proceedings of the seminar. Considerations of this kind, obviously, lie behind examination of the so-called practical issues—birth control, etc.—to which we referred earlier.

NATURAL LAW

It was inevitable in a seminar on ethics between Protestants and Catholics that the subject of natural law would come up. However, as in the exchanges on pluralism, there was an unexpected diversity and "openness" of opinion. Differences of emphasis and approach by no means followed confessional lines.

In his introduction to *Natural Law and Modern Society*, John Cogley defines the subject this way: "Fundamentally, the idea of natural law . . . is based on a belief that there exists a moral order which every normal person can discover by using his reason and of which he must take account if he is to attune himself to his necessary ends as a human being. Three propositions, then, are included in the definition: (1) there is a nature common to all men—something uniquely human makes all of us *men* rather than beasts or angels; (2) because that 'something' is rationality, we are capable of learning what the general ends of human nature are; and (3) by taking thought we can relate our moral choices to these ends."[5] Protestants and Catholics have

---

[4] Talcott Parsons, *Religious Perspectives in College Teaching* (Edward W. Hazen Foundation, n.d. [1951?]), p. 37.

[5] (Cleveland, 1963), pp. 19–20.

tended at times to differ regarding the capacity of man rationally to discover a "moral order" and then to act upon his knowledge. Certain schools of Protestant thought have inclined to emphasize the pervading sinfulness of all man's perceptions. What man takes to be the "objective moral order" is only a projection of his own limited interests and ambitions. There is only one reliable source of action—the living, acting God revealed in Jesus Christ. Protestants have laid stress upon the "open" and relative character of Christian ethical behavior. Some contemporary Protestant ethical thought has developed this theme still further in the direction of "contextual" or "situational" ethics. The Christian, it is argued, must take his bearings from the Word of God and the given social situation in which he finds himself, rather than from an overarching, abstract "moral order."

Catholics, on the other hand, have generally adhered to a long-standing tradition of natural law formulated by such a thinker as Thomas Aquinas. They have sometimes been troubled by the relativism and apparent intuitionism of so much Protestant ethical thought. They have asserted the need and the possibility of positing a minimum standard of right action, which is available to all men regardless of whether they are Christian or not. Natural law requirements by no means exhaust the demands of the Christian life, but they serve as a prerequisite to it.

Many of the seminar participants seemed to be groping toward a new formulation of the "natural law problem," hoping to combine insights and emphases developed out of both Protestant and Catholic traditions. There were intimations that this spirit of groping, so evident in the discussions, was a reflection as well as an adumbration of a kind of tentative conciliation. As one Catholic put it, Protestants have emphasized the "existential" or situational aspect of ethical behavior, while Catholics have concerned themselves with the "categoric," or the more abstract, objective aspect. He pointed out that both extremes have had unfortunate effects, and each tradition needs the other.

He claimed, and he was joined in this by some Catholics *and* some Protestants, that we now begin to see a genuine convergence or consensus. What has caused this convergence among Protestants and Catholics on an approach to ethics? A Catholic theologian put it this way: "Perhaps one reason for the convergence is because of the tendency of man to overstate his position—a manifestation of original sin. There was overstatement by the Medievalists and then by the Reformers. These overstatements are corrected by life, by experience." But how, it was asked, do we judge the direction of life and experience? Can we in fact perceive the emergence of commonly acceptable general principles of moral behavior? What historic factors have contributed to their emergence?

A Catholic sociologist asserted that modern men—religious or not—are forced by the life situation in which they find themselves to acknowledge a process of sociological causation. There is, he said, "a general developmental structure of the world," and this structure imposes itself upon the consciousness of men, determining to some extent their course of action. The process at work here could, he claimed, be taken as a definition of the influence of experience, though it was never completely clear from the discussion just where specifically he felt the process was leading, and how it was shaping action.

A Protestant concurred that there is a convergence at work, but one more of method than of content. According to him a growing awareness in Protestant circles indicates an attachment to some kind of natural law theory. Protestants seem to acknowledge that there is a universal obligation upon all men to be concerned with questions like, "What ought man to be?" There is not necessarily a commitment to any particular answer, but only a commitment to the fact that questions like this one must be raised and discussed. Moreover, this particular scholar said he had analyzed various Protestant thinkers, like Karl Barth and Reinhold Niebuhr, and he said he could find no logical relation between their theology and their ethical judgments. Inevitably, he claimed, they fall back, like all men, on some kind of "natural law method," if not on any explicit doctrine of natural law.

At the same time, a spirit of caution was injected regarding the existing state of the discussion on natural law. The sentiment of certain Protestants is summarized in the comments of Professor Kenneth Underwood, one of the speakers. "In the churches an attempt is being made to meet the moral confusion of men in the complex and varied organizations of modern life by an emphasis on 'the law.' Even Protestants who have scorned the Catholic's stress on natural law ethics now recognize that some ground for moral action capable of shaping our common life must be found. Yet Protestant ethicists have not been greatly impressed by current Catholic reinterpretations of the law for our society.[6] Can our dialogue on the law keep before us the deciding judge, the corporation executive, and the presidential office so that perspective, social structure, and personal judgment are fully respected in the law? Both Protestant and Catholic models of the law and the moral actor . . . still lack the causal complexity, the psychological depth, the social dramaturgy, the historical uniqueness to catch the style and tone of personal action in our new society."

Finally, the amazing flexibility of the general discussion of natural law was underscored by the comment of a Catholic from abroad. He related that at a recent conference of Catholic jurists in France, the participants to a man re-

[6] See, for example, John Courtney Murray, S.J., *We Hold These Truths; Catholic Reflections on the American Proposition* (New York, 1960); and John Cogley, *Natural Law and Modern Society* (Cleveland, 1963).

jected the traditional theory of Thomistic natural law. This
is particularly remarkable, as someone pointed out, in the
light of the renewed interest in natural law, not only among
American Protestants, but also among American legal
thinkers.

Although his comments were soon swallowed up in the
rush of discussion (as were so many), one Protestant's inter-
jection raised afresh the pertinent question of specifically
Christian ethics as opposed merely to natural ethics. "The
ethical situation," he said, " is not exhausted by natural law
and the context. We have to relate also the Cross, the absolute law of love, and the Sermon on the Mount to this.
This is a third factor. What I do not understand is what is
peculiarly Christian about political decisions made in a
Christian context as compared with a secular environment."
In part, at least, his concerns were addressed in the consideration of the Christian conscience, for in that exchange,
more than in any other, specifically theological and confessional debate took place. It was, generally speaking, in the
discussion on conscience that the terms "Protestant" and
"Catholic" seemed to make some sense in identifying differing positions.

CONSCIENCE

The exchange was opened by some remarks on conscience
by a Catholic theologian. In the first place, he reviewed
briefly some traditional views of conscience. While the
positivist understanding "leaves out everything important,"
it is useful as a starting-point: "conscience is the concentrated experience of the race." We must combine this notion
—certainly true so far as it goes—with the claim of Socrates
that conscience is the "rule of reason" which presents us
with an ideal toward which to aspire. This notion of the
ideal is elaborated by Cardinal John Henry Newman's more
strictly theistic formulation: "I have to be faithful to the

endowments God has given me." Man, according to Newman, begins with potentialities granted by God, and he is called upon to actualize them. This is the ideal centered in God toward which the conscience prods man. Conscience, then, amounts to an "interior witness of the existence and law of God." Its three salient characteristics are that (1) it transcends itself, and judges the actual in terms of the ideal or potential; (2) it is dynamic (essentially oriented toward the potential); and (3) it is the source of special emotional feelings in relation to action. Conscience at its heart, according to this theologian, provides "dictates" or "directives," and these, in turn, are linked to natural law. Conscience, in other words, is universal and it is rooted in certain universal ideal directives which guide and inform the ethical life of man.

This treatment of conscience drew the battle lines for much of the subsequent debate. A Protestant responded that the analysis was far too "imperative" in that it spoke of conscience exclusively in terms of exhortation. It neglected the peculiarly liberating and enabling character of the Christian conscience. The conscience, he said, "becomes aware of its vocation toward the other"; it catches the individual up in what God *is* doing, not merely in what God commands that we do. It is, in short, more "indicative" in its thrust than "imperative." Thus, the context of action, the situation in which man actually finds himself, becomes decisive, rather than abstract "directives." We are in a situational rather than an abstract world, and it is there that we must seek the meaning of the conscience.

Thenceforth the discussion ranged around the conflict between the "indicative" (contextual) and the "imperative" (principial) aspects of conscience. On the one hand, it was argued that psychology and sociology demonstrate that man operates in relation to a "rank order of values." These stand above the actor, so to speak, and direct his action. Conscience operates on the basis of these general premises. In fact, they help the actor to define his place in the world. There is no "situation" apart from the overarching value premises. Beyond that it was asserted that "indicative conscience," one that is caught up in the activity of God in relation to the other, is endowed with the "gifts of the Holy Spirit." It is the "enlightened conscience," infused with the theological virtues. Such a conscience is not to be confused with the average individual who lives at a lower level of virtue. That person must rely upon "natural" guidelines which may be informed by sociological and psychological insight.

On the other hand, it was reasserted time and again that God's concrete action in the world made plain in revelation, rather than in "natural" principles or social science, was of central significance for conscience. One Catholic agreed that his own tradition had been "too analytical." It had, he said, failed to see conscience in a *theological* context. The reason for this is the too-ready separation of natural law from the law of grace. As a result, he concluded, Catholics "have never had a creative conscience which opens man up and gives him freedom." They have seen the conscience as something oppressive which does not permit men to grow. He urged in a conciliatory spirit that conscience be viewed as *both* indicative *and* imperative.

The same essential tension appeared in various ways throughout the discussion. The point was made, for example, that there is no necessary content implied in conscience. It is quite wrong, the argument ran, to link the conscience either to a specific theological understanding of "what God is doing in the world," or to a set of abstract principles. Rather, conscience is "the imperative to do the best that I know." With such a conception—quite apart from the question of content—we have a basis for pluralism and tolerance.

This point of view, however, encountered opposition. Tolerance is not based upon conscience as such, but upon a "recognition of fallibility." Every conscience is informed by some kind of content—it is related to values or ideals. The point is that the mature individual realizes the limitations of his values to ideals; he realizes that while he does have some reliable perceptions of what is good, he does not and cannot know all there is to know. He therefore remains open-minded, or tolerant of the perceptions of others. With this emphasis the consideration of conscience returned to the underlying problem of pluralism and tolerance.

CONCLUSION

From a brief consideration of these three facets of the theme "Conscience in a Pluralistic Society," it becomes apparent how interrelated with each other they all are. Precisely because of this one of the difficulties in preparing this report was the interpenetration of pluralism, natural law, and conscience throughout all of the discussions. To unravel the conversations and organize them under three such headings is at best artificial and at worst misleading. It is important, therefore, to reflect generally on all three themes together.

There was a tendency on the part of those who looked at conscience *through* natural law, or at least strongly in relation to it, to favor a kind of organic or developmental understanding of the contemporary situation. The "organic metaphor" was sometimes employed to describe the structure and process of the world, on its way toward deeper and wider uniformity. This developmental process shapes, so it was argued, the kinds of ethical decisions with which Christians are confronted. Man lives in relation to a grand metaphysical scheme—ultimately, the eternal order of God, and he is called upon to conform to that scheme. Thus, when conscience and natural law were taken as indissolu-

bly linked, the tendency was to favor uniformity as opposed
to pluralism. This was true, as we have indicated, of both
certain Protestants and Catholics.

On the other hand, when the question of conscience
was divorced from natural law, or seen as removed from it,
there was a corresponding tendency to favor what was referred to as a "dramatic" view of history. Implied in this,
of course, was a greater emphasis upon the "openness" or
pluralism in history. As we pointed out, conscience was
informed by fluid situations and contexts, rather than by
established principles and structures. It was suggested, for
example, that God is the first pluralist simply because he
created man and the world apart from himself! Though
these two different emphases inclined to divide along confessional lines, it is by no means clear, as I hope the general
analysis has made apparent, that Protestant and Catholic
are *necessarily* divided in this way. There is evidence,
pointed to at the beginning, that much overlapping exists
between both sides in these matters.

If the seminar accomplished nothing else, it helped to
identify some of the central concerns that must constitute
further discussions. It also indicated that much hard and
careful thinking is in order. Certainly, one came away from
the encounter convinced of the accuracy of Professor Parsons' words: "simple tolerant 'good will' and avoidance of
prejudice is not enough . . ."

David Little
Yale Divinity School

COLLOQUIUM PARTICIPANTS

COLLOQUIUM PROGRAM

COLLOQUIUM PARTICIPANTS

Rev. Savas Agourides, *Holy Cross Greek Orthodox Theological School, Brookline*

Rev. Joseph T. Alves, *Catholic Family Counseling Services, Boston*

Dean Bernhard W. Anderson, *Drew University, New Jersey*

Professor James Barr, *Princeton Theological Seminary*

Rev. Gregory Baum, o.s.a., *St. Michael's College, Toronto*

His Eminence, Augustin Cardinal Bea, *President, Secretariat for Promoting Christian Unity*

Professor Harrell F. Beck, *Boston University School of Theology*

Very Rev. Henry G. J. Beck, *Immaculate Conception Seminary, New Jersey*

Professor Harold J. Berman, *Harvard Law School*

Professor Peter A. Bertocci, *Boston University*

Professor Morton W. Bloomfield, *Harvard University*

Professor William J. Bouwsma, *University of California*

Dr. Scott F. Brenner, *United Presbyterian Church, Philadelphia*

Dr. Edgar S. Brown, Jr., *Lutheran Church in America, New York City*

Rev. Raymond E. Brown, s.s., *St. Mary's Seminary, Baltimore*

Rev. Walter J. Burghardt, s.j., *Woodstock College, Maryland*

PROFESSOR J. LAWRENCE BURKHOLDER, *Harvard Divinity School*

MR. DANIEL J. CALLAHAN, *The Commonweal, New York City*

REV. EDWARD R. CALLAHAN, S.J., *Weston College*

PROFESSOR RICHARD M. CAMERON, *Boston University School of Theology*

REV. JAMES J. CASEY, S.J., *Boston College*

MR. PAUL CHAPMAN, *Packard Manse, Stoughton*

REV. DAVID CLARK, *Harvard Divinity School*

DEAN JOHN B. COBURN, *Episcopal Theological School*

REV. JOHN J. COLLINS, S.J., *Weston College*

REV. JOSEPH I. COLLINS, *Harvard-Radcliffe Catholic Club*

REV. JOHN J. CONNELLY, *St. John's Seminary, Brighton*

PROFESSOR GILES CONSTABLE, *Harvard University*

REV. DON H. COPELAND, *World Center for Liturgical Studies, Boca Raton*

PROFESSOR J. HARRY COTTON, *Harvard Divinity School*

REV. THOMAS COWLEY, O.P., *St. Dominic's Priory, Washington, D.C.*

PROFESSOR GERALD R. CRAGG, *Andover Newton Theological School*

PROFESSOR EDWARD CRANZ, *Connecticut College for Women*

PROFESSOR FRANK M. CROSS, JR., *Harvard Divinity School*

MR. JOSEPH E. CUNEEN, *Cross Currents, New York*

REV. CHARLES CURRAN, *St. Bernard's Seminary, Rochester*

HIS EMINENCE, RICHARD CARDINAL CUSHING, *Archbishop of Boston*

REV. MARTIN D'ARCY, S.J., *Boston College*

PROFESSOR W. D. DAVIES, *Union Theological Seminary*

Mr. Michel S. Despland, *Harvard Divinity School*

Rev. Joseph A. Devenny, s.j., *Boston College*

Rev. Philip J. Donnelly, s.j., *Weston College*

Professor Edward A. Dowey, Jr., *Princeton Theological Seminary*

Rev. Robert F. Drinan, s.j., *Boston College*

Rev. Avery R. Dulles, s.j., *Woodstock College, Maryland*

Professor Nils Ehrenstrom, *Boston University School of Theology*

Rev. Gerald Ellard, s.j., *St. Mary's College, Kansas*

Professor Rollin Jonathan Fairbanks, *Episcopal Theological School*

Professor William W. Farmer, *Perkins School of Theology, Dallas*

Professor Nels F. S. Ferré, *Andover Newton Theological School*

Professor Joseph F. Fletcher, *Episcopal Theological School*

Professor Georges Florovsky, *Harvard Divinity School*

Professor A. L. Gabriel, *University of Notre Dame*

Professor Deno Geanakoplos, *University of Illinois*

President Herbert Gezork, *Andover Newton Theological School*

Rev. R. Jerrold Gibson, *Harvard University*

Professor Myron P. Gilmore, *Harvard University*

Professor S. MacLean Gilmour, *Andover Newton Theological School*

Professor Eugene Van Ness Goetchius, *Episcopal Theological School*

Professor Erwin R. Goodenough, *Yale University*

PROFESSOR NORMAN K. GOTTWALD, *Andover Newton Theological School*

REV. ANDREW M. GREELEY, *Chicago, Illinois*

PROFESSOR HARVEY H. GUTHRIE, JR., *Episcopal Theological School*

REV. JOHN J. HARMON, *Packard Manse, Roxbury*

REV. LOUIS J. HARTMAN, C.SS.R., *Catholic University of America*

RT. REV. GEORGE G. HIGGINS, *National Catholic Welfare Conference*

REV. HENRY HORN, *University Lutheran Church, Cambridge*

PROFESSOR DOUGLAS HORTON, *Dean Emeritus, Harvard Divinity School*

VERY REV. JOHN JADAA, *St. Basil's Seminary, Methuen*

PROFESSOR RICHARD B. KALTER, *Berkeley Divinity School, New Haven*

REV. PHILIP J. KING, *St. John's Seminary, Brighton*

PROFESSOR JOHN KNOX, *Union Theological Seminary*

PROFESSOR HELMUT KOESTER, *Harvard Divinity School*

PROFESSOR STEPHAN KUTTNER, *Catholic University of America*

PROFESSOR GERHART LADNER, *University of California at Los Angeles*

REV. JOHN LAFARGE, S.J., *America, New York City*

RT. REV. FRANCIS J. LALLY, *The Pilot, Boston*

MR. H. DARRELL LANCE, *Harvard Divinity School*

MR. RALPH LAZZARO, *Harvard Divinity School*

PROFESSOR PAUL L. LEHMANN, *Union Theological Seminary*

REV. LOUIS LEKAI, S.O. CIST., *Cistercian Monastery, Dallas*

REV. WILLIAM LEONARD, S.J., *Boston College*

Mr. David Little, *Harvard Divinity School*

Rev. H. Ganse Little, Jr., *Harvard Divinity School*

Mr. Herbert D. Long, *Harvard Divinity School*

Professor Robert E. Luccock, *Boston University School of Theology*

Mr. Robert Maddox, *Harvard Divinity School*

Professor Harvey K. McArthur, *Hartford Seminary Foundation*

Mr. S. Dean McBride, *Harvard Divinity School*

Rev. R. A. F. MacKenzie, s.j., *Regis College, Toronto*

Rev. John L. McKenzie, s.j., *Loyola University, Chicago*

Rev. Frederick R. McManus, *Catholic University of America*

Rev. Robert E. McNally, s.j., *Woodstock College, Maryland*

Mr. John Mannion, *National Catholic Liturgical Conference*

Very Rev. Dom Hilary Martin, o.s.b., *Priory, Portsmouth, Rhode Island*

Rev. Armand A. Maurer, c.s.b., *Pontifical Institute of Mediaeval Studies, Toronto*

Rev. John H. Miller, c.s.c., *Catholic University of America*

Dean Samuel H. Miller, *Harvard Divinity School*

Professor Paul S. Minear, *Yale Divinity School*

Rev. George T. Montague, s.m., *St. Mary's University, San Antonio*

Professor Bruce Morgan, *Amherst College*

Professor O. Hobart Mowrer, *University of Illinois*

Professor Lucetta Mowrey, *Wellesley College*

Dean Walter G. Muelder, *Boston University School of Theology*

REV. ROLAND E. MURPHY, O.CARM., *Catholic University of America*

RT. REV. EDWARD G. MURRAY, *Sacred Heart Church, Roslindale*

PROFESSOR RICHARD R. NIEBUHR, *Harvard Divinity School*

VERY REV. EAMONN O'DOHERTY, *St. Columban's Seminary, Milton*

REV. JAMES A. O'DONOHUE, *St. John's Seminary, Brighton*

MR. JAMES O'GARA, *The Commonweal, New York City*

PROFESSOR LLOYD G. PATTERSON, JR., *Episcopal Theological School*

PROFESSOR WILLIAM PECK, *Williams College*

PROFESSOR RAY C. PETRY, *Duke Divinity School*

PRESIDENT NATHAN M. PUSEY, *Harvard University*

REV. JOHANNES QUASTEN, *Catholic University of America*

REV. J. RICHARD QUINN, *St. John's Seminary, Brighton*

REV. ROBERT F. QUINN, C.S.P., *The Paulist Fathers, Catholic Information Center, Boston*

REV. HANS A. REINHOLD, *The Oratory, Pittsburgh*

MR. R. EUGENE RICE, *Harvard Divinity School*

PROFESSOR CYRIL RICHARDSON, *Union Theological Seminary*

MR. HERBERT W. RICHARDSON, *Harvard Divinity School*

MOST REV. THOMAS J. RILEY, *Auxiliary Bishop of Boston*

PROFESSOR JAMES M. ROBINSON, *Southern California School of Theology at Claremont*

PROFESSOR FRANCIS M. ROGERS, *Harvard University*

RT. REV. FRANCIS S. ROSSITER, *St. John's Seminary, Brighton*

RT. REV. J. JOSEPH RYAN, *St. John's Seminary, Brighton*

PROFESSOR MARTIN A. SCHMIDT, *San Francisco Theological Seminary*

Rev. Stefano Schmidt, *Secretariat for Promoting Christian Unity*

Professor Paul Schubert, *Yale Divinity School*

Professor George R. Seltzer, *The Lutheran Theological Seminary, Philadelphia*

Rev. Shawn G. Sheehan, *St. John's Seminary, Brighton*

Professor Henry M. Shires, *Episcopal Theological School*

Rt. Rev. Patrick W. Skehan, *Catholic University of America*

Professor Robert H. L. Slater, *Harvard Divinity School*

Rev. G. S. Sloyan, *Catholic University of America*

Professor Charles W. F. Smith, *Episcopal Theological School*

Professor H. Shelton Smith, *Duke University*

Mr. Max L. Stackhouse, *Harvard Divinity School*

Rev. David M. Stanley, s.j., *State University of Iowa*

Rt. Rev. Matthew P. Stapleton, rector, *St. John's Seminary, Brighton*

Rev. Theodore M. Steeman, o.f.m., *Harvard Divinity School*

Professor Douglas Steere, *Haverford College*

Professor Krister Stendahl, *Harvard Divinity School*

Rev. P. Thomas Stransky, c.s.p., *Secretariat for Promoting Christian Unity*

Rev. Anselm Strittmatter, o.s.b., *St. Anselm's Abbey, Washington, D.C.*

Professor Richard E. Sullivan, *Michigan State College of Agriculture and Applied Science*

Rev. John L. Thomas, s.j., *St. Louis University*

Professor Bard Thompson, *Lancaster Theological Seminary, Pennsylvania*

PROFESSOR KENNETH W. UNDERWOOD, *Wesleyan University*

REV. GERALD F. VAN ACKEREN, S.J., *St. Mary's College, Kansas*

REV. CHARLES K. VON EUW, *St. John's Seminary, Brighton*

REV. JOHN J. WALSH, S.J., *Weston College*

MR. ROY B. WARD, *Harvard Divinity School*

REV. GUSTAVE WEIGEL, S.J., *Woodstock College, Maryland*

PROFESSOR AMOS N. WILDER, *Harvard Divinity School*

RT. REV. J. G. M. WILLEBRANDS, *Secretariat for Promoting Christian Unity*

SISTER WILLIAM, *Radcliffe Institute for Independent Study*

PROFESSOR GEORGE H. WILLIAMS, *Harvard Divinity School*

MR. E. DAVID WILLIS, *Harvard Divinity School*

VERY REV. DAMASUS WINZEN, O.S.B., *Mount Saviour Monastery, Elmira, New York*

PROFESSOR WILLIAM J. WOLF, *Episcopal Theological School*

PROFESSOR C. CONRAD WRIGHT, *Harvard Divinity School*

PROFESSOR G. ERNEST WRIGHT, *Harvard Divinity School*

REV. SAMUEL J. WYLIE, *Church of the Advent, Boston*

COLLOQUIUM PROGRAM

Wednesday, March 27th
7:00 P.M.—Reception for Participants
Busch-Reisinger Museum

8:00P.M.—The First Stillman Lecture
Sanders Theatre
Welcome—President Pusey
"The Academic Pursuits and Christian Unity"
His Eminence, Augustin Cardinal Bea

9:00 P.M.—Brahms' *Requiem*
Sanders Theatre
Handel and Haydn Society

Thursday, March 28th
8:30 A.M.—Prayer Service
Andover Chapel
Rev. Jerrold Gibson

9:00 A.M.—
Morning Seminars for invited guests. Each of the four seminars will run through the three days of the Colloquium.

1. Biblical Studies: Record and Interpretation
Braun Room
Speakers: Rev. Raymond E. Brown, S.S.,
St. Mary's Seminary
Dr. W. D. Davies,
Union Theological Seminary
Discussion Leader: Dr. Krister Stendahl,
Harvard Divinity School

2. Symbol and Sacrament
                              B.D. Room, Library
   Speakers: Rev. Gerald Ellard, S.J.,
              St. Mary's College
              Dr. Cyril Richardson,
              Union Theological Seminary
   Discussion Leader: Dr. J. Harry Cotton,
                        Harvard Divinity School

3. "Reformatio"
                  Center for the Study of World Religions
   Speakers: Dr. Gerhart B. Ladner, University of
              California at Los Angeles
              Dr. Martin A. Schmidt,
              San Francisco Theological
              Seminary
   Discussion Leader: Dr. Giles Constable,
                        Harvard University

4. Conscience in a Pluralistic Society:
   Theological and Sociological Issues
                                        Jewett House
   Speakers: Rev. John L. Thomas, S.J.,
              St. Louis University
              Dr. Kenneth W. Underwood,
              Wesleyan University
   Discussion Leader: Mr. David Little,
                        Harvard Divinity School

4:00 P.M.—"Theological Reflections on the Second Vatican
           Council"
                                        Sanders Theatre
           Rev. Gregory Baum, O.S.A.,
           St. Michael's College

8:00 P.M.—The Second Stillman Lecture
                                        Sanders Theatre
           Welcome—Dean Miller
           "The Second Vatican Council and
           non-Catholic Christians:
           Preparation and the Work in the
           First Period"
           His Eminence, Augustin Cardinal Bea

9:00 P.M.—Memorial Church Choir
                                        Sanders Theatre

Friday, March 29th
   8:30 A.M.—Prayer Service

                                              Andover Chapel

         Rev. Jerrold Gibson

   9:00 A.M.—*Morning Seminars*

   4:00 P.M.—"Interpretation of Scripture in
           Biblical Studies Today"

                                        Sanders Theatre

         Dr. James M. Robinson, Southern
         California School of Theology at Claremont

   8:00 P.M.—The Third Stillman Lecture

                                        Sanders Theatre

         Welcome—Dr. George H. Williams
         "The Second Vatican Council and
         non-Catholic Christians:
         Evaluation and Prognosis"
         His Eminence, Augustin Cardinal Bea

   9:00 P.M.—The Old North Singers

                                          Sanders Theatre

Saturday, March 30th
   8:30 A.M.—Prayer Service

                                              Andover Chapel

         Rev. Jerrold Gibson

   9:00 A.M.—*Morning Seminars*

   4:00 P.M.—"Conscience and Introspection"

                                        Sanders Theatre

         A Panel Discussion:
         Rev. Charles E. Curran,
         St. Bernard's Seminary
         Dr. Paul L. Lehmann,
         Union Theological Seminary
         Rev. David M. Stanley, S.J.,
         State University of Iowa
         Dr. Krister Stendahl,
         Harvard Divinity School

7:00 P.M.—Reception and Dinner

Harvard Club of Boston

Presiding—Dean Miller
Speakers—President Pusey
Rev. Gustave Weigel, S.J.,
Woodstock College

SPECIAL INFORMATION

Masses—Will be held at St. Paul's Church, Bow and Arrow
Streets, Cambridge, at 7:00 A.M., 8:00 A.M., and 5:30 P.M.
daily. On Saturday, there will be a 5:45 P.M. Mass, rather than
one at 5:30 P.M. Facilities are available for visiting Priests to
offer Mass at any time (there are six altars). Please write or see
Father Joseph I. Collins.

Luncheon—Will be served for the participants following the
Morning Seminars.

The Afternoon Lectures—Will be open to the public. No tickets
will be required for admission. Presiding Chairmen will be as
follows: on Thursday afternoon, Dr. Douglas Horton; on Friday
afternoon, Dr. Amos Wilder; on Saturday afternoon, Dr. G.
Ernest Wright.

INDEX

INDEX